2024 EDITION

PERSONALITY
WINS

Who Will Take the White House and How We Know

By Merrick Rosenberg
with Richard Ellis

Personality Wins (2024 Edition)
Who Will Take the White House and How We Know
© 2023 by Merrick Rosenberg with Richard Ellis

Published by Take Flight Learning
https://takeflightlearning.com/

Cover Design by Nathan Davis

Paperback ISBN: 978-1-959554-02-8
Hardback ISBN: 978-1-959554-04-2
Ebook ISBN: 978-1-959554-03-5

Published in the United States of America

To my incredible wife, Traci, thank you for holding the space for me to be the highest version of myself.

To my team at Take Flight Learning, this book and everything I do would not be possible without you.

To my parents, who paid for my Political Communications degree from George Washington University, look, I'm using it!

Merrick

To Mom and Dad, thank you for believing in my writing career. I feel grateful to come from a home filled with laughter, bickering, love, and stories worth repeating.

I told you that History degree would come in handy!

Rich

Acknowledgements

You know what happens when you are surrounded by a great team? You accomplish things that you could never do alone. To the staff at Take Flight Learning, this book exists because of the passion and dedication you show all throughout the year.

To Jeff Backal, an Eagle who always has his eye on the prize. To Dolores Woodington, my resident Owl who keeps this Parrot safe. To Andy Kraus, Rick Kauffman, Jim Di Miero, and Steven Farber — you provide the wind that enables the birds to fly around the world. To Kerry Bayles, Jason Meucci, and all the facilitators of Taking Flight Learning training programs around the world, you magically bring the birds to life. To Chris Askew, your artistic vision makes the birds shine. And to Cathryn Plum, I deeply appreciate your Owl-like attention to detail, which keeps this Parrot on track. Cyndi Lamon, Alex Woodington, Josh Levoff, and Mimi Thompson, you keep things moving behind the scenes and I appreciate everything you do. One more special thank you goes out to Barry Woodington, who generously put his researching Owl to work.

Finally, there are two people who truly helped make this book a reality. To Traci Rosenberg, beyond being a sounding board and a cheerleader, you make it possible for me to follow my dreams. I think I owe you several months of feeding the dogs and our parrot.

And from Richard to Heather Wilk, your unwavering support and storytelling brilliance helped us find the way through challenging chapters. You have braved Park City snow, rain, hail, and everything between just to be there for me. Thank you for being my muse every step of the journey.

Table of Contents

Section I:
The Winning Personality

The Landslide That Wasn't

IT WAS THE UPSET OF THE CENTURY to anyone who accepted the conventional wisdom about how to predict a U.S. presidential election. There was no way that Donald J. Trump could defeat Hillary Rodham Clinton to become the next president of the United States...or at least, that's what most experts and polls were predicting.

Two days before the election, Princeton University data scientists gave Hillary Clinton 99 percent odds of beating Trump. Their model had correctly called forty-nine out of fifty states in the 2012 election.

The Los Angeles Times, Moody's, Fox News, The Associated Press, *The New York Times*, Reuters/Ipsos, ABC News, Bloomberg, *The Economist*, the betting markets, and nearly every other news source you can think of called the election in favor of Clinton.

There was such over-the-top confidence in Clinton that op-eds from October had headlines like, "Hillary Clinton will win. But what kind of president will she be?" Other articles worried about what to call Bill

Clinton after Hillary's inevitable victory. First Man? First Gentleman? First Partner? First Dude? It was worth considering since Hillary would win by a "landslide."

Every pollster and pundit gave Hillary monster odds of trouncing Trump. But there was a difference between what the numbers said and what people did.

Excited About Hillary

"Hillary Clinton faces an enthusiasm gap," said Berkley Professor Robert Reich, who served as Secretary of Labor in Bill Clinton's administration. "I don't know many people who are extremely excited about her candidacy."

Even Republican presidential candidate Dr. Ben Carson, who has all the charisma of a Valium prescription, threw shade in an op-ed: "The political elites and their loyal media are desperate because they are seeing the large enthusiastic crowds for Donald Trump and the meager crowds for Hillary Clinton, and they know that there will be a huge enthusiasm gap on election day."

CNN ran an entire news segment about Hillary's enthusiasm gap. One clip showed Clinton trying to look tough and cover her heart with one hand, Obama-style. In Clinton monotone, she said, "We've got to defend the American worker's right to organize and bargain for better wages and benefits. We're going to get incomes rising here in Western Michigan and across this state."

Seconds later in the clip, Trump boasted, "We will stop the jobs from leaving your state." He was in his element. Something about his approach, his communication style, and his demeanor generated, well, enthusiasm.

But where did this enthusiasm come from? Were his policies more carefully defined? Not really. Did he have a more compelling resume than Clinton? That's not it either. So why did one candidate create raving fans and another create an "enthusiasm gap"?

The Lesser of Two Personalities

Polls captured what people do *if* they had to vote, which they don't. Just over 61 percent of voting-age Americans went to the polls in 2016.

Despite what all polls and data scientists said, the media focused on the personalities of Clinton and Trump. We heard it after every debate. We read about it in the blogosphere. We watched it on every twenty-four-hour news station.

"She's too robotic."

"He's too brash."

"She's too dispassionate."

"He's too aggressive."

While Trump generated enthusiasm, he lacked likability. In fact, a shocking number of Americans disliked the personalities of *both* candidates. For about two-thirds of Americans, voting *against* Clinton or Trump was the main reason for supporting their opponent. Many people couldn't bring themselves to vote for their party's candidate.

The people who disliked Trump were concerned about his "temperament" and "unpredictability." Many Clinton haters said, "I just didn't like her."

Were political pundits and everyday Americans onto something? Does personality *really* make a difference in the election process?

The answer is a resounding YES.

It's All About Personality

On November 8, 2016, Donald Trump defeated Hillary Clinton with 304 electoral votes to 227. The polls and pundits were wrong.

For those who say, "Yeah, but Hillary got more actual votes than Trump," that's true. But in the end, Donald Trump put his hand on the Bible and was sworn in as the forty-fifth president of the United States. This book is about why candidates win elections, not how to reform electoral politics.

Why did Trump fill convention centers and stadiums while Clinton could barely pack a high school auditorium or community center? The answer is hidden in plain sight.

If you looked at the personalities of Trump and Clinton instead of their polling numbers, 2016 was completely predictable. In fact, every election—and we mean every election—since Franklin Delano Roosevelt's first run in 1932 was predictable.

Personality has won the day in twenty-three straight elections. Let that sink in for a moment. Regardless of whether the country was at war or peace, personality determined the outcome. Regardless of whether one candidate was an incumbent or both were running for the first time, personality determined the outcome. Regardless of whether the economy was booming or flailing, personality determined the outcome. For 88 years of elections, personality has determined who takes the White House.

We've Been Thinking about Elections All Wrong

As a nation, we act as if elections are about party, platform, and policy because we'd like to think they determine how an enlightened democracy elects its leader. But that doesn't square with the facts.

If you want to know what will happen in 2024, forget about those, "When I am president, here's what I am going to do" plans. Instead, focus on what matters: the candidates' personalities.

We can hear it now: "What about die-hard party loyalists? Don't they always vote party first?" Sure, many voters will only vote for their party's nominee. They've done it before and will do it again.

Of course, we hear about the infamous "undecideds." These folks can swing to either side of the political spectrum, as the term "swing voters" implies. What variable pulls them to one side of the pendulum versus the other? You're about to discover that it's the personalities of the candidates.

To be clear, we're not trashing policies! They are critical to the health of our government and society. We're just saying that people don't vote for presidential candidates based on their policies. We vote for who they are, not what they say they will do.

If we want to understand how our democracy works, we need a model that matches reality and predicts elections. And if you want that, well, the heck with politics, platform, and party. It's all about personality!

Section II:
Which Bird Are You?

Personality in Everything

At President Ronald Reagan's first State of the Union address in 1982, he opened the way that only the Gipper could:

> President Washington began this tradition in 1790 after reminding the Nation that the destiny of self-government and the 'preservation of the sacred fire of liberty' is 'finally staked on the experiment entrusted to the hands of the American people.' For our friends in the press, who place a high premium on accuracy, let me say: I did not actually hear George Washington say that.

This is the most important annual speech on the president's calendar, and Reagan started with a joke that pokes fun at himself and the media. What would prompt him to do that? Look no further than Reagan's personality.

Personality is reflected in everything we do. We see it in our daily actions. We see it in characters from books and movies. We see it in our spouse and our coworkers. We also see it in the way candidates run for office and in the way a president speaks and governs. Reagan had a "big" personality that lit up rooms and helped him win elections.

In 2020 election coverage, the personalities of the candidates took center stage. Donald Trump held rallies with sound-bite slogans like "Lock her up!" and "Build the wall!" Biden couldn't get through a public address without botching the story of a war hero or mixing up the First and Second Amendments. And Elizabeth Warren sold T-shirts with the slogan, "Warren has a plan for that."

If personality is that important in presidential elections, let's take a step back to discuss what we mean (and don't mean) by "personality."

What is Personality Anyway?

Allow us to nerd out briefly. The American Psychological Association (APA), which is presumably filled with people who understand human behavior, says that "personality refers to individual differences in characteristic patterns of thinking, feeling, and behaving." So, personality is a combination of what people experience inside and what others see on the outside.

Many behaviors reflect personality, but some don't. Anyone can be respectful, honest, courageous, or reliable regardless of their personality. Likewise, anyone can be mean, deceitful, cowardly, or reckless. There is a big difference between personality and concepts like values and ethics. We will leave the latter to philosophers. There are also vast differences between personality, intelligence, and mental well-being. We will leave those topics to psychologists.

Skills like creativity, leadership, and negotiation aren't exclusive to one type of personality. For some, creative art looks abstract and messy.

For others, art must be perfectly realistic, like a portrait that resembles a photograph. Personality does not determine *how creative* people will be, but it absolutely shapes how they will go about *being* creative.

The same is true about leadership. Personality does not determine how successful someone will be as a leader, but it does shape how that individual will lead.

For example, Richard Branson's fly-by-the pants leadership style at Virgin Group was different from the way that Steve Jobs led Apple. Branson, known to be democratic, unpretentious, and upbeat, treated his employees with dignity. In public, he was never afraid to be the butt of a joke. He dressed up in a $10,000 wedding gown for the launch of Virgin Brides in 2006. He also wore a space suit to the press conference announcing Virgin Galactic, his space travel company.

Jobs, on the other hand, was famed for being autocratic, brash, and unforgiving. Neither employees nor business partners were spared from his profanity-laced tirades and penchant for public humiliation. He took himself and his accomplishments very seriously. In 2007, Jobs introduced the first iPhone in the same black turtleneck and blue jeans he wore daily. On stage at MacWorld, he said that Apple was going to "reinvent the phone" six times. He said the word "revolutionary" twelve times and "breakthrough" seven times.

Although Branson and Jobs had almost opposite personalities, they both built multibillion-dollar companies. They just went about it differently. The same is true for the White House. Presidents with different personalities have led the country to prosperity. As we discuss the personalities of the presidential candidates throughout this book, it's important to note that we are not talking about their odds of succeeding in office. We're addressing how likely they are to win an election.

Doesn't Integrity Matter?

We don't view politicians the way we view coworkers, friends, and partners. In friendships and romantic relationships, integrity comes first and personality second. Nobody wants to be in a relationship with someone who lies, cheats, or steals. Presidential candidates get *way* more leeway than people in our personal lives!

Why? Maybe they get a pass on character because we're naturally skeptical of anyone who wants power. Is it so surprising that people who want power lie to get it?

It would be great if presidential candidates didn't rattle off lies and get caught by FactCheck.org and PolitiFact. But as long as the U.S. is safe and the economy is healthy, we cut presidents slack.

Most people wouldn't be happy with a spouse who is truthful 90 percent of the time, yet most of us can live with a president who only stretches the truth 10 percent of the time. As the old joke goes, how do you know if a politician is lying? His lips are moving.

Americans elected presidents with the nicknames Tricky Dick and Slick Willy. We didn't care. For better or worse, character doesn't seem to matter when America chooses a president.

About That Personality Training
Your Boss Made You Take

If you work for a corporation, there's a good chance you've taken a personality assessment and done some personality styles training. You spent the day looking at reports, learning a model, and boiling your personality down to a few letters. Maybe you took the Myers-Briggs Type Indicator and discovered that you are an ENTJ. Or perhaps you completed a DISC profile and learned that you are a D.

If you don't know what any of that means, don't worry. Three months after the training, neither do most of the people who have learned them!

If you do happen to remember your personality type, you must use it every day. The insights you gained about your style guide how you communicate and interact with the people in your life. It is your secret power that helps you get along with everyone. Right?

Probably not.

Most likely, the results of those personality assessments are filed in a drawer, never to be seen again. You have no idea what other people's letters are, and you don't even remember your own. You can't read people's personalities even though someone at your company paid a lot of money for those acronyms.

To understand the presidential candidates—and everyone around us, for that matter—we need a better model. We need something that you can learn in seconds and never forget. It needs to be intuitive, so you don't have to memorize anything. It should be visual, so you can see the personality styles in everyone you meet. It has to be practical and easy.

Let's discard the DISC letters introduced by Dr. William Marston in his 1928 book, *The Emotions of Normal People*, and replace them with something that doesn't need to be memorized. Five years from now, you'll still be able to use this model because it's just that memorable and simple.

Enter the four birds.

Welcome to the Birdhouse

In *Taking Flight!* and *The Chameleon*, books by yours truly, Merrick Rosenberg, four birds were introduced to symbolize the personality styles. Instead of the alphabet soup of letters used in so many personality assessments, the birds make it easy to learn about yourself and others.

It's time to use your imagination. Take a moment to think about an **Eagle**. Picture how that Eagle stands and looks out over the forest. Visualize that Eagle flying at 10,000 feet. Now picture a person with the traits of an Eagle. What characteristics come to mind?

Maybe you thought of someone who is confident, assertive, direct, and decisive. You may have thought of words like visionary, daring, or take-charge. And if results-oriented came to mind, you're right on target. Eagles are all business. They call it like it is and make things happen. *Spoiler alert: George W. Bush, Donald Trump, and Bernie Sanders are Eagles. Bush was the "decider" after all. And Trump and Sanders are pretty blunt and direct.*

What about a **Parrot**? Visualize this brightly colored bird amongst a flock of her friends. What are the first words that come to mind? Talkative, perhaps? Maybe social, outgoing, and fun? If those words came to mind, you're feeling the right vibe.

Parrots are also optimistic, enthusiastic, and fun-loving. They typically have contagious smiles and their wild ideas inspire people to take risks and try new things. They love the spotlight and revel in being the life of the party or the center of attention. *Spoiler alert #2: Can you feel John F. Kennedy, Ronald Reagan, Bill Clinton's and Parrot energy? Their toothy grins and charisma can be seen and felt across a crowded room.*

How about a **Dove**? Imagine the soothing sounds of these gentle birds as you identify their traits. What comes to mind? Maybe you selected words like calm or peaceful. As the universal symbols of love, harmony, and compassion, they seek to help others. As for conflict, no thanks. It tears at the fabric of collaboration and togetherness.

Doves are usually more reserved and in no rush to change or disrupt the status quo. They're great listeners and want to be there for you and everyone in their life. *Spoiler alert #3: Picture Jimmy Carter or Dwight Eisenhower. Both spoke a lot about their personal values and duty to the community.*

Finally, what is the first word you think of when you picture an **Owl**? If you're like most people, the word "wise" or "wisdom" comes to mind. From the Owl of Athena in ancient Greek mythology to Owl in Winnie the Pooh, this bird has been characterized as thoughtful and knowledgeable throughout history.

We're not saying that the Owl personality is the smart one. Remember, intelligence doesn't correlate to style. Still, the logical and observant nature of the Owl radiates wisdom.

What other words come to mind? You may have thought of analytical, detail-oriented, or accurate. They love to ask questions. Even the sound they make is a question! "Hooooooo?" Accident or just happy coincidence? We'll let you decide.

Know this: Owls are all about plans and tactics. If they are going to do something, you can bet that they have a plan for it. *Spoiler alert #4: George H. W. Bush and Richard Nixon were Owls…. They had plans galore.*

Notice how you were able to identify the traits of the Eagles, Parrots, Doves, and Owls. The birds embody the four personality types, making them easy to remember and apply. Soon, you'll be able to identify the styles of people around you as well as the presidential candidates.

You may already be thinking about which bird you, your spouse, your kids, and your coworkers are. Before you start playing personality whisperer, a few things to note.

First, we have all four styles. We each have varying levels of Eagle, Parrot, Dove, and Owl, and many of us are so strong in two styles that a personality assessment would reveal that we're a combination of two. (If you would like to take the assessment to identify your bird style, go to TakeFlightLearning.com/profile to purchase an online profile.)

Second, we can display any behavior regardless of our personality. Some situations require us to be flexible and take on the styles that are less natural to us. Picture a Parrot talking to an IT person because she encountered the "blue screen of death." When this technician asks what the Parrot was doing prior to this catastrophe, the Parrot may want to reply, "I don't know. It just died."

Most Parrots have no interest in troubleshooting a problem or explaining the specifics of what they were doing just before the breakdown. An Owl in the same situation might say, "I wrote down the last ten actions I took before the blue screen. I just emailed them to you in a bulleted list, starting with the earliest action and ending with the most recent."

In order to communicate more effectively, the Parrot could explain her actions in detail, as if she were an Owl. We can all be flexible when we need to be. The more flexible we are, the more effective we are. When we lack flexibility, we get into trouble.

Third, people can change over time. Life experiences can impact us so profoundly that our personality changes over time. Imagine the structured, disciplined Owl who becomes more carefree and Parrot-like in retirement. Picture the Dove who has had enough of people stepping on him and starts to act more Eagle-like. He learns to stand in his power and assert his needs with conviction. Our personalities don't change quickly, easily, or dramatically, but they can change a bit over time. *Spoiler Alert #5: Joe Biden's personality changed between his time as Vice President and his election campaign in 2020.*

Fourth, some traits are shared by all presidential candidates. Whatever their style, candidates for president tend to be confident, ambitious, optimistic, active, competitive, courageous, dutiful, idealistic, outspoken, and even a bit narcissistic. Wouldn't they need to be a bit conceited to think that they should be *the one* to run the world's most powerful nation? While some of these traits relate to a specific style, in the rarified air of the presidency, some traits transcend style.

Birding Practice

Before we reveal the styles of the presidential candidates, we'd like to show you how we came to our decisions. Let's go birdwatching to see how personality predictions are made. (Vests, khaki hats, and binoculars are optional.)

We'll name some folks from each style. See if you can figure out which bird they are.

First up, Simon Cowell. Recall the early days of American Idol. He was brutal. His bluntness regularly offended his fellow Dove judge, Paula Abdul, and his feedback sometimes made contestants cry. You want honesty? You got it. He didn't pull any punches. He stated exactly what he thought of people's abilities. He's toned it down in recent years but is still one style to the core.

Which bird?

Yep, you guessed it. He's an Eagle. He's straight to the point and about as dominant as they get. So are Jeff Bezos, Michelle Obama, Arnold Schwarzenegger, and Serena Williams.

How about legendary television personality, Mr. Rogers. With a soft voice and genuine compassion, he taught 1970s kids to be kind and respectful. What style does that sound like? You got it. He's a Dove. So are Princess Diana, Beyoncé, Howard Schultz, and Pharrell Williams.

Let's take a fictional character: Hermione Granger from the Harry Potter books. She knows all the spells, does all the homework, and always raises her hand in class. She saves Harry and Ron by knowing her magic and formulating clever plans.

What style? She's an Owl all the way. Other Owls include Bill Gates, Warren Buffet, Jerry Seinfeld, and yes, Emma Watson herself.

Next up, three late-night TV hosts whose parents named them James: Jimmy Fallon, Jimmy Kimmel, and James Corden. What style do you think they share? They think fast on their feet, sport big smiles, and exude positivity. They bring laughter to millions and have conversations for a living. What a perfect job for a…Parrot. Notice how easily you are identifying people's personalities. *Saturday Night Live's* Kate McKinnon is also a Parrot. So are Miley Cyrus, Kevin Hart, Jennifer Lawrence, and Katy Perry.

Personality in Action

Let's see how the styles play out in the real world with two actors whose personalities drove their approach to the craft. Compare Daniel Day Lewis to the late Robin Williams. We can agree that they're both outstanding actors. But they went about it differently.

Robin Williams was so dynamic, off-the-cuff, and unpredictable that when he played the Genie in Disney's *Aladdin*, he ad-libbed many of the lines. Williams did his thing, and the illustrators had to depict whatever he said. The magic was in his spontaneity.

In the more serious movie *Good Will Hunting*, Williams improvised while playing the therapist Dr. Maguire. In one scene about accepting imperfections in a partner, Maguire tells Matt Damon's character that his late wife farted so loudly in her sleep that she once woke up the dog, which woke her up. That was ad-libbed. No one knew he would say that, which is why Damon's character broke into genuine laughter. For Williams, making things up on the spot brought the scene to a new level.

Daniel Day Lewis, the only man who has ever won the Oscar for Best Actor three times, is a method actor. He learned Czech so he could speak English with a Czech accent in a movie adapted from Milan Kundera's *The Unbearable Lightness of Being*. He tracked and skinned animals, built a canoe, learned to fire a flintlock rifle, and then carried his rifle to Christmas dinner while preparing to be Hawkeye in *Last of the Mohicans*. Allegedly, while playing Abraham Lincoln, he sexted Sally Field who was playing Lincoln's wife, Mary Todd. Thankfully, she understood his approach and responded in character.

Daniel Day Lewis spends months embodying the character he'll play. Robin Williams made up his lines on the spot. Their styles are completely different, but they are both acting geniuses. Can you guess their bird styles?

If you guessed that Williams is Parrot and Lewis is an Owl, we agree with you. And that's how it's done. Once you know the styles, you can quickly and intuitively read them in others. By the time you finish this book, you will become what the Audubon Society refers to as a Master Birder.

Dead People Can't Take Personality Assessments

Identifying the style of a celebrity is one thing, but this book hinges on accurately identifying the presidential candidates. We can't make them take a personality assessment, especially if they're no longer with us.

So, how did we do it? We based our determinations on a variety of sources. We watched videos of debates and speeches. We tuned into their tone, body language, and connection to the audience. We examined what they said and wrote and looked at the decisions they made. We studied what presidential scholars, authors, and journalists said about them. We reviewed interviews with their colleagues. Using all this information, we linked each candidate to the four styles.

For example, British journalist Paul Johnson once said, "The most intimidating world leader was Lyndon Johnson." Does that sound like a Dove? Of course not. It's a clue that he may be an Eagle.

Jimmy Carter said, "The measure of a society is found in how they help their weakest and most helpless citizens." Doves are compassionate, caring, and giving, so that's a decent clue.

In addition to studying what candidates said, we tuned into how they said it. Parrots like Robin Williams don't have a monopoly on humor. The *way* that Williams delivered a joke—with a big grin, dynamic body language, funny accents, and sheer delight—screamed Parrot. An Owl comedian who is more logical and less animated, like Jerry Seinfeld, can be just as funny but in a different way.

Point being, we examined the available evidence and never based our call on a single statement or incident because there are always anomalies. Instead, we looked at overall behavior patterns and how people perceived them *in their own time.*

Who we are in Public Versus Private

In 2016, a common defense of Hillary Clinton went like this: she seems stiff and impersonal on TV, but she's lovely and charming in private. That's probably true.

If you've taken a personality assessment, it may have contained a description of your private self versus your public self. You might act differently at work than at home. Sometimes, the same holds true for presidents.

Senator Bob Dole was supposedly a jovial Parrot in his private life but seemed like a rigid Owl in public. Al Gore was an Owl policy wonk on TV but supposedly a more relaxed guy in private. George W. Bush, "the Decider," went hardcore Eagle in public. At home and in less guarded moments, he supposedly was a fun, light-hearted Parrot.

We identify the style of each presidential candidate based on their public self, but we give a nod to their private identity if it's different.

How Personality Strengths Turn into Weaknesses

In *The Count of Monte Cristo*, novelist Alexander Dumas wrote, "Any virtue carried to the extreme can become a crime." And so it is with personality. When we use our style at a healthy level, the strengths drive our success and enable us to develop healthy relationships. When we overuse our strengths, they become our weaknesses.

Overused, Eagle directness becomes insensitive. Dial up Parrot optimism, and it becomes impractical. Too much focus on accuracy for the Owl turns into perfectionism and analysis paralysis. Even an excess of Dove kindness can become smothering. It's not that a style is good or bad. We just need to use our styles at a healthy level instead of pushing them into the red zone, where strengths become weaknesses.

Trump, who you surely recognize is an Eagle, spent much of his election campaigns and the presidency in overuse mode. Even after taking the White House in 2016, he went into hardcore overuse mode about the size of his inauguration day crowd on January 20, 2017. His pride and overriding need to win could not tolerate the idea that Obama had a bigger crowd, even when the photo evidence made that clear. Competitiveness helped Trump win the election, but in overuse mode, it turned a momentous occasion into a controversy. *Spoiler Alert #6: Eagle overuse probably lost Trump the 2020 election.*

Trump was hardly the only president to carry their personality to extremes. As you'll see, even revered presidents like Franklin D. Roosevelt and John F. Kennedy spent time in overuse mode. We are *all* susceptible to the extremes of our personality—it just matters a bit more when the overuser has America's nuclear launch codes.

The Big Assumption

Most of us grew up learning a version of the Golden Rule: "Do unto others as you would have them do unto you." If you want people to be kind to you, be kind to them. If you want people to be honest with you, be honest with them. Treat others how *you* want to be treated.

But what if we told you that the Golden Rule is *not* meant to be applied to all areas of life? In matters of personality, the Golden Rule can do more harm than good.

Picture an Eagle who values candor and hurts a Dove's feelings with "harsh" words. Or imagine an Owl who provides so many instructions to his Parrot spouse that she feels untrusted. When we treat others the way *we* want to be treated, we assume that they have the same needs we do. Our intentions are good, but others may react negatively because their personality-driven needs aren't being met.

Let's apply this to elections. Why are some politicians determined to share their detailed plans for everything troubling America while others speak in sound-bite slogans? Because they operate under The Big Assumption:

If it's important to me, it's important to everyone.

They assume that people like what they like, want what they want, and need what they need. If they value something, others must value it too. The public must desire information the way they desire to see it, read it, and process it.

Candidates fall prey to The Big Assumption when they believe that if an issue is important to them, it's important to everyone. In turn, they communicate how *they* would want information shared with them. Overall, they run their campaigns to appeal to themselves because they believe that will inspire the electorate to vote for them.

Consider how Hillary Clinton applied The Big Assumption to her candidacy. To this day, her personal website shares "a comprehensive progressive vision for America's future" from her 2016 campaign. It covers forty-one different issues with at least five policies for each! Clinton assumed that voters might need to read over 200 policy ideas because, well, that's how Clinton would evaluate a candidate. But not everyone cares about policies. By imposing the needs of her personality on others, Clinton made The Big Assumption.

For Dove and Owl candidates, The Big Assumption can be devastating. After the debates between Al Gore and George W. Bush, the pundits said that Gore seemed stiff and dispassionate as he spouted statistics, plans, and future policies in relentless detail. Effectively, the pundits criticized Gore for being an Owl. He suffered from The Big Assumption. How can voters make a decision without *all* of that information?

Ironically, The Big Assumption can often work *for* Eagles and Parrots during presidential campaigns. A big-picture vision is easy to consume and digest, but detailed plans are hard to swallow. When these energizing personalities treat the public like they themselves would like to be treated, they inspire voters with action-oriented slogans and catchy messaging.

Recall Donald Trump's Make America Great Again campaign compared to Hillary Clinton's 'Let me tell you exactly what I am going to do about every issue in excruciating detail' strategy.

Some candidates, like Bill Clinton and Ronald Reagan, seemed to intuitively understand and transcend The Big Assumption. Instead of speaking strictly in their own style, they flexed to the diverse needs of their audiences. Watch videos of their speeches, and you'll find Eagle, Parrot, Dove, and Owl moments. With chameleon-like adaptability, they appealed to everyone, not just people who shared their personality.

How Does Personality Elect Presidents?

You can see that personality is visible throughout the election process, but how does it sway voters? That's the question that we'll examine in the next two sections, starting with the Founding Fathers.

Section III:
The Early Years

Personality in Everything

In an era of unelected kings and queens, General George Washington was an enigma. After leading the Continental Army to victory against the British, Washington easily could have ruled over the former colonies as "King of America." Some revolutionary factions wanted that. Yet once the Revolutionary War officially ended in 1783, Washington resigned his commission, eager to retire to his Mt. Vernon estate.

Across time, rebel and revolutionary leaders had always capitalized on military victories to seize political power. Who was Washington to break this historical precedent?

Washington's personality is critical to understanding the early years of the republic and the nature of its presidential campaigns. His words and actions influenced how presidential candidates were expected to behave. In turn, those expectations shaped which personality styles were best positioned to win the presidency.

Essentially, Washington was forced into power after the 69 members of the electoral college unanimously elected him the first president of the United States of America on February 4, 1789. Washington didn't campaign for the role or put himself on the ballot. After receiving the news, the general compared his feelings to those of "…a culprit who is going to the place of his execution."

As Ron Chernow writes in his biography of Washington, the general doubted his ability to be a successful president. He felt he could never meet the public's high expectations. He feared being subject to public critique. Clearly not an Eagle.

The president-elect also loathed the festivities, parades, and ceremonies that greeted him on the road from Mt. Vernon to the first inauguration in New York. He wanted no pomp and ceremony. He pleaded with New York Governor George Clinton for a "…quiet entry devoid of ceremony." Clearly not a Parrot.

Washington's first inaugural address aired all his anxieties and doubts. "Among the vicissitudes incident to life," read the first line, "no event could have filled me with greater anxieties" than the call to lead the nation. He felt he was accepting an "order" and acting in "obedience to the public summons," as he explained later in the address. He was quiet and trembly throughout the speech according to observers.

Can you imagine a modern president starting their inaugural address by telling the public how much they dread the job?

That leaves two possibilities: Owl or Dove? Thomas Jefferson, who had a long and complicated relationship with Washington, provided the most telling description of his personality in a letter to Virginia politician Walter Jones, written 15 years after Washington passed:

> Perhaps the strongest feature in [Washington's] character was prudence, never acting until every circumstance, every consideration was maturely weighed; refraining if he saw a doubt, but, when once decided, going through with his purpose whatever obstacles opposed. His integrity was most pure, his justice the most inflexible I have ever known, no motives of interest or consanguinity, of friendship or hatred, being able to bias his decision.

A leader who weighs all the information and data, commits single-mindedly to a plan, and never allows himself to be biased by emotions or relationships? That is an Owl.

Jefferson also noted that "...no General ever planned his battles more judiciously" than Washington, but if the plan was thwarted, "he was slow in re-adjustment." Owl again. They prepare fastidiously but hate changing anything on the fly.

In addition, the first president's "...heart was not warm in its affections; but he exactly calculated every man's value, and gave him a solid esteem proportioned to it." Classically unbiased Owl who cares about merit.

And if that isn't Owl enough, Jefferson noted that "...in public when called on for a sudden opinion, he was unready, short, and embarrassed." Owls do not like being put on the spot. They prefer to reflect carefully before giving an opinion.

As for why Washington didn't use his position of immense power and prestige to seize control of America, Jefferson nodded again to his personality: "[Washington] has often declared to me that he considered our new constitution as an experiment on the practicability of republican government, and with what dose of liberty man could be trusted for his own good: that he was determined the experiment should have a fair trial, and would lose the last drop of his blood in support of it."

As an Owl, Washington was skeptical of this risky, untested form of government but believed in running a real experiment. In fact, said Jefferson, he was "naturally distrustful of men, and inclined to gloomy apprehensions." He couldn't be more Owl!

That, in short, is how we deciphered the personalities of early presidents. Their personalities shined through contemporary descriptions, speeches, debate transcripts, and quotes. Their actions in office often signaled their personalities as well.

We could explore the legendary stories of Washington's honesty and exactness in business for further evidence, but the picture is clear enough. Washington was an Owl and an extremely reluctant president with a loud inner critic. These traits seemed to shape what voters and their elected representatives expected from a presidential candidate—at least until the 1932 election.

The Quiet Birds

In the first 152 years of the United States, Owls and Doves dominated the presidency. In total, there were 13 Owls presidents and 12 Doves. Only three Eagles and two Parrots led the nation.

The question is why Owls and Doves outcompeted Eagles and Parrots in this era. Maybe American culture favored the more restrained, contemplative personalities of Owls and Doves.

The first six presidents—George Washington, John Adams, Thomas Jefferson, James Madison, James Monroe, and John Quincy Adams—were all Owls. In a vulnerable new nation experimenting to replace absolute rule by monarchs with a rules-based democratic order, perhaps that was no coincidence. Owls are sticklers for the rules and well-suited to interpret and rigorously apply a confusing document like the Constitution. Doves, too, are protective of institutions and the values on which they stand.

Another reason Owls and Doves dominated the presidency is that candidates weren't supposed to promote themselves! Washington set a precedent that wanting executive power was unbecoming of the office. It was considered inappropriate for candidates to appeal to voters directly during a campaign. Local allies and surrogates spoke on their behalf and hosted parades and rallies while the candidate remained at home receiving important visitors.

Newspapers commented on the candidates' personalities, but papers of the time were known to be highly partisan. Campaigns invented catchy songs and printed and distributed materials touting their candidate. Still, reading or hearing that someone is charismatic, for example, is very different from experiencing their charisma in person. Few American voters experienced the candidates' personalities the way we do now.

To win the presidency before 1932, a domineering Eagle or self-aggrandizing Parrot had to emulate Owls and Doves or create a competitive playing field. As you'll see, that is what the first Eagle and Parrot presidents did.

Old (Flexible) Hickory and the Red Fox

In the first 104 years of the U.S. presidency, there was only one Eagle (Andrew Jackson) and one Parrot (Martin Van Buren). Jackson's personality was problematic in an election, and he knew it. As CBS reporter John Dickerson recounts in his book *Whistlestop,* Jackson realized that to win the presidency, he had to act like he didn't want it. He also had to hide many of his Eagle tendencies.

PRESIDENTS FROM 1789-1928

	GEORGE WASHINGTON		ANDREW JOHNSON
	JOHN ADAMS		ULYSSES S. GRANT
	THOMAS JEFFERSON		RUTHERFORD B. HAYES
	JAMES MADISON		JAMES GARFIELD
	JAMES MONROE		CHESTER A. ARTHUR
	JOHN QUINCY ADAMS		GROVER CLEVELAND
	ANDREW JACKSON		BENJAMIN HARRISON
	MARTIN VAN BUREN		GROVER CLEVELAND
	WILLIAM HENRY HARRISON		WILLIAM MCKINLEY
	JOHN TYLER		THEODORE ROOSEVELT
	JAMES POLK		WILLIAM HOWARD TAFT
	ZACHARY TAYLOR		WOODROW WILSON
	MILLARD FILLMORE		WARREN HARDING
	FRANKLIN PIERCE		CALVIN COOLIDGE
	JAMES BUCHANAN		HERBERT HOOVER
	ABRAHAM LINCOLN		

PRESIDENTS FROM 1789-1928

ANDREW JACKSON
JAMES GARFIELD
THEODORE ROOSEVELT

MARTIN VAN BUREN
WILLIAM HOWARD TAFT

GEORGE WASHINGTON
JOHN ADAMS
THOMAS JEFFERSON
JAMES MADISON
JAMES MONROE
JOHN QUINCY ADAMS
JAMES POLK
ANDREW JOHNSON
GROVER CLEVELAND
BENJAMIN HARRISON
WOODROW WILSON
CALVIN COOLIDGE
HERBERT HOOVER

WILLIAM HENRY HARRISON
JOHN TYLER
ZACHARY TAYLOR
MILLARD FILLMORE
FRANKLIN PIERCE
JAMES BUCHANAN
ABRAHAM LINCOLN
ULYSSES S. GRANT
RUTHERFORD B. HAYES
CHESTER A. ARTHUR
WILLIAM MCKINLEY
WARREN HARDING

Mainstream politicians and journalists viewed Jackson, infamously a hothead, brawler, and duelist, as a threat to the rule of law—and not without reason. He had overstepped his authority as a U.S. general by, for instance, invading Florida without permission, breaking treaties with Native Americans, and executing mutineers. But he achieved major military victories, like the 1815 Battle of New Orleans against the British, which cemented his reputation as a war hero and effective leader.

Once he set his eyes on the presidency, Jackson held his infamous temper, made a point of acting statesmanlike, and positioned himself as an ally of the people against the elite. This was a political innovation and savvy strategy for an Eagle in this era.

In 1824, Jackson lost the election despite carrying 43% of the popular vote (a story for another time). After decisively winning office in 1828, however, Jackson ended his charade of docility. He became the first and only president to ever be censured by the Senate—a rather Eagle distinction.

"Old Hickory" wanted to unilaterally dissolve the Bank of the United States, which he considered an unconstitutional, rich man's entity. In 1832, he vetoed a bill to renew its charter. Then in 1833, he instructed Treasury Secretary William J. Duane to withdraw all federal deposits from the bank. When Duane refused, Jackson dismissed him and installed a treasury secretary who would do his bidding.

When hard-core Eagles want something done, they don't worry about rules or appearances. They do whatever is necessary. Gone was the Owl and Dove façade that won the presidency.

Jackson's strong-arm tactics led to the bank's demise in 1836 and may have caused an economic crash in 1837. The Senate censure, adopted 26 to 20 in 1834, asserted that Jackson "…has assumed upon himself authority and power not conferred by the Constitution and laws, but in derogation of both."

Jackson wasn't having it. In a response he insisted be published in the Senate journal (it wasn't), he claimed, "It was settled by the Constitution, the laws, and whole practice of the government that the entire executive power is vested in the President of the United States." That sure sounds like a militant Eagle accustomed to wielding supreme authority on the battlefield.

Had the first six presidents of the United States been Eagles in Jackson's image, there's a good chance the executive branch would have grown in power. Jackson was the lone Eagle president until Eagle-Parrot James Garfield won in 1881. He, like Jackson, refrained from self-aggrandizement and stayed home while others stumped on his behalf.

Martin Van Buren, Jackson's endorsed successor, was the only Parrot to win the presidency until Grover Cleveland in 1885. Van Buren knew how to play the Owl and Dove game. Nicknamed the Red Fox of Kinderhook (his birthplace) and the Little Magician, Van Buren was known as a charming conversationalist and clever political operator. He could draw out other people's opinions without revealing his stance on anything.

When the dominant Democratic-Republican Party splintered over Jackson's loss in 1824, Van Buren became Jackson's hype man and built the new Democratic Party to ensure Old Hickory's victory in 1828. Van Buren had a head start on the other splinter, the smaller Whig Party, which didn't coalesce until 1833 and couldn't muster as many members anyway.

If personality won in Van Buren's case, it's because he had the Parrot knack for building a coalition that could not lose in 1836 by sheer force of its numbers. Interestingly, Richard Nixon would one day benefit from the splintering of the Democratic Party that Van Buren created. Nixon's personality wasn't a winner in its time either.

The point is that Jackson and Van Buren didn't win the presidency by being proud Eagles and Parrots. Rather, they flexed their personalities to the culture and campaigning style of their age.

Inventing the Campaign Trail

Every candidate followed the precedent of staying home during presidential campaigns until 1840, when General William Henry "Old Tippecanoe" Harrison, a Dove-Owl, traveled around delivering his own speeches. His was also the first campaign to feature mass rallies, parades, and big donations to candidates.

Still, Harrison's campaign needed to recruit an army of surrogate speakers to canvas the nation for one simple reason: the realities of transportation.

The first American railroad began its regularly scheduled service in 1830. There were approximately 23 miles of railroad in 1830; 2,808 in 1840; and 9,021 in 1850. Travel times reflected that. In 1800, it took six weeks to travel from New York to the western edge of Illinois, according to the 1932 *Atlas of the Historical Geography of the United States*. In 1830, it still took three weeks. Not until 1857 could someone get from New York to Illinois in a day. No wonder few candidates followed Harrison's winning model.

Once the railroads spanned nationwide, however, most candidates still didn't hit the campaign trail. Not even Teddy Roosevelt, an Eagle-Parrot with a beaming personality and adventurous streak, took to the rails. He stayed in Washington fulfilling his duties as vice president while others stumped on his behalf.

The norms of campaigning wouldn't shift permanently until Franklin D. Roosevelt's candidacy in 1932. FDR felt pressure to show that despite his polio, he could lead the nation with vigor. Thus, he flew to Chicago to accept the Democratic nomination in person—something candidates never did before—and gave 60 speeches around the country.

Personality Won

For the first 139 years of U.S. presidential elections, Owls and Doves overwhelmingly won. The cultural expectations for a U.S. president, campaigning norms, and the media environment seemed to favor these personalities. The expected charade of not wanting the presidency was more of a challenge for a driven Eagle or effusive Parrot than a calculating Owl or deferential Dove.

Even after Harrison broke the taboo on self-promotion in 1840, candidates were slow to start tooting their own horns. And still, trains and print media could only amplify personality so much.

Between 1904 and 1928, Owls and Doves beat Eagles and Parrots. Doves and Owls won in the world of private politicking, impersonal campaigning, and slow-speed communications.

But things were about to change.

Section IV:
The Ultimate Personality Contest

The Pattern of U.S. Elections

The time has come to reveal the pattern behind the past 23 U.S. presidential elections. This pattern holds true regardless of whether a candidate is new or an incumbent. It has nothing to do with peace, war, or the state of the economy. This pattern is not influenced by the candidates' previous experience or whether they come from the military, government, or business. None of that seems to matter.

As you just learned, personality won between 1789 and 1928. Owls and Doves founded the U.S. and overwhelmingly held the presidency. The few Eagle and Parrot presidents flexed their personalities to demonstrate Owl and Dove qualities—at least until they took office. Then suddenly, the personality pattern flipped.

So, here's the pattern: In general elections since 1932, the energetic, bigger personalities of Eagles and Parrots have beaten the more reserved, soft-spoken Doves and Owls. With two notable exceptions, Eagles and

Parrots have won whenever they have gone head-to-head against Doves and Owls.

There have been Dove and Owl presidents in the past eight decades. But Doves and Owls have won only when they've faced off against other Doves and Owls. Jimmy Carter, a Dove, is a prime example. He defeated Gerald Ford, another Dove. Both candidates had a shot. We were destined to have a Dove president.

The next time around, when Carter faced the larger-than-life personality of Ronald Reagan, The Great Communicator won. A Dove can win against another Dove but loses against a Parrot. This pattern of Eagles and Parrots beating Doves and Owls has happened over and over and over again. For the Owls among us, you can add in 19 more "overs."

The are two anomalies. In 1968, Republican Owl Richard Nixon beat Hubert Humphrey, a Democratic Parrot nominee, and George Wallace, an independent Eagle who split from the Democratic Party. The Parrot and Eagle divided the personality vote. The other anomaly is Joe Biden, currently a Dove-Parrot, who beat arch-Eagle Donald Trump in the 2020 election.

What Changed in 1932?

In a word: radio. When Franklin Delano Roosevelt went on the Lucky Strike Radio program on April 7, 1932, the U.S. was in the throes of the Great Depression. FDR, then governor of New York, had a shot at becoming the Democratic candidate, who would then challenge President Herbert Hoover in November.

It was only FDR's fourth time on the radio. He opened with Eagle confidence and vision:

These unhappy times call for the building of plans that rest upon the forgotten, the unorganized but the indispensable units of economic power for plans like those of 1917 that build from the bottom up and not from the top down, that put their faith once more in the forgotten man at the bottom of the economic pyramid.

This became known as the "Forgotten Man" speech. Millions of distressed Americans heard FDR speak up for the farmers, factory workers, and small-town merchants who were suffering while Hoover's "top-down" plan bailed out large corporations and banks. This speech positioned FDR as a leader of the Democratic Party and a tough advocate for the people.

With radio, FDR could speak directly to the public in his famous fireside chats. Radio would help FDR win four straight elections. It was the first medium that allowed tens of millions of Americans to hear a candidate's voice from anywhere in the country.

For the first time, a candidate could inspire and energize the entire population. For the first time, Americans could make snap judgments about candidates' personalities. Radio upended how Americans understand, assess, and compare presidential candidates. Cultural norms that had long insisted on humble, reluctant presidents couldn't stand up to the dynamic, spirited candidates who took to the airwaves.

The next time you hop on the phone with a stranger, notice how much information you get from the tone, cadence, pace, rhythm, and level of excitement in their voice. Notice how much detail they share and the amount of small talk they engage in. Those cues are more than enough to determine whether you're speaking to an Eagle, Parrot, Dove, or Owl.

A few decades after radio emerged, television gave personality an even bigger platform. On September 26, 1960, John F. Kennedy and Richard Nixon faced off in the first-ever televised debate between two presidential candidates. The 70 million people who watched the debate on TV thought that the young Kennedy, with his good looks, charm, and presence, beat Nixon.

60 Minutes founder Don Hewitt said that Kennedy was "looking tan and fit...this guy was a matinee idol," whereas Nixon looked "like death warmed over." To be fair, he was in pain and had been hospitalized recently. Chicago Mayor Richard J. Daley, whose city hosted the debate, supposedly said of Nixon, "My God, they've embalmed him before he even died."

Meanwhile, people who listened to the debate on radio thought that it was a draw or that Nixon had won! His Owl plans and logic scored points with listeners but didn't register with viewers who saw a shifty, anxious, ashen guy sweating next to the bronze, athletic Kennedy.

TV debates became a permanent fixture of presidential politics. There was no going back to the radio days. There was no going back to the print-only days. There was no going back to an era where party leaders could reduce the presidential candidate pool to Owls and Doves who would bow to precedent and staunchly adhere to the Constitution and its rules. The brave new world of public attention wars, in-your-face campaigning, and high-speed soundbites meant that backroom Democrats and Republicans couldn't filter out Eagles and Parrots anymore. Power was shifting from the parties to individual members with big vision, bold ideas, and charismatic energy.

In the following decades, presidents would spend more and more time on television and master it. In 1984, *The New York Times* wrote of Reagan, "He and his aides have also achieved a new level of control over the mechanics of modern communication—the staging of news events for maximum press coverage, the timing of announcements to hit the largest television audiences."

In 2008, technology changed yet again. Barack Obama became the first candidate to run a campaign on social media. His 3 million Facebook followers were quadruple what John McCain had, and his Twitter following was 23 times greater than McCain's. Obama could have commanded attention on any medium, but on social networks, he was unstoppable.

The Digitized Candidate

Social media has given candidates the power to project their personalities anytime, anywhere, with images, video, audio, and text. TV stations can crop sound bites and throw a positive or negative spin on what candidates say, but social media is unmediated. Whatever a candidate wants to say is precisely what the public will see or hear. When Donald Trump had direct access to more than 88 million Twitter followers, he could announce executive orders, start trade wars, and move stock markets while sitting on the toilet (hypothetically—we have no proof that he was a toilet tweeter).

Twitter, Facebook, Instagram, TikTok, and Trump's Truth Social are the perfect mediums for confident Eagles and self-promoting Parrots who know how to construct their own pithy sound bites. Their outrage, humor, and aggression are concise and go viral easily. Owl logic and Dove empathy, which are more understated, don't hook people the same way. They raise questions rather than provide juicy, quotable answers.

Put simply, today's mass media favors Eagles and Parrots and gives us a one-dimensional view of presidential candidates. The more we tune into mass media, the more we know about candidates' personalities and the less we know about their policies.

America's Owl and Dove founders mistrusted Eagle and Parrot leaders whose personalities seemed more befitting of a royal dictatorship than a rules-based democratic order. Now though, most Americans have no direct experience with living under authoritarian rule. When they judge presidential candidates by their tone, body language, and an IV drip of addictive tweets, they don't see a would-be tyrant. In fact, they seem to prefer assertive, dominant, and enthusiastic presidents over calm, analytical, and policy-driven leaders. But why?

Electability and Candidate Likability

You can hear it in the dynamism, volume, and range of their voices. You can see it in their big grins and contagious smiles. You can experience it in the wild applause they get. Eagle and Parrot leaders energize crowds and make us want to vote. They have an "it" factor, a magnetic quality that's hard to define. The softer, calmer Doves and Owls just don't have this quality. Before 1932, that didn't matter because candidates stayed home while others stumped on their behalf.

Compared to Doves and Owls, Eagles and Parrots seem to arouse emotions, horde attention, and create feelings of loyalty. In addition, they signal two qualities we value in a president: electability and likability.

Eagles and Parrots score high on electability because they command attention. They exude confidence and inspire belief in their grand ideas. The media reports on the energy they create at their rallies. The more excited they are, the more excited their followers get. That passion translates into action in the voter booth.

Doves and Owls are less electable in modern times because their communication doesn't cater well to short-form media. They obsess over their plans and explain in painstaking detail what they will do if elected president. Plans don't inspire emotion and they don't motivate the electorate to vote. To Americans who treat politics like a spectator sport, the Dove and Owl candidates basically say, "Get ready for four boring years!"

Parrots and Doves score high on likability because they tend to be personable, smiley, and appealing. They're friendly and easily connect with people. When you think of someone who's a "people person," it's probably a Parrot or Dove.

Eagles score low on candidate likability because they are relatively candid and uncompromising. They say what they mean and don't worry about the impact on others. Their words can come across as harsh, and they occasionally offend the electorate.

Owls also score low on candidate likability because they are relatively low-key and matter-of-fact. They don't exude emotion and excite the electorate. They offer plans in vast detail, but plans don't create connection or build rapport.

During a campaign, electability is more important to voters than likability. Unlikable yet electable Eagles beat likable yet unelectable Doves every time. A candidate who is both electable and likable—an Eagle and Parrot combo or an Eagle and Dove combo—has the best odds of winning an election and being liked in office.

It's important to note that while Eagles and Owls score low on *candidate* likability, this has nothing to do with *personal* likability. Outside the confines of an election, they can be funny and quite engaging. George W. Bush, Bob Dole, and Al Gore are prime examples of this.

Looking back to 2016, how did a two-minute news segment or tweet capture Owl Hillary Clinton's facts, data, and nuanced plans? Not well. She seemed unelectable and was described as unlikable. All the qualities that would have made her a shoo-in before 1932 made her a long shot in modern America. But Donald Trump's Eagle vision—to Make America Great Again—was ubiquitous on hats and hashtags. Trump may not have been likable to many voters, but he was electable.

American voters recognize self-confidence, extraversion, and toughness when they get quick hits of presidential candidates on radio, TV, and social media. They also recognize introversion, detachment, and scholarliness from snapshots, but they don't like these qualities in a leader. Instead, reserved candidates come across as boring, weak, and uninteresting. And although they might deeply care about the public and have better ideas for advancing American prosperity, voters find them too cold and too docile.

Essentially, American voters link big personalities to competence when the best proxy for competence is a president's performance on radio, TV, and digital media. Eagles and Parrots don't necessarily make better presidents than Doves and Owls. But a majority of American voters think they will.

The Most Likable POTUS

Eagles fall into the electable but not likable box during the election, but are they likable as presidents? No, they are not. Eagles win elections, but they are often unpopular once in office. They do what they think needs to be done and don't care whether others like it.

Let's look at the data. Gallup began conducting presidential approval polls in 1937. Since then, there have been four Eagle presidents who did not have a secondary Parrot style: Harry Truman, Lyndon Johnson, George W. Bush, and Donald Trump. These former presidents received four of the five lowest Final Approval Ratings in Gallup's records. At the bottom of the list, Nixon bowed out with just 24% approval. Not surprising. Truman ended his presidency at 32%. Both Carter, a Dove-Owl who became cynical and hopeless under pressure, and Bush were at 34%. Trump also ended at 34% and became the first president on record never to register a 50% or higher approval rating. Johnson closed out at 49%.

Add some Parrot energy to the Eagle, though, and likability rises dramatically. Three presidents since 1927 had strong Eagle and Parrot personalities, and two of them clocked the highest Final Approval Ratings. Franklin Delano Roosevelt departed at 65% and Bill Clinton left office at 66%. John F. Kennedy, the other Parrot-Eagle, had the highest Average Approval Rating at an incredible 70.1%.

As for Joe Biden, a likable Dove-Parrot, he started his presidency with a relatively high approval rating—57% at one point. However, he lost approval as his actions in office undermined perceptions of competence (more on that in Amtrak Joe's own chapter).

The Eagle-Parrot and Parrot-Eagle combos are not only electable but also well liked once they are in office. This makes them easy to elect twice (or four times).

In Defense of the Birds

To be clear, we are discussing likability only in the context of presidential elections. Owls and Eagles can be very likable when they're not trying to become the leader of the free world. Indeed, you know many who are. They just may not strike the broader electorate as likable.

Also, it might seem like we've crushed the dreams of millions of Dove and Owl kids who want to be president someday. We're not saying that Doves and Owls can't win the presidency. We are saying that in modern history, Eagles and Parrots win in head-to-head contests with Doves and Owls. Perhaps this knowledge will encourage Doves and Owls to become more chameleon-like and appeal to all four styles.

Some of America's best presidents have been Doves and Owls. George Washington, an Owl with a smidge of Eagle, defeated the British and successfully led the United States through its early, turbulent years because he was an exceptional planner. "There is nothing so likely to produce peace as to be well prepared to meet the enemy," wrote Washington in a letter discussing his war strategy. As president, he didn't make decisions quickly. Washington said, "Decision making, like coffee, needs a cooling process."

Thomas Jefferson, the third president and the main author of the Declaration of Independence, was an Owl with some Parrot. He was known to speak in a soft voice and gave few public addresses. If he had been forced to debate his contemporaries on TV, he would have seemed shy and awkward.

Abraham Lincoln, a Dove with a tinge of Parrot, spoke with empathy and humility. After the Battle of Gettysburg, where the Union dealt a decisive blow to the Confederacy, Lincoln gave his most famous speech. Yet he downplayed his words as nothing compared to the actions of the slain soldiers: "The world will little note, nor long remember what we say here, but it can never forget what they did here."

Lincoln was wrong. His words were immortalized in monuments and history books. Can you imagine one of our Eagle or Parrot presidents reminding you that their words don't matter?! Never.

All three of these presidents are immortalized on Mt. Rushmore yet would have poor odds of winning a modern election. Theodore Roosevelt, the sole Eagle on Mt. Rushmore, was known to be a patron and political ally of the artist who led the project. He had his merits, but c'mon....

The lack of Dove and Owl presidents in the 20th and 21st centuries may be a detriment to the country. Every eight years since 1982, Siena College Research Institute has polled presidential scholars on who they think the best and worst presidents are. The top 10 list is split relatively evenly between Eagle, Parrot, Dove, and Owl leaders.

Personality doesn't determine a president's success, but it does affect how a president will go about being successful. Unfortunately, some of history's best presidents had personalities that could not get elected today—unless they went against people like themselves.

First Impressions about Personality are Surprisingly Accurate

Eagles and Parrots have an advantage over Doves and Owls because modern voters base their choices on first impressions that are shockingly accurate—at least about personality.

In 1993, Stanford social psychologist Nalini Ambady wanted to see if people could form accurate impressions of strangers based on tiny slices of information. She showed students three 10-second clips of professors—with the audio off—and asked them to rate the nonverbal behavior of the professor.

Based on those short clips, the participants could accurately predict the ratings these teachers received from students who took their courses for an entire semester. When Ambady shortened the clips from 10 seconds to five seconds and then again to two seconds, students were still shockingly accurate. They could tell which professors were liked most or least.

It took students two seconds to gauge likability.

What about elections? In 2005, researchers from Princeton University asked people to rate the competence of Senate and House candidates from past elections based on black-and-white headshots of the winner and runner-up. The candidates they perceived as more "competent" won 71.6% of Senate races and 66.8% of House races. Even when people were given just one second to view the two candidates' faces, they predicted who would win 67.6% of the time. So, what were they tuning into? The personalities of the candidates.

A similar study from Tufts University found that American undergraduates can predict Canadian elections based on nothing more than headshots of the candidates. Interestingly, candidates who looked "powerful" to the students—meaning, they seemed like Eagles—were more likely to have won their races. Conversely, those who looked "warm"— more like Doves—were less likely to have won.

It took students seconds to gauge electability.

Snap impressions cut across cultures, but voting preferences do not. American and Japanese voters, for example, get the same impressions of each other's candidates in studies. But whereas Americans think that Japan's powerful-looking candidates won their elections, the Japanese actually voted for the warmer-looking candidates. It seems that the Personality Wins Model might just work in reverse in Japan because their electorate has different values.

46

The point is that our snap impressions of personality are pretty darn accurate and stable. When Hillary Clinton's and Mitt Romney's teams tried to make them more likable, it was too little, too late. Voters' minds were made up.

Even so, we don't necessarily trust our first impressions. We think we need more information than we actually use, so we desire more information even when we won't use it. This new information is subject to the psychological principle known as confirmation bias, our tendency to interpret new evidence as confirmation of previously held beliefs.

In 2018, researchers from the University of Chicago ran studies on how people judge art, vegetable juice, social traits like character and intellect, potential lifelong partners, and job applicants. Participants were assigned to two groups. "Experiencers" would sample (or had sampled) the thing to be judged until they'd reached an opinion. "Predictors" would estimate how many samples, how much evidence, or how much time they'd need to form an opinion.

The conclusion was sobering: People think they will collect and evaluate more information before drawing conclusions than they actually do. In every case, the experiencers used less information to make a judgment than the predictors thought they would.

Note that these studies are all based on what people see in photos and videos, not on what they read. These impressions are made possible by the TV and YouTube era.

Now, think about how these findings apply to a presidential election. Voters see photos or video clips of the candidates and instantly recognize who the Eagles, Parrots, Doves, and Owls are without using those words. Regardless, they'll read articles and watch town halls, rallies, news coverage, and debates thinking that additional information might change their minds. In reality, they're unlikely to discard or ignore what they intuitively know about the candidates' personalities.

When we think we're assessing "the issues" during a debate, we're more likely gauging personalities or reaffirming what we already think. Ditto with news reporters. Personality is all they talk about after a debate, and the candidates know this. In the few minutes candidates have to speak, they don't say much of substance about their platforms. Instead, they try to say something that will look like a win in the post-debate highlight reel.

So we assess personality quickly and form stable perceptions of the candidates. Those quick, intuitive hits ultimately drive voting preferences.

This discussion might make Americans sound shallow. Don't we care about compassion? Yes, in our relationships. What about thoughtfulness? Yeah, in our coworkers. Aren't plans better than vision? When you're going on vacation, they sure are. Wouldn't we rather have candidates who believe in peace and dialogue? Not when the news tells us that the world is dangerous and unpredictable. Why isn't logic attractive? Because for most people, emotion trumps logic.

This Is Where We Handle Your Questions and Objections

It's bold to claim that personality has been the deciding factor in American presidential elections since the founding of the country. It's even bolder to claim that we can use personality to help predict the winner of the 2024 election. We expect some pushback! So, allow us to address questions that have been raised by friends, family, colleagues, and other people, especially since publishing the original *Personality Wins* in 2020.

1. *Most individuals consistently vote either Democrat or Republican. What does personality have to do with their decisions?*

It's true that the bulk of Americans vote along ideological lines. In 2016, 94% of Democrats voted for Hillary Clinton while 92% of Republicans voted for Donald Trump, according to a Pew survey. Independents, whose votes were split almost equally between the two parties, represented 34% of the electorate. Of them, 42% went Clinton and 43% went Trump.

Swing states tend to have an equal proportion of Democrats and Republicans, so the one-third of voters that aren't chained to a party often play a powerful role in deciding the outcome of U.S. elections. The 2020 election demonstrated just how powerful.

Predictably, 95% of Democrats voted Biden, and 94% of Republicans voted Trump. However, 52% of independents swung Biden—a 10% gain over 2016! Still, 43% marked Trump on the ballot. In other words, a higher proportion of independents voted for a mainstream candidate.

Once the election is down to two candidates in the general election, it's easy to compare their personalities. In televised debates, social media, and news coverage, their personalities are on full display. Their policies, not so much.

Sometimes, the turnout of registered voters plays a big role in determining the winner. In certain swing states, elections can sometimes be won by several thousand votes out of millions cast. Well, 2020 had the highest voter turnout of any election in the 21st century, with 66.8% of eligible citizens going to the polls or mailing ballots.

However, there is no definitive relationship between personality and voter turnout. In years when Eagles and Parrots were up for election, turnout wasn't necessarily higher than when the choices included Owls and Doves. Perhaps 2020 was exceptional because the media framed the contest between Biden and Trump as an existential event for democracy.

That narrative, fair or not, drove turnout and a double-digit shift in independent support for the Democratic candidate.

2. *I disagree with your assessment of so-and-so's personality style.*

Cool, have at it. We did our best and stand by our determinations.

3. *What about the popular vote versus the Electoral College?*

In this book, we look at who gets into office, not who wins the popular vote. The Electoral College doesn't diminish or raise the importance of personality. It simply shapes campaign strategy.

For example, in 2016, six states had more registered Democrats than Republicans yet cast more votes for Trump than Clinton. These were Florida, Kentucky, Louisiana, North Carolina, Pennsylvania, and West Virginia. New Hampshire was the only Republican-majority state where Clinton won.

The Trump and Clinton campaigns disproportionately spent their time and advertising budgets in these big swing states. So, their undecided voters got more exposure to the candidates' personalities than undecided voters in, say, reliably Democratic California. Trump lost the popular vote because large numbers of voters in swing states still cast their ballots for Clinton.

Let's say the U.S. abolished the Electoral College. Candidates would put less effort into those big swing states and focus on reaching as many undecided voters as possible nationwide. Undecided voters would still distinguish between candidates based on their personalities.

4. *What about race, prejudice, and sexual orientation?*

You've probably heard people question whether Americans are too prejudiced to elect a black woman or a gay man. We don't deal with

PERSONALITY WINS

those questions in this book. Rather, we consider voters' perceptions of each candidate's personality.

Keep in mind that candidates with big personalities have overcome prejudices before. Many Americans were prejudiced against Catholics when JFK won the presidency in 1960. People questioned whether a black man with a Swahili-Arabic name could win in 2008 and 2012. Obama did it anyway. Although Hillary Clinton didn't take the White House, she proved that a female nominee could win the popular vote.

5. *What about speechwriters?*

Since speechwriters provide the text for the candidates and presidents, can we use their words to identify someone's personality? Yes, we can. Politicians pick speechwriters who capture their voice. Nixon would no sooner hire a comedian to write jokes throughout his speeches than Jimmy Carter would have approved a speech filled with aggressive, threatening language.

Speechwriters help us understand the candidates' personalities because they try to convey the essence of their boss. Plus, politicians usually edit and change these speeches.

6. *Does the Personality Wins Model apply to the primaries too? Or any other type of American election?*

No. The Personality Wins Model applies only to the general election for president, not the primaries.

Primaries are more intimate than general elections. The candidates go to Iowa and New Hampshire to meet voters in person at diners, community centers, town square gazebos, state fairs, and private homes. Doves and Owls can shine in these small group settings.

This same dynamic makes the Personality Wins Model inapplicable to Congressional races. To win a seat in the House, you must turn on the Dove or Owl and meet people one-on-one and door-to-door. Usually, we don't get to know our Congressional candidates in national media. We get to know them through firsthand experience, conversations with friends, social media, and local newspapers.

In a general election, though, we experience candidates through national TV, social media, and major newspapers and magazines. Those mediums favor drama, conflict, one-liners, and click-bait headlines, all of which fall in the comfort zone of Eagles and Parrots, but not Doves and Owls.

7. *Is your system better than random? Better than other predictions?*

As far as we know, no other pattern has been consistent over 23 consecutive elections. But we're not alone in developing prediction models that work for multiple elections.

Allan Lichtman, a political historian at American University, correctly predicted the last 10 presidential elections based on 13 key factors with yes-no answers. Lichtman's system gives a slight nod to personality, as two of the 13 factors are "incumbent charisma" and "challenger charisma."

The stock market predicts winners too. Dan Clifton of Strategas Research Partners found that market activity in the three months prior to voting predicted 19 of the 22 elections between 1928 and 2012. If stocks are up, the incumbent party wins. If the market is down, the other party wins. In 2020, the markets plunged as COVID-19 shut down the economy, but by the time of the election, the S&P 500 had surpassed its pre-pandemic high. That didn't carry Trump to a second term.

A spookier system is Spirit Halloween's Presidential Mask Index, which has accurately predicted the last six presidential elections based on the top-selling candidate mask. In October 2016, when all the polls were predicting Hillary's landslide, Spirit Halloween was calling the election in favor of Trump. People mocked the Mask Index, but, hey, it was accurate six times in a row. Although the Mask Index didn't make an appearance in 2020, it would have heavily favored Trump according to an analytics firm that tried to approximate the index using Google Search Trends.

Here's one that stands above many of the other prediction methods: In the last 23 elections, the taller candidate won 15 times. That's better than a coin toss.

To the Races

Before we look forward, we are going to look back at the previous 23 presidential elections. In the chapters ahead, we'll examine how personality has played out in the past so we can understand what it means for the future.

Section V:
Off to the Races

Personality in Action

THE PRESIDENTIAL CANDIDATE'S PERSONALITY has played a role in determining the outcome of elections since the beginning of the United States. But what does that actually look like? Why do some candidates win in landslides, while others squeak by? Why do some candidates win their first race but lose their second? What do Eagles, Parrots, Doves, and Owls do to get themselves elected—or not?

Now that you know the four personalities, it's time to see them in action.

Intentionally or not, presidential candidates said and did things that conveyed their personalities. Their speeches, one-liners, debates, gaffes, slogans, conversations, and decisions will help you see their personalities on full display. Presidential history is full of moments that American voters could never forget. If you think U.S. presidents were the boring politicians from your history textbooks, you're in for a treat.

You probably studied presidents like FDR, Eisenhower, and LBJ, but do you really know them? What made them tick, and what made them act the way they did? Why did they win, and what do they tell us about future presidential elections?

Those are the questions we set out to answer. The Personality Wins Model lives in these historic characters and campaigns.

We'll focus on the stories that make us say, "That's an <Eagle, Parrot, Dove, or Owl> in action." You'll see why Eagles and Parrots have beaten Doves and Owls in general elections since 1932. And you'll see how The Big Assumption leads candidates to impose their personalities on the electorate.

Before we reach 2024, you'll meet candidates who resemble Joe Biden and his Republican contenders. These historical politicians will help us answer the question of today: Why did Joe Biden win in 2020, and how is he likely to fare in 2024?

Before We Begin

Culture, communication, and norms have changed over the last 88 years. Back in the day, Americans had different standards for entertainment. They didn't own smartphones with a never-ending stream of funny cat videos, captivating TED Talks, and fist-pumping toddler memes. In 1932, "show business" consisted of live theater and some radio segments.

Candidates who sounded exhilarating to Americans in the 1930s and 1940s might sound convoluted and long-winded to us now. They spoke in full, rich sentences instead of tweets, abbreviations, and GIFs.

Politics only became more of a show business with the rise of partisan TV and arguing for entertainment. In the 1930s, there was no national program where panels of experts tried to one-up each other's ideas. You'll notice that when old-school candidates attack each other, *they don't sound that mean.*

So, before you think, "Is that *really* Parrot charisma?" put yourself in the time and place.

Alright, let's do this.

1932, 1936, 1940, 1944: The Sphinx

"Be sincere; be brief; be seated."

- Franklin Delano Roosevelt

Hooverville

IT WAS A TERRIFYING MOMENT, a change of fortunes so vast, so fast, and so damaging that the U.S. was caught off guard. It began on October 29, 1929, "Black Tuesday," when the U.S. stock market crashed. 650 banks soon failed, and hundreds more followed. Americans lined up to get their money out, but to no avail. The Dust Bowl Drought struck the Midwest, causing massive crop failures. Starvation and malnutrition proliferated. The Roaring Twenties, the pinnacle of wealth and extravagance in the U.S. up to that point, gave way to the worst economic disaster in American history.

Good thing America had a logical, thoughtful president ready to fix its problems, right?

Maybe not.

President Herbert Hoover didn't seem to believe that the American economy could collapse under *his* watch. He was dead set against intervening.

In June of 1930, a group of political activists met with Hoover to advocate for an infrastructure initiative that might counter the effects of the Great Depression.

"Gentlemen," said Hoover, "You have come sixty days too late. The depression is over."

Over? Not even close.

Amos Pinchot, a lawyer and activist who attended that meeting, wrote it about several years later. Hoover insisted that he knew better than the advocates—that *he* had better data: "The Census and Labor Department reports, and other information to which, as he reminded us, he had better access than we, would presently show that things were quite different from what we feared."

Things *weren't* different than what they feared. Hoover was an Owl in denial who *hated* being wrong and refused to act until he understood the situation better, which he did too late. Flustered by the pace of events, he interpreted the data to fit his belief that governments should keep out of private affairs. Hoover had Owl-like data with an Owl-like plan, and by God, he was going to stick to it.

Hoover's hyper-rational, inactive response seemed cold and callous to suffering Americans. By 1932, a quarter of Americans were unemployed, and one million men wandered the nation in search of work. The homeless lived in shack towns called Hoovervilles, and the jackrabbits people caught for food were called Hoover Hogs.

Presidential biographer William A. DeGregorio said Hoover, "... concentrated on detail rather than on the broader significance of a problem. He was a dull speaker, rarely lifting his eyes from the prepared text."

To see the trees but not the forest is a common Owl tendency. To read from a script rather than speak fluidly from notes is also very Owl—they don't want to get anything wrong.

Americans, however, were ready for big ideas and a can-do spirit. They needed a president who could mend their battered morale and *just do something*. There was one candidate who was dynamic, likeable, and electable. Hoover's Owl didn't stand a chance.

The Prophet

Born in 1882 to a wealthy New York family, Franklin Delano Roosevelt was raised to be a gentleman and leader. By the time he was an undergraduate at Harvard, he confided to a friend that he planned to follow in his cousin Teddy Roosevelt's footsteps. FDR said he would become secretary of the navy, governor of New York, and then president, in that order. And he did.

That is the bold confidence of an Eagle.

FDR was ambitious, nontraditional, and adventurous. He also had the temperament of a happy-go-lucky, mischievous, and persuasive Parrot. Although this combination of traits could make him seem grandiose, this wasn't necessarily a flaw for a candidate who would run for president four times—first during the country's worst economic crisis and later during the world's bloodiest international conflict.

Roosevelt had one liability as a candidate. In 1921, he was struck with polio and lost the use of his legs. So, when the July 1932 Democratic Convention was held in Chicago, FDR flew there to quell fears about his sickness and accept the nomination in person. To do so was, "unprecedented and unusual," FDR told the audience, "but these are unprecedented and unusual times."

It was the kind of commanding Eagle-Parrot performance that FDR would bring to the White House. As he told his Democratic colleagues, "Let it also be symbolic that in so doing I broke traditions. Let it be from now on the task of our Party to break foolish traditions."

FDR was *not* bound by rules and ideology the way Hoover was. He would toss convention out his campaign railcar if that's what it took to revive confidence in America.

FDR closed his July acceptance speech with words that changed American history: "I pledge you, I pledge myself, to a new deal for the American people." What he said next was quite a personality tell: "Let us all here assembled constitute ourselves prophets of a new order of competence and of courage. This is more than a political campaign; it is a call to arms."

Vagueness didn't matter because FDR's readiness to do something was better than Hoover's reluctance to do anything. FDR's campaign song, "Happy Days Are Here Again," captured his vision of restoring the good times.

It was Eagle bigness. It was Parrot inspiration. It was just what American needed to hear.

Owl for President

As a candidate, Hoover took FDR's New Deal *very* literally, as Owls are prone to do. He didn't grasp that it was an extension of FDR's personality rather than a defined policy.

As Hoover told a crowd in New York's Madison Square Garden, "It is not the change that comes from normal development of national life to which I object, but the proposal to alter the whole foundations of our national life…. They are proposing changes and so-called new deals, which would destroy the very foundations of our American system."

To warn about risks to a "system" is very Owlish. Hoover seemed offended by the idea that FDR could win the campaign with appeals to emotion. "We must go deeper than platitudes and emotional appeals of the public platform in the campaign," said Hoover, "if we will penetrate to the full significance of the changes, which our opponents are attempting to float upon the wave of distress and discontent from the difficulties we are passing through."

Essentially, Hoover was warning, "Careful! FDR is going to break everything," to which the public yelled back, "Everything is already broken!"

FDR won the election by a fat margin. It was the beginning of an (almost) unbroken trend in which Eagles and Parrots beat Owls and Doves.

The Eagle-Parrot-in-Chief

On March 4, 1933, FDR gave his first of four Inauguration Day speeches. It was the famous battle call of an Eagle-Parrot:

> This great Nation will endure as it has endured, will revive and will prosper. So, first of all, let me assert my firm belief that the only thing we have to fear is fear itself—nameless, unreasoning, unjustified terror which paralyzes needed efforts to convert retreat into advance. In every dark hour of our national life a leadership of frankness and vigor has met with that understanding and support of the people themselves which is essential to victory.

63

Five days later, FDR launched the Hundred Days, a fury of legislative action during which Congress passed sweeping bills to revive the economy. FDR compared himself to a quarterback, calling the plays and throwing touchdown passes.

No one, least of all FDR, was sure what the New Deal would entail. By 1936, FDR had expanded the government more than any prior President. Legacies of that first term alone include the end of Prohibition (cheers!), the Federal Deposit Insurance Corporation (FDIC), the Securities and Exchange Commission (SEC), the Federal Housing Administration, the National Labor Board, and Social Security, among other agencies and programs we still depend on (and fight about) today.

FDR had the Eagle drive to execute and the Parrot words to convince everyone that they should go along with him. His personality was uniquely suited to a crisis that required a brazen, visionary, and aspirational response.

Fireside Candidate

In office, FDR began to show more of his Parrot side. The nation, enthralled by his flurry of action, gradually mirrored the optimism he projected. And, thanks to radio, the public came to know FDR more intimately than any prior president.

FDR gave his first fireside chat on March 12, 1933, eight days after taking the White House. Radio was FDR's direct, unfiltered way of speaking to the American people. He updated the nation and discussed his policies in casual, clear language.

Harry Butcher of CBS coined the term "fireside chat" in a press release announcing the second such address. The way FDR spoke, it felt like you were cozied around the president at home, warmed by a wood fire.

FDR gave roughly thirty fireside chats between 1933 and 1944. His single most popular broadcast, on May 27, 1941, was about the rising danger of World War II. Out of a population of 82 million Americans, 54 million tuned in. No modern politician—not even President Trump with his massive Twitter following—gets that percentage of Americans to tune in at the hour of his or her choosing.

No president before FDR could project his personality to the American people quite like this. Now that Roosevelt had the power of radio, it seemed that few Republicans could win in 1936—least of all Alfred "Alf" Landon, an oilman and the governor of Kansas.

Alf

A traditional fiscal conservative, Alf had a dilemma. He couldn't criticize FDR's New Deal because it was popular. But he could paint FDR as a powermonger and spendthrift who was thwarting the checks and balances of American government. Sounds logical.

In his 1936 speech accepting the Republican nomination, Alf denounced the speed and uncertainty of the New Deal programs: "We knew they were being undertaken hastily and with little deliberation." He added, "The record shows that these measures did not fit together into any definite program of recovery. Many of them worked at cross-purposes and defeated themselves. Some developed into definite hindrances to recovery."

If you're still wondering about Alf's personality, munch on this line: "A government is free in proportion to the rights it guarantees to the minority." Landon has boiled freedom down to a formula!

Alf's Owl personality is apparent in his priority: "Our party holds nothing to be of more urgent importance than putting our financial house in order." His strategy was to lambast the way Democrats were spending the nation's way out of the Great Depression. He tried to take down FDR by critiquing how the president did too much with too little forethought and too much money. For an Owl, planning and practicality are everything.

To his credit, Alf generated some Dove energy and tried to seem more supportive of the American people than the detached and seemingly indifferent Hoover.

What did FDR do in response? He tapped into his Parrot playfulness and made fun of Alf and the Republicans. His most memorable campaign sound bite, on September 29, 1936, in Syracuse, New York, made the audience burst into laughter. Just imagine the regal FDR switching into a whiny, pleading voice meant to mock his rivals. He couldn't help breaking into ear-to-ear smiles as he jabbed his opponents:

> Let me warn you and let me warn the nation against the smooth evasion which says, "Of course we believe all these things; we believe in social security; we believe in work for the unemployed; we believe in saving homes. Cross our hearts and hope to die, we believe in all these things; but we do not like the way the present Administration is doing them. Just turn them over to us. We will do all of them—we will do more of them, we will do them better; and, most important of all, the doing of them will not cost anybody anything.

FDR nailed it. Alf and the Republicans wanted to hit the brakes—to analyze where they had come from and where they should go next—to suggest they could do the same things as FDR, only more efficiently and cost-effectively.

To the Eagle-Parrot Roosevelt, there was no time to stop and run the numbers, and Americans agreed. FDR carried over 60 percent of the popular vote and all but eight electoral votes. Not since 1820 had any candidate won that decisively.

Above the Law

After clobbering Herbert Hoover and Alf Landon, tradition held that FDR would pass the reins to a new democratic candidate. But FDR, as he so brashly stated in 1932, didn't pay heed to "foolish traditions." By refusing to say whether he'd run for a third term, FDR earned his nickname, "The Sphinx," after the mythical creature that spoke in riddles.

Lucky for FDR, historical forces were working in favor of a third term. In 1936, Adolph Hitler kicked off the invasions and treaty-breaking that would lead to World War II. In 1937, Japan launched its brutal invasion of China and began to challenge U.S. supremacy in the Pacific. The Spanish Civil War, which lasted from 1936 to 1939, gave the world a terrifying preview of what modern war would look like.

Meanwhile, FDR was drawing comparisons to Europe's dictators. Furious that the Supreme Court had shot down some of his New Deal bills, FDR proposed a plan to add one justice to the court for every sitting justice over seventy years old. It was a not-so-subtle plan to stack the court. To friends and foes, it seemed like FDR considered himself above the law. When Eagles don't get their way, watch out. They like to win and will find creative ways to do so.

When the 1940 Democratic Convention arrived in July, Roosevelt couldn't be seen as wanting or demanding the nomination, as that would fuel the narrative that he was becoming too power-hungry. He wanted the convention to *want* him. It was a mix of Eagle strategy and his Parrot need for popularity.

At a healthy level, Parrots can be incredibly persuasive. When the confidence dial gets turned up, they can become self-centered and manipulative. FDR didn't attend the convention in Chicago this time. Instead, he asked Senator Alben Barkley of Kansas to deliver a message from him to the convention about *not* desiring to continue in office and wishing the candidates well. Immediately after Barkley read FDR's note, cheers of "We want Roosevelt!" broke out. He made it appear as though they were begging for him to do it. And he was happy to oblige.

Roosevelt was perhaps the last presidential candidate to play the charade of being duty-bound and reluctant, like literally *everyone* who ran for the White House after George Washington. Of course, his opponents saw through the act.

The convention nominated FDR, adding to the suspicion that FDR was consolidating power in the style of Europe's rising dictators. The Republicans had a better attack narrative than four years ago. They also had a personality up for the job.

The Heroic Loser

In the late 1930s, a small but influential group of Republicans from Wall Street and the media industry grew alarmed at their party's isolationist stance. They recognized that the U.S. could not avoid the brewing conflicts in Europe and the Pacific. Rather than settle with the Republican frontrunners, they courted business executive Wendell Willkie, a pro-business internationalist, to be their candidate. There was just one problem. Willkie was a Democrat, and FDR was likely to run for a third term.

The ambitious Willkie switched his party affiliation in 1939 and stepped up for the Republican nomination insisting, "I didn't leave my party, my party left me." Fundamentally, his platform was no different from FDR's, although Willkie claimed to be infuriated by FDR's anti-business New Deal measures. And, he made a big deal out of FDR's unprecedented run for a third term.

Willkie, a successful lawyer, had become chairman of Commonwealth and Southern, one of the country's largest utility holding companies, in 1934. He was only forty then. People just *liked* Willkie and believed in him. In April 1940, he gained political momentum as a funny yet knowledgeable contestant on the radio quiz show *Information Please*.

After announcing his campaign for president, the charismatic Willkie attracted hordes of unpaid volunteers. Allegedly, he made so many speeches that he had to travel with a doctor to avoid losing his voice. Allies including Russell Davenport, editor of *Fortune*, and Henry Luce, owner of *Life* and *Time* magazines, ensured that Willkie received positive press coverage in the run-up to the Republican convention in July 1940.

During Willkie's acceptance speech in his hometown of Elwood, Indiana, he said, "Here I give you an outline of the political philosophy that is in my heart." This was not another rational Owl, like Hoover or Landon. This was a man powered by emotion. This was a candidate who had an "electric personality and a magnetic energy about him," as his grandson David Willkie said.

Willkie viewed himself as part of a movement, not as a lone candidate. "We go into our campaign as into a crusade," he asserted.

Can you see the similarity between Roosevelt and Willkie?

Willkie insisted he'd go to war with Germany if necessary while painting FDR as the hawk who "has courted a war for which the country is hopelessly unprepared—and which it emphatically does not want." He compared FDR's polarizing leadership to the kind that led France to a rapid defeat against Nazi Germany earlier that summer. Never mind Willkie's logic (or lack thereof). He was tapping the fear and division over war.

The year 1940 was becoming a contest between two titanic personalities with indistinguishable platforms. Wendell was a Parrot-Eagle who, like FDR, gained momentum by energizing and motivating crowds. He was so confident in his stage presence that he proposed debating FDR publicly around the country. Neither Hoover nor Landon would have ever suggested such a thing. Videos of Willkie show him standing on top of his campaign car, arms outstretched, waving his hat at the rally crowds flooding the city streets. That's Parrot enthusiasm in action. It's contagious.

So, who wins when an Eagle-Parrot fights a Parrot-Eagle for the White House? When personalities are equally matched, it's a toss-up. Factors besides personality can come into play. Someone with Eagle and Parrot qualities was going to win...and one did. Maybe voters felt that tried-and-true FDR would be the wiser choice when war with Germany seemed inevitable.

Although Roosevelt won the election, Willkie and his big personality have aged well. After losing to FDR, he broke with Republican isolationists to help the president prepare for war. This act of conscience cost Willkie a future in the Republican Party. His testimony to Congress in favor of FDR's Lend-Lease program ensured that Britain received desperately needed military aid. During the war, Willkie convinced FDR to let him travel worldwide to strengthen relationships and campaign for a global effort against fascism. It was the perfect job for the Parrot-Eagle, who attracted big crowds wherever he went.

When Willkie passed away in 1944, Eleanor Roosevelt praised him in her eulogy. "Americans," wrote the First Lady, "tend to forget the names of the men who lost the presidency. Willkie proved the exception to this rule."

The Little Man on the Wedding Cake

It should come as no surprise that Franklin Delano Roosevelt, a dynamo of American spirit throughout the Great Depression and World War II, would take the White House for a fourth time. Based on personality, the governor of New York, Thomas E. Dewey, didn't stand a chance against FDR.

Dewey built his reputation in the 1930s as a sharp, methodical prosecutor who took down New York mobsters like "Lucky" Luciano, the father of American organized crime. After winning seventy-two convictions out of seventy-three prosecutions between 1935 and 1937, Dewey converted his notoriety into political capital. He became governor of New York in 1942.

In private, Dewey was supposedly a likeable, funny guy. In public though, he was remembered as cold, stiff, and remarkably unlikable. (*Teaser: Mitt Romney drew comparisons to Dewey during his campaign against Barack Obama*).

Someone once nicknamed Dewey, "the little man on the wedding cake," and it stuck. His dark suits, stiff demeanor, and trim mustache were sources of endless ridicule.

Dewey lacked FDR's force-of-nature personality, but as an objective Owl, he didn't let emotion and prejudice get in the way of good leadership.

A 1985 piece in *The New York Times* about Dewey's protégés notes that as a prosecutor and district attorney, Dewey hired the best people regardless of race, heritage, or gender. They included Italians, Irish, Jews, African Americans, and women who Wall Street law firms wouldn't hire.

Still, Dewey had an Owl flaw that would make him an easy snack for FDR's Eagle. "The big tragedy about him, and no one would believe it, was lack of self-confidence," Judge Whitman Knapp, a protégé of Dewey, told the New York Times in 1985. "His instincts were absolutely superb, but he didn't have the self-confidence to expose his soul. So the public got the picture of the fellow on the bridal cake."

Dewey tried to take down FDR with nitpicky Owl attacks, one of which backfired royally. His campaign falsely claimed that FDR, after leaving his dog Fala behind on the Aleutian Islands in 1943 after their reconquest from Japan, sent a Navy destroyer to pick Fala up at a cost of millions of dollars.

In his address about the matter on September 23, 1944, FDR spoke with Eagle seriousness and a Parrot's wit, acting as if the insults to Fala were a grave matter:

"These Republican leaders have not been content with attacks on me, or my wife, or on my sons. No, not content with that, they now include my little dog, Fala."

The audience burst into laughter.

"Well, of course, I don't resent attacks," adds FDR, "and my family doesn't resent attacks—but Fala does resent them."

He remained deadpan in his delivery as the crowd laughed even harder. It was a disciplined and clever performance, the kind that an Eagle-Parrot excels at.

72

"You know, Fala is Scotch, and being a Scottie, as soon as he learned that the Republican fiction writers, in Congress and out, had concocted a story that I had left him behind on the Aleutian Islands and had sent a destroyer back to find him — at a cost to the taxpayers of 2 or 3 or 8 or $20 million—his Scotch soul was furious. He has not been the same dog since."

Some commentators think this speech took out Dewey. FDR was trying to win a war against Germany, Italy, and Japan, while Dewey was obsessing over how much FDR doted over his dog. Dewey's Owl was no match for the experienced Eagle-Parrot.

FDR's fourth term was short-lived. He died on April 12, 1945, passing the presidency to his VP, Harry S. Truman.

Undefeated FDR

Franklin Delano Roosevelt is the only American president who was elected four times. It should come as no surprise that Willkie, the Parrot, received more votes than any of the three Owl contenders who ran against the towering Eagle-Parrot.

Unlike prior presidents who kept the press at a distance, FDR worked hard to get positive coverage. According to biographer Jean Edward Smith, FDR shook hands with all 125 reporters who attended his first press conference on March 8, 1933. He chitchatted with them for forty minutes. He didn't say anything substantive but still left a good impression. FDR held 337 press conferences during his first term alone and 998 total during his time in office.

FDR's personality was highly adaptable and likable. He was the decisive and determined leader Americans needed at the onset of the Great Depression. He connected with the people and spoke like a caring teacher during his fireside chats. He restored faith in government at a time when economic depression, the rise of fascism and communism, and horrors of World War II had eroded faith in humanity itself.

By taking his candidacy and presidency to radio, FDR forever changed how Americans elect their leaders. The Owls and Doves who thrived in early twentieth century elections could no longer do so. FDR set the template for how the big personalities of Eagles and Parrots could outmaneuver opponents and take the White House.

1948:
Give 'Em Hell Harry

"All my life, whenever it comes time to make a decision,
I make it and forget about it."

- Harry S. Truman

Inheriting World War II

WHEN PRESIDENT FRANKLIN DELANO ROOSEVELT DIED on April 12, 1945, his successor inherited more than just the U.S. presidency. He inherited World War II and the choice of whether to use the deadliest weapon humanity had ever created.

Could he handle the pressure? Harry S. Truman, relatively unknown on the national stage despite being the vice president, was about to show America what he was made of.

The son of a Missouri mule trader, Truman grew up as a farmer and a four-eyed, voracious reader. In retirement, Truman bluntly told a room full of schoolchildren that he was "kind of a sissy" growing up.

Truman was no coward, however. Due to his poor eyesight, he could have sat out World War I but didn't. Instead, he memorized the eye chart exam to sneak into the military and served valiantly as the captain of an artillery unit. He kept multiple pairs of glasses on him to ensure he'd never be caught helpless. The admiration he earned in the military launched his political career.

In his first elected role, as a county administrator based in Kansas City, Missouri, Truman was a budget wonk who spent entire news conferences running over the numbers on flipcharts. He ran for the U.S. Senate in 1934, defeating his Republican rival in Missouri. True to his number-crunching track record, Truman built a reputation rooting out waste and corruption in the defense industry. He was so darn stubborn and thorough about doing what he knew was right. No one questioned Truman's integrity.

Truman became FDR's running mate in 1944 because he was seen as a safe compromise. FDR's other options were considered too far left or too far right.

When Truman took command in 1945, the Allies were on the march to victory in Europe and East Asia. However, the Soviet Union was already jockeying to control Eastern Europe. Truman had the unenviable job of negotiating a post-war order with Winston Churchill, the Parrot-Eagle prime minister of the UK, and Joseph Stalin, the wily, sociopathic leader of the Soviet Union.

Truman was in the tough position of closing wars on two fronts, reestablishing an economy that would have to manufacture something other than weapons, and not triggering a third world war with the Soviets.

No sweat, right?

In his first address to Congress on April 16, Truman positioned himself as a tough, no-nonsense leader who would carry out FDR's plans.

"So that there can be no possible misunderstanding," said Truman, "both Germany and Japan can be certain, beyond any shadow of a doubt, that America will continue the fight for freedom until no vestige of resistance remains!"

What type of personality asserts in no uncertain terms that victory is inevitable?

That's an Eagle who also has a strong Owl component to his personality. Eagle-Owls know what they want, how they want it, and how they'll get it. With confidence and a plan, Truman was determined to fight Germany and Japan to unconditional surrender.

True to his word, Truman engaged U.S. forces to battle Nazi Germany to absolute defeat. Japan, unwilling to lay down arms, presented Truman with a difficult choice. Should he sacrifice an ungodly number of American lives in an invasion of the Japanese mainland? Or should he use the top-secret weapons that had been developed in New Mexico (and perhaps send a message to the Soviets)?

Truman ordered atomic bombs to be dropped on Hiroshima and Nagasaki. Soon after, the emperor surrendered on August 14, 1945, ending the war in the Pacific.

Underdog Candidate

Truman had a rough start. His perceived softness towards the land-grabbing Soviets and his trouble managing the post-war economy led the Republicans to retake Congress in 1946 for the first time since 1930. Their slogan, "Had enough?" captured how Americans felt after fifteen years of economic recovery and war.

Everyone assumed that Truman would get crushed in 1948. Thomas Dewey, the little man on the wedding cake, was back for round two. The pollsters said that he would beat Truman.

The 1948 Democratic National Convention was divisive and bitter. Truman's candidacy seemed inevitable, and no one was happy about it. At 2 a.m., after Truman finally earned the nomination, he took the stage for a speech that no one anticipated. The energy and applause were unlike anything Truman had mustered in office so far. The Eagle came out to win an election. After the customary thanks yous, here's how Truman opened:

"Senator Barkley and I will win this election and make these Republicans like it—don't you forget that! We will do that because they are wrong and we are right, and I will prove it to you in just a few minutes."

That's Eagle determination coupled with Owl argumentation. Truman gave some numbers and facts about economic growth, which is not what FDR did in his campaign speeches (Eagle-Parrot). After his takedown of Republican policies and lies, Truman made what was then an edgy comment: "I wonder if [the Republicans] think they can fool the people of the United States with such poppycock as that!"

Poppycock is a curse word that means "soft dung." Feel free to work that into conversation.

Profanity was well-suited for an Eagle-Owl who didn't give a [fill in four-letter word of your choice] what anyone else thought. Truman would eventually call the egomaniacal General Douglas MacArthur a "dumb son of a bitch" and refer to Richard Nixon as "a shifty-eyed goddammed liar."

Anyway, southern white supremacists who felt threatened by Truman's pro-Civil Rights record broke ranks to support Strom Thurmond as their Dixiecrat candidate. Henry Wallace, FDR's former VP who was ousted in favor of Truman, decided to run too. No one thought the Democrats could win after their butt-kicking in 1946. Now that the party was broken in three, their odds looked terrible.

Give 'Em Hell Harry

American pundits hardly considered the race between Harry Truman and Thomas Dewey to be a contest. Whatever Dewey lacked in personality, he had an advantage: *everyone* expected him to win. He also had a disadvantage: *he* expected to win.

In 1948, Dewey's speech accepting the Republican nomination was caught on video. He tried to wear a smile, but he looked like an overly starched white shirt.

Nothing Dewey said in that speech would make a modern highlight reel. Dewey was infamous for loading speeches with platitudes while failing to convey human emotion, a struggle for public Owls. A political cartoon from the period portrays Dewey as a hand-cranked calculator robot that moves on parallel tracks wearing roller skates. Next to him, Truman is running with a blindfold on.

Dewey's campaign tried to be agreeable and appealing to everyone. It seemed as if Dewey was so certain of victory that he didn't bother to campaign. He didn't want to risk a spat with Truman that could backfire. So, Dewey just sat on his fat lead, playing it safe. Owls tend to be natural risk managers, more afraid of loss than ambitious for gain.

One journalist supposedly summed up the Dewey campaign platform as, "Agriculture is important. Our rivers are full of fish. You cannot have freedom without liberty. The future lies ahead." His Owl campaign felt matter of fact and bland to voters, who were looking for some spice. (*Teaser: This quip was resurrected in 2016 to mock Hillary Clinton.*)

Meanwhile, Truman wasn't winning allies. Moved by Eagle conviction, he signed an executive order on July 26, 1948, that desegregated the United States military. Critics thought that would sink Truman if a divided Democratic Party hadn't already.

Nevertheless, Truman campaigned intensely. His Eagle seemed to find excitement in being the underdog. The more the papers pontificated on why Truman would lose, the harder he fought. He covered 31,000 miles by train and spoke directly to some six million Americans.

Reporters were perplexed by how many people attended Truman's rallies. At one stop, Truman promised to "give 'em hell." The expression became the best-known words of his campaign. Can you imagine a Dove promising to "give 'em hell?" Probably not.

Truman also had a campaign tune that was adapted from a song titled, "I'm Just Wild About Harry." The song included the lyrics:

> FDR had his new deal and Truman now will follow through
> My country's wild about Harry,
> and Harry's wild about, cannot do without,
> both my country and me.

The country wasn't "wild" about Harry, but compared to Dewey, Truman was a fireworks show. Neither candidate was likable, but one was electable. Once again, the Eagle beat the Owl.

Truman's underdog ticket kept the White House with 303 electoral votes and 49.6 percent of the popular vote. A famous photograph taken at a St. Louis train station after the upset showed Truman defiantly holding up a two-day-old copy of the *Chicago Tribune*, which went to press without waiting for the official results.

"Dewey Defeats Truman," said the headline. The toothy grin on Truman said it all—winning was nice, but for that Eagle-Owl, nothing was more satisfying than proving all the doubters wrong.

Hated but Brave

Truman's colorful use of profanity became famous during his presidency. Unfortunately, his leadership skills did not.

After a music critic wrote a mean review of first daughter Margaret Truman's singing, Truman wrote the guy a note scrawled on White House stationary.

"Some day I hope to meet you," Truman wrote, and "[w]hen that happens you'll need a new nose, a lot of beefsteak for black eyes, and perhaps a supporter below!"

The salty Truman may seem endearing now, but in his time, he was considered crude and unpresidential. And his luck ran out after winning the 1948 election.

In August 1949, the Soviet Union tested its first atomic bomb, aided by spies inside America's Manhattan Project. Soon after, Mao Zedong's Communist forces defeated their Nationalist opponents and declared the People's Republic of China. Truman was blamed for "losing" China to communism. In June 1950, war broke out in Korea, and Truman felt pressured to respond.

On Truman's order, General Douglas MacArthur landed on the southern tip of Korea and pushed the communists north. MacArthur, notoriously overconfident, drove the Korean communists to the Chinese border. In response, Chinese forces poured across and fought MacArthur back. Truman was losing control of MacArthur, who wanted to take the war to China and talked seriously about using nuclear weapons.

So, Truman relieved MacArthur of his command, which was an *extremely* unpopular move at home. It was brave, however. Historians now praise Truman for asserting his authority over the military. By doing so, Truman may have prevented World War III. Eagle-Owl leaders have the personality to make those difficult, unpopular decisions that won't garner respect until long after they're gone.

The Korean War was fought to a draw on the thirty-eighth parallel, where Korea remains divided to this day. With an approval rating hovering in the twenties and thirties, Truman chose not to run for a second term. For an Eagle, it's less embarrassing to quit than to be defeated badly. It was a relief to the Democratic Party, until they met their opponent.

Truman was one hell of a campaigner, but as an Eagle-Owl, he had the two most unlikable personality styles. He couldn't surprise America a second time.

1952, 1956:
Ike

"Morale is the greatest single factor in successful wars."

- Dwight D. Eisenhower

The Compassionate Commander

In June 1944, the Allies launched the largest seaborne invasion in history. Everyone knew it was coming, including Nazi Germany, which controlled continental Europe and was determined to keep it. Few people knew where the D-Day forces would land. Arguably, just one person understood the scope of the preparations for this decisive battle. That person was Dwight D. Eisenhower, Supreme Commander of the Allied Expeditionary Force.

Texas-born and Kansas-raised, Eisenhower attended the U.S. Military Academy at West Point and narrowly missed his chance to serve in World War I. Eisenhower became a sophisticated military planner under the tutelage of General Fox Conner in Panama and at the War Department in D.C., where he learned the intricacies of Washington politics. After Japan struck Pearl Harbor on December 7, 1941, few officers were more prepared to lead the war effort than Eisenhower.

Compared to the other generals, Eisenhower cared far more about the morale and well-being of his troops. Under his command, officers received the same food and quarters as enlisted men. He believed that everyone risking life and limb in Europe ought to be treated with dignity. Which personality style does that sound like?

No commander was organized, detail-oriented, and systematic quite like "Ike," as he was known. The Nazis, well-entrenched from Normandy to Berlin, could not be overcome by brute force. The Allies needed a patient, methodical thinker like Eisenhower to find and exploit their weaknesses. He planned and directed D-Day with its many moving parts and details to coordinate. Maybe a second bird type comes to mind.

Ike's recipe for success was three parts Dove and two parts Owl.

Eisenhower had earned the trust of President Franklin Delano Roosevelt, Prime Minister Winston Churchill, and his mentor, U.S. Chief of Staff George Marshall. He somehow wrangled the massive egos of France's leader-in-exile, Charles De Gaulle, and Britain's Field Marshall Bernard Montgomery. Perhaps only a strong Dove could have navigated so many Eagle personalities.

In his pre-invasion letter to the troops, Eisenhower wrote, "I have full confidence in your courage, devotion to duty and skill in battle." It was fatherly and reassuring.

He also drafted an "In Case of Failure" letter: "The troops, the air and the Navy did all that Bravery and devotion to duty could do. If any blame or fault attaches to the attempt it is mine alone." This is Dove-Owl accountability at its finest, internalizing the responsibility without blaming others.

D-Day succeeded and changed the momentum of the war, leading to the unconditional surrender of Nazi Germany on May 7, 1945.

Eisenhower had unified the Allies through deft personality management and skilled planning. Thanks to Ike, veterans returned home to their wives and sweethearts, who had been operating the factories. They moved into suburban homes built on assembly lines and had lots of kids. The carefree era of white picket fences, green lawns, the family car, and middle-class comfort had begun.

No American hero was more popular or well-liked than Eisenhower. And no candidate was so coveted by both political parties. The Democrats didn't yet realize that Ike was a Republican and would run as one.

Eisenhower was not hungry for power or fame. As he would say later, "Leadership consists of nothing but taking responsibility for everything that goes wrong and giving your subordinates credit for everything that goes well." Spoken like a humble Dove.

Eisenhower was unlike any of the presidents or candidates we have met so far. He was a Dove-Owl whose personality scored high on likability but relatively low on electability. He was a war hero, but not a dynamic personality like FDR, Truman, or Willkie. This would have been a liability in most elections, but not this one.

Wit Without Charm

On paper, Illinois Governor Adlai Stevenson was an ideal candidate for president. A Princeton-educated lawyer who assisted the secretary of the navy and joined the first U.S. delegation to the United Nations, Stevenson had an unblemished record of government service. There was just a slight problem.

Stevenson "possessed the very reverse of 'charisma,'" wrote essayist Joseph Epstein in *Commentary* magazine. Think about that. After Eagles and Parrots had beaten Doves and Owls in five straight elections, the Democrats ran a candidate who had the "reverse of charisma." Still, he could "elevate" people and "somehow make them feel good." Said Epstein, "…he struck a chord of affection in people in a way few other American political figures have ever managed to do."

Stevenson had a self-deprecating, intelligent style of humor that, to the kinds of people who wrote essays in high-brow magazines, was endearing.

Stevenson famously hated Richard Nixon, Eisenhower's running mate. "Mr. Nixon's defenders insist that although there are certain things in his record that aren't very pretty, he has nevertheless shown the capacity for growth," said Stevenson. "And if elected will develop the character for the job. I think it unlikely, however, that the American people will want to send Mr. Nixon to the White House just on the chance that it might do him a world of good."

It's not laugh-out-loud humor, but it's clever. Just because Stevenson was witty, that doesn't mean he was a Parrot. His observational style of humor resembles George Carlin's, who was known for jokes like, "Anyone driving slower than you is an idiot. Anyone driving faster than you is a maniac." Stevenson similarly played off logic.

Stevenson, like Eisenhower, was a Dove-Owl. Their similarities and differences are striking. Ike's Dove side built a tightly knit, high-morale military. His Owl strengths became adapted to war planning. Stevenson, too, was well-liked, kind, and humble. He expressed his Owl side through rigorous governance and thought-provoking humor.

Having the same personality doesn't mean that two people will have the same life experiences. But it does mean that they're likely to make similar impressions on the public in a presidential election. Ike and Stevenson's personalities—not their track records—scored high on likability and relatively low on electability. In any case, electability would not be an issue, as a Dove-Owl would be sworn in as the thirty-fourth president of the United States either way.

Dove War I

Eisenhower, former leader of the most powerful military alliance ever assembled, ran his campaign with Dove steadiness and Owl discipline. Not once did he mention his opponent, Adlai Stevenson, by name. Instead, he commented on the vulnerable Truman, whose popularity was tanking.

At the 1952 Republican Convention in Chicago, Eisenhower's Dove came out in force. Before speaking, he scanned the audience, acknowledging individuals with eye contact, smiles, and nods. He raised his arms to rile the crowd once but didn't attempt to match or elevate the energy of an already amped audience. Dignified and calm, he looked more human than Dewey but lacked the commanding presence of Truman or FDR.

Eisenhower didn't need to play tough guy the way some Eagles do in presidential elections. He was the real deal. As he told the Republican Convention, "…you have summoned me on behalf of millions of your fellow Americans to lead a great crusade—for Freedom in America and Freedom in the world. I know something of the solemn responsibility of leading a crusade. I have led one. I take up this task, therefore, in a spirit of deep obligation."

These are the words of a Dove-Owl commander. Like George Washington, he felt an "obligation" to serve, not a craving for power. His strategy to win, even more Dovish, came from his time in the military:

> Before every attack it has always been my practice to seek
> out our men in their camps and on the roads and talk with

them face to face about their concerns and discuss with
them the great mission to which we were all committed.

In this battle to which all of us are now committed it will
be my practice to meet and talk with Americans face to
face in every section, every corner, every nook and cranny
of this land.

Ike ran to listen, not to tell Americans what they should want. After
the convention, Ike sought the support of his Republican primary contender, Ohio Senator Robert Taft, who was reluctant to help. Eisenhower
desired consensus and unity so much that he agreed to adopt a document drafted by Taft outlining his positions on an assortment of issues.
To Doves, group unity is more powerful and valuable than independent
action.

Stevenson's acceptance speech was strikingly similar to Eisenhower's,
and even more Dove-like. He looked like a schoolkid who received a nice
compliment from an intimidating teacher. His smile betrays a shyness
unfamiliar to voters who spent thirteen years with FDR and seven with
Truman. His stiff wave—more of a hand raise and a pause—was the gesture of a guy saying, "Hey! Look! I'm over here...."

Stevenson didn't sound like a nominee for president; he sounded
like the guy meant to introduce the nominee. Self-deprecating to a fault,
he said, "I should have preferred to hear those words uttered by a stron-
ger, a wiser, a better man than myself." The opening of his speech was
about why he didn't deserve the nomination nor seek it. *Yawn*.

To his fellow Democratic contenders, Stevenson offered a juicy
olive branch: "...I am profoundly grateful and emboldened by their
comradeship and their fealty, and I have been deeply moved by their

expressions of good will and of support." He goes on to congratulate his Democratic colleagues for debating the issues without any name calling and meanness. Only a Dove thanks his competitor for being kind after a debate.

You'll remember that FDR and Truman framed their campaigns as battles and crusades. So did Eisenhower. Stevenson, taking a gentle dig at Eisenhower, does the opposite: "I hope and pray that we Democrats, win or lose, can campaign not as a crusade to exterminate the opposing Party, as our opponents seem to prefer, but as a great opportunity to educate and elevate a people whose destiny is leadership."

Stevenson was so passive that he made Ike look like the more aggressive of the two personalities. Welcome to the Dove cage match.

Why Did Ike Win?

If 1952 was a toss-up between two Dove-Owls, why did Eisenhower win?

Being a celebrated war hero certainly didn't hurt, but a few differences between the campaigns probably affected how the public perceived their personalities. Eisenhower and Nixon became the first presidential ticket to use TV extensively. One in three homes had a TV by the election year. Eisenhower's simple ads, which showed him answering questions about issues, put his kind, smiling face in homes around the country.

By contrast, Stevenson's TV spots were Owl-heavy. His long-winded speeches were jumbled with erudite language that made Stevenson seem like an "egghead," as commentators remarked. His balding, round head helped that label stick. While Ike was promoting his likeability, Stevenson didn't do anything to help his likeability or electability.

The United States also was stuck in the Korean War without a resolution in sight. No president could afford to let the communists win, and no president could afford to start a nuclear war now that the Soviets had the bomb. Korean casualties were in the millions, and by 1953, almost 40,000 American would be killed and another 100,000 wounded.

Would the next president escalate the war or end it? There was no appetite for a protracted conflict after World War II.

Stevenson was in a tight spot because this Dove wasn't about to bash President Truman, a fellow Democrat, for his management of the war. (*Teaser: notice that Eagle Trump had no problem bashing fellow Republican George W. Bush for the wars in Iraq and Afghanistan*). Eisenhower wasn't about to either because that's not what Doves do.

Eisenhower, ever the Owl planner, tested a campaign sound bite. During a speech in San Francisco on October 8, 1952, he said, "Without weakening the security of the free world, I pledge full dedication to the job of finding an intelligent and honorable way to end the tragic toll of America's casualties in Korea."

A media and psychological warfare expert who served on Eisenhower's staff confirmed that this line played well with the public. He wanted Ike to deliver the message more forcefully, but Ike didn't want to be hedged into a promise he couldn't fulfill. Urged by his campaign staff, he took a bolder position in Detroit six days later, pledging that if elected, "I shall go to Korea."

It had the vagueness you'd expect from an Eagle or Parrot, not Eisenhower. What would he do when he arrived in Korea? He didn't say.

Stevenson couldn't make the same promise. Would that have stopped an Eagle from making the same claim? Hell no.

Thanks to Ike's reputation as the man who ended World War II, the public read it the way his campaign strategists hoped: Ike would end the war, in person. Those five words rocketed Ike's campaign just weeks before the election. By adding some Eagle boldness to his campaign, he gained an edge.

Eisenhower won a landslide victory over Stevenson.

The Organizer-in-Chief

The Oval Office hadn't been occupied by a Dove-Owl leader in decades. Both Eisenhower and Stevenson campaigned on how much of a mess Washington had become. It was time for Eisenhower to set the White House in order.

"For years I had been in frequent contact with the Executive Office of the White House and I had certain ideas about the system, or lack of system, under which it operated," said Eisenhower. "With my training in problems involving organization it was inconceivable to me that the work of the White House could not be better systematized than it had been during the years I had observed it."

He needed a structure in place to fight the Cold War. So, he created new positions and systems: White House chief of staff, the Congressional Relations Office, presidential assistant for national security affairs (now the national security advisor), and the National Security Council, among others. The Dove-Owl turned the executive branch into the smooth-running machine that would fit his methodical nature.

To outsiders, Eisenhower's "hidden hand" leadership strategy was indecipherable. Critics thought that Secretary of State John Foster Dulles and Chief of Staff Sherman Adams were running the show. *That's what Eisenhower wanted*: to seem apolitical and slightly ineffectual. As a Dove, perhaps Ike didn't want to be perceived as for or against any Americans and their political ideology. Clearly, he didn't need the spotlight—Doves don't want it or seek it.

Ike's apolitical persona buoyed his approval ratings and gave him leeway to solve charged issues. For instance, Eisenhower never outwardly said that Congress should confront Joseph McCarthy, the Wisconsin senator who exploited the Red Scare to run a communist witch hunt. In public, Ike was casual, optimistic, and intentionally vague. Behind the scenes, where Doves and Owls thrive, Ike plotted against McCarthy. The Owl war planner was still there.

Eisenhower held his first televised press conference in 1955 during the Formosan Strait Crisis, a conflict between Communist China and the Nationalist government in Taiwan. The media were worried that Ike might intervene—potentially with nuclear weapons. He had no intention of nuking China, but he needed the Soviets and Chinese to *think* that was an option so that they wouldn't escalate the conflict. Press Secretary Jim Hagerty asked Ike to not answer questions about the crisis.

"Don't worry Jim," said Eisenhower, "if that question comes up, I'll just confuse them." And he did. To contemporaries, Ike's nonanswer about a U.N.-brokered cease-fire made him seem noncommittal and unclear about his position on the conflict. In reality, Ike played the media and foreign opponents masterfully. They had no idea how Ike would react if they increased the pressure on Taiwan. It was a public relations victory for the wise Owl.

Dove War II

Between the 1952 and 1956 elections, American culture and politics grew turbulent. *Brown v. Board of Education of Topeka*. Rosa Parks. The Montgomery Bus Boycott. Race relations in the U.S. were coming to a head, and neither party had the courage to confront the issues—least of all the Democrats, who still depended on the Deep South to win elections.

Abroad, the Cold War raged. The U.S. detonated its first hydrogen bomb in November 1952, and the USSR followed suit in 1955. The U.S. intervened in Iran, Vietnam, and Guatemala, and tensions between mainland China and Taiwan continued to flare. These were also the glory years of Elvis Presley, Marilyn Monroe, and James Dean (until their untimely deaths).

Back for round two, Adlai Stevenson tried to channel some Eagle energy. He went after Ike for being a "part-time" president, though he refused to specifically mention cases where Eisenhower was absent was due to a heart attack. Consider how Dove-Owl that is: I'll attack you for being absent but *specifically* exclude cases where you had a legitimate medical excuse. Stevenson didn't want to take advantage of Ike's health issues, but he did want to stoke fears of a trigger-happy Vice President Nixon becoming president and taking charge of the H-bombs.

TV ads were now essential to campaigning, and the Republicans spent twice as much as the Democrats on them. By the end of the race, the Republicans had $5 million left in the war chest, and the Democrats could barely afford an ad. Ike dominated the American living room again.

Interestingly, campaign ads in 1956 began to touch on information overload. An Eisenhower ad shows a cartoon voter being bombarded with arguments: Lower taxes or higher taxes, employment or unemployment, peace or war, and so forth.

The overwhelmed voter finally says, "Woah!!! Stop. I've tried. I've listened to everybody on TV and radio. I've read the papers and magazines. I've tried, but I'm still confused. Who's right? What's right? What should I believe? What are the facts? How can I tell?"

If only that voter saw what we have today. A man appears on the screen to comfort the voter. "If it's any consolation, you're not alone," he says.

The man shows that he was listening to the voter and his concerns, as a good Dove would. He concludes, "Beyond all the words, beyond all the claims and promises, there's actually just one big thing on which people base their final decision: the man."

The video becomes all about the personality and identity of Ike, who has "...captured the admiration, trust, and devotion of Americans from all walks of life." Interviews with voters drive this message of how great Ike is, as a person. This was among the early instances where a campaign effectively said, forget the issues. Eisenhower's slogan said it all: "I still like Ike." Essentially, vote for the guy with the better personality!

In future elections, we will see this strategy again. Doves promote their values. They make it all about the belief system of the person voters are electing. But when they overplay the Boy Scout card against tough Eagles and visionary Parrots, it's not compelling enough.

Stevenson's ads lacked charisma and charm. One shows him having a staged, rambling conversation with John F. Kennedy, the young senator from Massachusetts and rising Democratic star. It's not surprising that Stevenson tried to intellectualize a TV ad.

Before an audience of journalists, Stevenson criticized the Republicans: "They have merchandised the American people—tried to sell them a bill of goods, to put it in language the advertising business can understand."

For better or worse, personality had, since 1932, become an ever-growing factor in presidential elections. The year 1956 seemed like another tipping point. Stevenson, clinging to old ways, was frustrated with the notion that voters would pick candidates based on their "slick slogans and advertising arts." Stevenson was resisting change and trying to preserve tradition, as Dove-Owls often do. It may have lost him another election.

Eisenhower's Legacy

Since Eisenhower left office in 1961, America has *not* had another Dove or Owl president serve two consecutive terms. The apolitical, fatherly tone he brought to the White House has been absent. In both spirit and policy, he was a unifier.

It is worth noting that while in the White House, Ike's Dove ways occasionally backfired—most notably in the nuclear arms race. In 1957, the Soviets launched Sputnik, the world's first outer space satellite. It was a not-so-subtle message that the USSR could deliver nuclear payloads to the U.S. mainland. Ike downplayed the threat of Sputnik, but scared Americans weren't calmed. They wanted an Eagle's firm response, not a Dove's soothing consolation. Recall how FDR rallied the nation during the most turbulent years of his presidency.

Footage from high-altitude U2 spy planes showed Eisenhower that, indeed, there was no missile gap. The U.S. was ahead, but Ike couldn't say how he knew that without endangering this valuable source of intelligence (until the Soviets shot down a U2 in 1960). He was too much of an Owl to sacrifice a strategic advantage for his political gain.

For years to come, Eagle and Parrot candidates would milk the missile gap to present themselves as tough, competitive leaders. The U.S. and USSR would stockpile more than enough missiles to end human civilization. The intent to build bigger, better missiles became yet another proxy for personality. No president would dare copy Ike's rational, calm response to the nuclear race.

Eisenhower ended his second term in Dove-Owl form, with prayers for peace, trust, and mutual respect, and a warning. In his paternal way, Ike cautioned that the "conjunction of an immense military establishment and a large arms industry is new in the American experience." The Supreme Allied Commander of WWII warned against allowing this "military-industrial complex" undue influence and power that would corrupt democratic life.

Eisenhower, the warrior Dove, had charted a steady course for America in the first decade of the Cold War. His successors would struggle to find what Ike most desired: "balance between actions of the moment and the national welfare of the future."

1960:
Jack

"Conformity is the jailer of freedom and the enemy of growth."

\- John F. Kennedy

The Rock Star

It's 1960, and a camera is pointed at the entryway to American Serb Hall in Milwaukee, Wisconsin. The black-and-white footage captures Jacqueline Kennedy walking through the door. Next, a policeman barges through, nightstick pointed ahead, scanning for trouble. Finally, Massachusetts Senator John F. Kennedy swaggers in as he removes his coat. The fans lining the entryway go wild.

No campaign up to this point had generated such passion—or at least none had captured it on video.

There's no barrier between Kennedy and his charmed admirers as he weaves through the crowd, shaking hands with a wide grin. He seems to have little regard for his safety. Admirers jostle for position and reach over strangers' shoulders in hopes of shaking the candidate's hand. A lucky woman yells out, "I can't wash my hand for a year!"

Kennedy doesn't seem like a politician. He's treated like a rock star. The women in the footage look smitten. Allegedly, Kennedy's right hand would become so swollen from handshakes that he'd have to ice it during his primary campaigning.

John takes his place beside Jackie Kennedy on stage. The camera pans to the audience, showing it from JFK's perspective. The hall is packed and singing a campaign song. By this point, John F. Kennedy wasn't a stranger to stardom. His campaign seemed to be based on one discernible principle: maximize attention.

Not since FDR had a presidential candidate delighted so much in the spotlight. In 1957, a friend of Kennedy's said he was overdoing the magazine profiles. JFK begged to differ. They'll "help take the 'V' out of VP," he said.

Kennedy had the charisma of a Parrot and the cutthroat determination of an Eagle. Wisconsinites only saw the smiling, lovable Parrot.

Like Roosevelt, Kennedy was groomed for office. Born in 1917 to Boston multimillionaires, Kennedy came from the elite of the elite. His intensely competitive family prized athleticism and frequently debated politics at the dinner table. Joseph P. Kennedy, John's father, took his money out of the stock market just before the 1929 crash. As a result, the Kennedy children grew up with servants, sailboats, and summer homes instead of the Great Depression.

John attended the prestigious Choate Rosemary Hall boarding school and graduated from Harvard in 1940. After Japan attacked Pearl Harbor in December 1941, Kennedy wanted to serve in combat, but his long history of health problems meant he'd be denied. Joseph used his political clout to get John into a naval officer program with a forged bill of health.

JFK took command of a small torpedo boat in the Pacific. In 1943, a Japanese destroyer rammed Kennedy's boat in the middle of the night, when everyone was asleep. The collision killed two men. Kennedy led the survivors on a three-mile swim to the nearest island. He towed a badly burned crewmate to safety, exacerbating the chronic back pain that had prevented him from joining the armed forces in the first place.

Kennedy had been negligent and violated naval rules—he was supposed to always have a crewmember on watch. An inquiry discovered this lapse in leadership, but the Navy preferred to make a hero of Kennedy rather than an example. Kennedy received the U.S. Navy and Marine Corps Medal for Valor along with a Purple Heart for his injuries sustained in combat.

As Parrots do, JFK used humor to reframe a bad situation. When a reporter later asked about how he became a war hero, JFK said, "It was absolutely involuntary. They sank my boat."

Most people in the 1940s couldn't enter politics as a twenty-something. Would-be politicians needed money. That was no problem for JFK, whose father had provided each of his eight children with trust funds. John bankrolled his run for the House of Representatives in 1946 and then was elected to the Senate in 1952.

Years later, to deflect complaints that his father's money bought the presidential primary, JFK joked, "I just received the following wire from my generous Daddy: Dear Jack, Don't buy a single vote more than is necessary. I'll be damned if I'm going to pay for a landslide."

The young JFK gained notoriety not for his policies, but for being a celebrity. Not surprising for a Parrot. His marriage to Jacqueline Bouvier received the kind of attention that British royal weddings get today. His good-looking family and glitzy lifestyle appealed to columnists and a curious public. Kennedy reveled in the spotlight. The male-dominated media ignored his track record of womanizing, so those behaviors remained hidden in the shadows. By the time Bill Clinton and Donald Trump ran for office, candidates could not expect that free pass.

In 1956 and 1958, no one campaigned harder for congressional Democrats than JFK. His Parrot was on full display as he cruised the country speaking on radio programs, giving speeches, and making political contacts. He was helping his party, but JFK was also a man on a mission: the presidency. It was a Parrot performance fueled by Eagle ambitions.

Unlike former candidates who aged their way into presidential contention, Kennedy was determined to skip the line and become the youngest person elected president in U.S. history. To do that, he would exploit the media in ways no prior candidate had.

First, he challenged his Democratic contenders to compete with him in the primaries, arguing that if they couldn't beat him, they couldn't beat the Republicans in November. Minnesota Senator Hubert Humphrey took the bait.

The trouble for Kennedy was religion. Should his Catholicism be a campaign issue or not? Should he distance it or embrace it?

JFK couldn't dodge the issue, so he instead embraced his Catholicism and ran ads implying that Humphrey was playing dirty by making the race about religion. Humphrey wasn't doing that, but the misinformation worked. JFK also threw tons of money, staff, and volunteers into the fray. Humphrey said he "felt like an independent merchant competing against a chain store."

Kennedy allied himself with West Virginia's coal miners and plant workers. Just like Trump would do fifty-six years later, Kennedy, a rich northeasterner, styled himself as the coal miner's champion. The news coverage and campaign ads spread images of Kennedy shaking hands and smiling with coal miners. Humphrey left the race humbled. As he discovered, JFK was a master of shaping public image to his own advantage. Parrot-Eagles don't let facts get in the way of a compelling narrative and competitive edge. Humphrey, a Parrot of the long-winded variety, couldn't keep up.

The Democratic Convention did the unexpected: they chose JFK over Senate Majority Leader Lyndon B. Johnson, who hadn't even bothered to campaign in the primaries. Not only that, JFK convinced Johnson to be his vice president.

Tricky Dick

Everyone remembers that John F. Kennedy was young to be running for president at forty-three years old. Few recall that Richard Nixon was only four years older and had already served two terms as vice president.

Nixon is the most complex candidate we explore in this book. *He wasn't likeable, inspiring, or trustworthy*, yet, spoiler alert, eventually he'd win the presidency. His close aides would remember him for his private nature, searing cynicism, and lack of faith in humanity.

Nixon was born in Yorba Linda, California in 1913. His parents owned a grocery store that barely stayed afloat. When Nixon was ten, his younger brother became ill and died. And when he was twenty, his older brother also became ill and passed away.

While his mother was well regarded for her kindness and compassion, his father was known to be angry and susceptible to conspiracy thinking. His response to a childhood of stress and tragedy was to bury himself in books and become an academic superstar.

In high school, Nixon earned a scholarship to Harvard, but his family could not afford room and board. Instead, he attended local Whittier College and then Duke Law School, where he was dubbed "Gloomy Gus." Yeah, not a Parrot.

He had no close friends in college. Kicking off Nixon's lifetime of unflattering cartoons, a Duke yearbook pictured students talking and laughing around Nixon, who sat solemnly alone. He was not good at small talk or connecting with people. Obviously, not a Dove either.

After earning his degrees, Nixon returned to Yorba Linda to practice law. When World War II broke out, he joined the war effort as a supply officer in the Pacific. During active duty, he rose to the rank of Lieutenant Commander. He also became extremely skilled at poker, which helped fund his 1946 Congressional campaign.

Although Nixon struggled to build relationships, he developed a strategy for connecting with people on the campaign trail. He recorded the names of politicians and everyday citizens along with details about their families on thousands of notecards. When he returned to a town, he'd study his notes and astound people by asking them about their children or spouse by name.

Yes, Nixon was an Owl. Self-critical and reflective—at least in his younger days—Nixon used his Owl strengths to overcome his complete lack of Parrot and Dove qualities.

In 1946, Nixon challenged Democrat Jerry Voorhis, a known anticommunist, for a seat in the House. Nixon managed to convince a debate audience that Voorhis was on the recommendation list of a communist-infiltrated political action committee (it wasn't true; he was on a different PAC's list).

Nixon won, and the Republicans seated him on the House Un-American Activities Committee, where his investigation of Alger Hiss, a State Department employee accused of spying for the Soviets, earned Nixon national fame. When Nixon ran for the Senate against Helen Gahagan Douglas in 1950, he studied and memorized her voting record. He seemed to know it better than she did. In debates, he used this extensive memory of Douglas's career to argue that she was voting in line with the communists. For Owl Nixon, it was all in the details.

This cunning campaign earned Nixon the nickname "Tricky Dick." It's one of the reasons why Republicans wanted Nixon on the 1952 ticket with Dwight D. Eisenhower. The kind, grandfatherly Ike needed an attack dog. And it didn't hurt that Nixon came from a state with an abundance of electoral votes.

In 1952, Nixon was accused of having a political slush fund that he spent on personal extravagances, and Eisenhower refused to defend him. Nixon went on TV to clear his record. He acknowledged that the one political gift he did receive was a dog: "It was a little cocker spaniel dog in a crate that he'd sent all the way from Texas. Black and white spotted. And our little girl Tricia, the 6-year-old, named it Checkers. And you know, the kids, like all kids, love the dog, and I just want to say this right now, that regardless of what they say about it, we're gonna keep it."

It was the first time a candidate had used TV to such powerful effect. Nixon's "Checkers Speech" won sympathy. How could people fault him for keeping his daughter's beloved dog? Critics should have learned the lesson from FDR's Scottie Fala: in the U.S., you do *not* attack a politician for loving his dog, even if that dog might have been a bribe.

Eisenhower never seemed to like his vice president. In 1956, Ike gave an ally permission to plot against Nixon and replace him with a different VP. It didn't work.

Towards the end of Ike's second term, Nixon was the presumed Republican nominee, and no one bothered to challenge him. At the 1960 Republican Convention in Chicago, Nixon looked uncharacteristically smiley though awkward working his way through the crowd. As he prepared to speak, his eyes nervously shifted from the lectern to the crowd and side to side.

His grin vanished as the speech began, and out came the Owl. His message to the American people reflected The Big Assumption: if it's important to me, it's important to everyone:

> And I urge you, study the records of the candidates, listen to my speeches and that of my opponent, and that of Mr. Lodge [his running mate] and that of his opponent. And then, after you have studied our records and listened to our speeches, decide—decide on the basis of what we say and what we believe which is best qualified to lead America and the free world in this critical period.

Nixon *is* the type who would "study" the records in detail. As he would soon find out, that's not what most American voters do.

A Tight Race

In July 1960, John F. Kennedy accepted the Democratic nomination for president. JFK didn't have much of a record to run on, but he had the right personality. His pitch to the nation, about a New Frontier, was as empty as his record. But Americans don't care about a candidate's plans—they care about how the candidate makes them feel, and JFK demonstrated that with his acceptance speech:

Beyond that frontier are the uncharted areas of science and space, unsolved problems of peace and war, unconquered pockets of ignorance and prejudice, unanswered questions of poverty and surplus. It would be easier to shrink back from that frontier, to look to the safe mediocrity of the past, to be lulled by good intentions and high rhetoric—and those who prefer that course should not cast their votes for me, regardless of party.

But I believe the times demand new invention, innovation, imagination, decision. I am asking each of you to be pioneers on that New Frontier.

It was a soaring vision of the future. Whatever the speech lacked in specificity and substance, it conveyed the big personality Americans vote for. What made it a true Parrot speech was the participatory spirit. JFK invited Americans to *join* him as pioneers in an uncharted future. Years later, Reagan would employ the same participatory spirit with his slogan, "Let's Make America Great Again."

Voting for JFK meant becoming part of something special. His campaign slogan, "A Time for Greatness," was total Parrot.

There were two faces to the Kennedy campaign. There was the inspirational, Parrot Kennedy, and there was the Eagle Kennedy who mobilized his trust fund, worth about $1 billion in today's dollars, to attack Nixon.

One of the Kennedy attack ads showed a picture of Nixon over the headline, "Would You Buy a Used Car from This Man?" We shouldn't fall for gimmicks, but then again, first impressions are often accurate. Nixon came off as a shady used car salesman, and Kennedy reinforced that image.

The Kennedy campaign also took advantage of a televised press conference in which Eisenhower was asked what policy ideas Nixon had contributed to his administration. Eisenhower thought about the question for a moment and then said, "If you give me a week, I might think of one." Ike laughed along with the reporters. Kennedy turned it into a TV ad that questioned Nixon's supposed experience.

Nixon's ads were stilted and uninspiring. One featured him talking about America's need for leaders who could achieve peace without surrendering an inch to the Soviets. He looked like a schoolkid taking his class photo. It was obvious that someone had directed him to take a photogenic, side-turned position on top of a desk. It didn't look natural at all.

Despite being a media darling and playboy, Kennedy was not as well-known as the vice president. So, Kennedy challenged Nixon to the first ever TV debate, thinking that could level the awareness gap. It did—and created a massive personality gap.

You may recall where we argued that the Kennedy-Nixon debate was a key development that made personality *even more* important in presidential elections. After radio, television was the next technology that gave Parrots and Eagles an edge over Doves and Owls. It highlighted their dynamic body language, charisma, and commanding presence.

Seventy million people watched the Kennedy-Nixon debate, which showed the handsome, magnetic Kennedy take on his Owl adversary. In black and white text, Nixon might have had a solid advantage. But black and white TV displayed a seemingly uncomfortable Nixon with sweat glistening on his chin.

The debate was *not* filled with the one-liners and headline grabbers that we take for granted today. Back then, debates were substantive, detailed policy conversations. One exchange was telling though.

Kennedy tried to use Parrot persuasion to level the playing field by getting Nixon to acknowledge him as *the* leader of the Democrats: "I think Mr. Nixon is an effective leader of his party. I hope he would grant me the same. The question before us is: which point of view and which party do we want to lead the United States?"

Journalist Howard K. Smith, the moderator, turned to Nixon and asked, "Mr. Nixon, would you like to comment on that statement?

"I have no comment," he replied. Perhaps it seemed illogical to Nixon to call JFK a leader of his party. Leadership experience was, after all, one of Nixon's differentiators. Still, this response made him look grouchy and unfriendly. In likability, there was no contest between Kennedy and Nixon.

Much focus was put on Nixon's ghastly appearance. Even if Nixon had been his usual healthy self, his personality would have seemed dour next to Kennedy's.

Nixon later reflected, "As for television debates in general, I doubt they can ever serve a responsible role in defining the issues of a presidential campaign. Because the nature of the medium, there will inevitably be a greater premium on showmanship than on statesmanship"

Unfortunately for Nixon, he wasn't much of showman. Historians don't seem to think the three subsequent debates mattered after that first impression of Gloomy Gus.

If Americans still weren't sure who to vote for, former President Harry Truman had a thought: "If you vote for Nixon, you might go to hell." Spoken like a true Eagle.

The campaign was close. Kennedy won by a mere 120,000 votes, but the Electoral College results were more definitive: 303 to 219. Kennedy did suspiciously well in Illinois, leading many to think that

Mayor Richard J. Daley committed voter fraud. A switch of just 4,500 ballots would have given Illinois to Nixon. In one district, there were more votes cast for Kennedy than there were people. Texas and California had some irregularities as well.

Nixon felt that he had been cheated out of the presidency, but he also thought that it would be dishonorable to contest the election. American democracy needed to appear, if not function, at its best during the Cold War. Adding insult to injury, Vice President Nixon had to certify JFK as the winner of the election in Congress. This was the first time in one hundred years that the losing candidate had to announce the victory of his opponent.

Nixon recorded the lessons he took away from the campaign in his memoirs: "From this point on I had the wisdom and wariness of someone who had been burned by the power of the Kennedys and their money and by the license they were given by the media. I vowed that I would never again enter an election at a disadvantage by being vulnerable to them—or anyone—on the level of political tactics."

Nixon the Owl sounded like a would-be movie villain. If he already believed people were out to get him, the 1960 race sealed that perspective. He had found even more anger and cynicism through victimhood. The Nixon of 1968 would be different from the one who ran in 1960. And the Nixon of 1972 would do anything to win.

We All Got Lucky

On January 20, 1961, JFK gave one of the most powerful inaugural addresses in U.S. history, and one of the shortest at just fourteen minutes long. Brevity is not typical for a Parrot. We remember it by these famous words: "And so, my fellow Americans: ask not what your country can do for you—ask what you can do for your country."

Like JFK's nomination speech, it was an invitation to participate in something great though undefined. JFK wanted America to know that they were in this presidency together.

JFK's Parrot ways had good and bad moments. Kennedy took the reins from a structured Owl. It didn't take long for him to dismantle Eisenhower's organizational systems, preferring an ad hoc, casual foreign policy operation to Ike's structured National Security Council and Cabinet. It's hard to say exactly how this affected international relations, but we have some clues.

Two months after taking office, Kennedy directed the CIA to topple Fidel Castro, the new, Soviet-friendly leader of Cuba. The Bay of Pigs invasion reflected overly optimistic Parrot thinking. It wasn't even close to succeeding and made a dangerous enemy of Castro.

The Bay of Pigs may have convinced Soviet Premier Nikita Khrushchev, an Eagle, that he was dealing with a lightweight. At their first meeting in 1961, the Soviet leader walked all over Kennedy. "He savaged me," the president later admitted to a reporter. You would *never* hear an Eagle like FDR admit that.

Some historians think that Khrushchev built the Berlin Wall two months later because he perceived Kennedy as too weak to do anything about it. Kennedy had tried to charm Khrushchev and build rapport, as Parrots often do in their personal relationships. Khrushchev went out to crush Kennedy.

And then came the Cuban Missile Crisis, probably the scariest moment of the Cold War. The U.S. had stationed intermediate-range ballistic missiles (IRBMs) in Turkey, within easy striking range of Moscow.

Khrushchev wanted to gain parity. So, he covertly moved IRBMs and 42,000 Soviet troops to Cuba, which welcomed them after Kennedy's coup attempt. Just ninety miles off the coast of Florida, Cuba put Soviet nukes within easy striking range of every major U.S. city.

Once the U.S. detected the missiles through aerial reconnaissance, the Kennedy administration pondered what to do in secrecy. Should they strike by air? Invade by land? Negotiate with Castro? Having exchanged Eisenhower's national security apparatus for Parrot's free-form structure, Kennedy was less prepared to act than he might have been.

Ultimately, Kennedy approved a naval blockade and, on October 22, 1961, revealed the situation to the American public. He promised the Soviets that any nuclear missile fired from Cuba would be met with "a full retaliatory response upon the Soviet Union."

Notably, Kennedy failed to speak to his administration's Soviet Union specialists until *after* this address. Kennedy was lacking in Owl methodicalness and risk management skills.

The two sides came to the brink of nuclear war, but a deal was reached. The Soviets would remove their IRBMs from Cuba, and Kennedy wouldn't invade the island. In exchange, the U.S. would remove its secret IRBMs from Turkey.

It's hard to trace a straight line from the Bay of Pigs to the Cuban Missile Crisis. However, it's fair to say that the Soviets took advantage of Kennedy's foreign policy miscalculations and disorganization. His care-free Parrot demeanor looked vulnerable to the wily Khrushchev.

Now, let's give credit where it's due. On May 25, 1961, Kennedy made good on the New Frontier with a bold promise: to land a man on the moon and return him safely to Earth before the end of the decade. Why? "No single space project in this period will be more impressive to mankind, or more important for the long-range exploration of space; and none will be so difficult or expensive to accomplish," said Kennedy. That is a Parrot rationale.

On September 12, 1962, at Rice University, Kennedy gave his most famous commentary on the moonshot:

> We choose to go to the moon. We choose to go to the moon in this decade and do the other things, not because they are easy, but because they are hard, because that goal will serve to organize and measure the best of our energies and skills, because that challenge is one that we are willing to accept, one we are unwilling to postpone, and one which we intend to win, and the others, too.

That's Parrot talk. Kennedy can't describe what benefit this will have for American society, besides filling it with pride and purpose. And for a Parrot, the "cool" factor is enough. *Let's do this because we can and because it'll be awesome.* Kennedy hoped the mission would have unintended benefits for technological innovation and education, and it did.

On November 22, 1963, President Kennedy and the First Lady were campaigning through Dallas, Texas, in an open motorcade. Just like in Milwaukee three years earlier, Kennedy didn't have much regard for his safety. He chose to be open and vulnerable, as Parrots often do. Two sniper's bullets ended Kennedy's life and started a wave of conspiracy theories. Lyndon B. Johnson took the oath of office that same day aboard Air Force One.

1964:
Landslide Lyndon

"There are no favorites in my office.
I treat them all with the same general inconsideration."

- Lyndon B. Johnson

The Johnson Treatment

On November 22, 1963, Lyndon B. Johnson became the first southerner to assume the Oval Office since before the Civil War. The progeny of Texan settlers and Confederate soldiers, Johnson became an unlikely champion for civil rights. His hardheaded, uncompromising personality left no partial victories or partial failures.

In his first address to Congress following Kennedy's assassination, Johnson demonstrated humility, sadness, and sympathy. But in that same speech, out came the Johnson that everyone knew—the action-ready, get-it-done Johnson.

In 1963, Kennedy had begun planning a massive poverty initiative, inspired by *The Other America*, a book by activist Michael Harrington, which argued that a fifth of Americans were living in poverty. Johnson would honor Kennedy by seeing his vision through.

113

"And now the ideas and the ideals which [Kennedy] so nobly represented must and will be translated into effective action," Johnson declared to Congress. "We will carry on the fight against poverty and misery, and disease and ignorance, in other lands and in our own."

Johnson called the nation to battle: "…it is our duty, yours and mine, as the Government of the United States, to do away with uncertainty and doubt and delay, and to show that we are capable of decisive action; that from the brutal loss of our leader we will derive not weakness, but strength; that we can and will act and act now."

Next, Johnson told Congress *exactly* what he expected from them:

"I urge you again, as I did in 1957 and again in 1960, to enact a civil rights law so that we can move forward to eliminate from this Nation every trace of discrimination and oppression that is based upon race or color. There could be no greater source of strength to this Nation both at home and abroad."

Johnson's presidency is about "effective action" and "decisive action." It's about "fighting" against society's ills. It's about doing one's "duty." It is about demonstrating "strength" in its myriad forms. In his first State of the Union address, Johnson went further: "This administration today, here and now, declares unconditional war on poverty in America."

Can you hear the Eagle?

Johnson viewed his world in competitive terms, as many Eagles do. War implies that there will be winners and losers. LBJ turned Kennedy's lofty Parrot visions into a mass mobilization of political will.

Of all the presidents to take on civil rights and poverty, none was better prepared than LBJ. He ascended the Democratic Party on ambition, work ethic, and an unmatched ability to get bills passed. LBJ is the first pure Eagle we've met—no Parrot, no Dove, no Owl. It was all Eagle, all the time.

Johnson grew up in the poverty-stricken Texas Hill Country, where he attended a one-room, one-teacher school. After failing to get into Southwest Texas State Teachers College, he ran off to California with five friends, worked odd jobs, and eventually hitchhiked home. While working on road crews, he became a drinker and fighter, which got him arrested. After cleaning up his act, Johnson gained admission to the Teachers College in 1927 and graduated in 1930, just in time for the Great Depression. His teaching salary was meager. Meanwhile, he built a reputation as an effective political volunteer and, in 1931, landed a job as a congressional aide.

Johnson's meteoric rise from aide to the youngest ever Senate Majority Leader had everything to do with his personality and timing. He was elected to the House in 1937 at the age of twenty-eight and suspiciously won a Democratic Senate primary in 1948 after colluding officials "discovered" a precinct that hadn't been counted and made "corrections" elsewhere. The brazen voter fraud earned Johnson the nickname "Landslide Lyndon." Eagles are ambitious, but Johnson was the type of overdrive Eagle who didn't believe that rules applied to him.

Johnson easily won his Senate race in Democratic Texas. He became whip two years later, Minority Leader two years after that, and finally, in 1955, assumed the most powerful role in the Senate. Most veteran Democratic leaders were knocked out of the Senate by Republicans in the 1950s, so LBJ filled the power vacuum. That's what Eagles do. Through drive and strategic maneuvering, they accumulate all the power and responsibility they can.

Johnson's ability to ram bills through the House and Senate became legendary. He didn't care about the policy specifics—he cared about getting a majority. His signature move was the "Johnson Treatment." At over six foot three, he towered above most senators and had no reticence about bullying them. Newspaper columnist Mary McGrory called it "an incredible, potent mixture of persuasion, badgering, flattery, threats, reminders of past favors and future advantages."

Johnson enjoyed power, prestige, and being feared. Allegedly, he was once pulled over by a cop for speeding.

After recognizing Johnson, the officer said, "My God!"

"Don't you forget it," replied Johnson.

He had the ego of an Eagle who was large and in charge.

Another story suggests that Johnson wasn't aware of how he came across to others. Angered that people weren't more enthusiastic about his legislative wins, he asked, "Why don't people like me?"

It was probably a rhetorical question, but the former Secretary of State Dean Acheson answered anyway: "Because, Mr. President, you're not a very likable man."

Emotional intelligence was not yet in vogue, but Johnson didn't have it. Like many Eagles, Johnson struggled to read the emotional states of others, but he was a master at gauging power dynamics.

His personality paid off at times. Senator Johnson's Eagle intimidation techniques helped him get the Civil Rights Act of 1957 passed. And on July 2, 1964, after wrangling the votes he needed to overcome a southern filibuster, President Johnson signed the Civil Rights Acts of 1964. The bill outlawed discrimination based on race, color, sex, religion, or national origin. It also illegalized discrimination in voter registration and banned segregation in schools, employment, and housing.

In May 1964, Johnson gave a speech at the University of Michigan that would define the other front of his war on poverty: The Great Society. What an Eagle name for a social justice agenda.

"The Great Society," said Johnson, "rests on abundance and liberty for all. It demands an end to poverty and racial injustice, to which we are totally committed in our time. But that is just the beginning."

It was a project of urban renewal, environmental protection, and education initiatives. How would he get it all done? "I do not pretend that we have the full answer to those problems," said Johnson. "But I do promise this: We are going to assemble the best thought and the broadest knowledge from all over the world to find those answers for America."

That is classic Eagle. He didn't know exactly how to do all this, but he'd put the right people on it. This "battle," as LBJ referred to it multiple times, would lead the eighty-ninth Congress to pass 180 major pieces of legislation.

Johnson was not content just to be a high-achieving politician. Behind the scenes, he needed everyone to know that he was the alpha male. His power moves sound like far-fetched stories from a high school football locker room. This was an Eagle who went way, way too far.

He would hold meetings while showering, shaving, or sitting on the toilet—he seemed to enjoy having his staff suffer the sights and smells. His belching, crotch-itching, farting, racist rants, and vulgarity are well-documented. His habit of groping women and making comments about their weight are well known too. He used to show off his penis, which he nicknamed Jumbo, to unlucky Congressmen who walked into the Capitol bathroom. "Have you ever seen anything as big as this?" he once asked an involuntary participant in his megalomania.

Yeah, *that's* the personality we have to thank for landmark civil rights legislation.

In 1964, with a sky-high approval rating, Johnson defeated segregationist George Wallace for the Democratic presidential nomination and named Hubert Humphrey his running mate. When Johnson called Humphrey about being VP, he allegedly asked, "Hubert, do you think you can keep your mouth shut for the next four years?"

"Yes, Mr. President," said Humphrey.

"There you go interrupting me again," LBJ said.

The Conservative Conscience

Of all the people the Republicans could have nominated for the presidency in 1964, no pick could have made the Democrats happier than Arizona Senator Barry Goldwater. An ultra-conservative at war with moderates, Goldwater and his protege, Ronald Reagan, would change the culture of the Republican Party. First, however, Goldwater would lose badly to LBJ.

Goldwater had the personality to win the presidency, but as they might have said in the sixties, this candidate *let his freak flag fly*. The only people saying crazier s**t than Goldwater in 1964 had discovered LSD. Johnson's campaign used Goldwater's gaffes to terrify the country out of voting Republican.

Goldwater descended from Jewish-Polish pioneers who established the first department store in Arizona. Born in 1909, three years before Arizona achieved statehood, he grew up working in that department store and dropped out of college to run it full-time once his father passed away. After serving in World War II, Goldwater was eager to avoid a lifetime in the store, so he entered city politics and ran successfully for the Senate in 1952.

He was a polarizing figure with a Jekyll-Hyde nature. He could be warm and hilarious in one moment; aggressive and warmongering in the next; optimistic in one appearance, grim in another. Goldwater had two distinct sides that never quite worked in tandem. *The New York Times* tried to explain him shortly after his nomination in July 1964. Notice the dichotomies:

> He will sometimes exert himself to be charming, or to be receptive to an idea, but he will do so only on his own terms and because it fits his mood and impulse. He will not, even for considerations which most politicians consider overriding, do either of those things when and if he does not feel like it.

Translation: there's something Parrot *and* Eagle about a candidate who can be charismatic, but only when *he* damn well feels like it. He was individualistic and stubborn.

Yet, says *The Times*, "There is a genuineness about Mr. Goldwater that is probably his most appealing quality. Even when he is offending someone's dearest political sensibilities he is, at least, direct about it."

He's blunt—an Eagle trait—yet somehow, that makes him likeable. Which bird had a bigger pull on his personality? Overall, the Parrot seemed to be more consistent. *Newsweek* described Goldwater as the rogue Republican personality who has "...broken all of the stereotypes. He has wit and charm. He is singularly unstuffy. He laughs readily and honestly at cartoons and jokes poking fun at him."

Goldwater was not just a conservative. He was *the* conservative, the evangelist of a new Republican Party.

Goldwater became a Republican star in 1960 with the publication of his book, *The Conscience of a Conservative*. It popularized doctrines that remain at the heart of conservative Republicanism sixty years later: small government, free markets, and individual responsibility. The

Democratic and Republican parties used to have a mix of liberals and conservatives. Goldwater was instrumental in purifying the Republican Party into a conservative one.

Once Goldwater won the nomination, Johnson's campaign exploited the senator's greatest weakness: *the things he said.* He gaffed liked Joe Biden and back-stepped his thoughts just as poorly. It seemed like an Eagle controlled Goldwater's mind, but a Parrot controlled his mouth.

Goldwater's record included doozies like, "Let's lob one into the men's room at the Kremlin" (i.e., let's nuke the Soviets when they least expect it). He suggested that nuclear weapons could be used to defoliate the jungles of North Vietnam so that American bombers could spot targets more easily. He thought that NATO's supreme commanders should have more "leeway" to use "tactical nuclear weapons of a very small nature" without phoning the White House for permission.

He suggested that more brinkmanship would be a good strategy for preventing war with the Soviets. As he told *Der Spiegel* in an interview, "Germany under Hitler would never have gone to war had the United States been a strong military nation and made it clear to our allies that any intervention by Hitler would mean intervention by us."

Goldwater seemed "trigger-happy," as many commentators said. And he was supremely confident in his perspective. There's that Eagle again. He used to tell his junior senator, John McCain, that if he'd taken the White House in 1964, "You wouldn't have spent all those years in a Vietnamese prison camp." Said McCain, "You're right, Barry. It would have been a Chinese prison camp." Even the hawkish McCain thought Goldwater would have spread the fight from Vietnam to China.

So, let's put Goldwater in context. The Cuban Missile Crisis happened three years prior. In August 1964, at least one U.S. destroyer was attacked in the Gulf of Tonkin, off the coast of Vietnam, by North

Vietnamese torpedo boats. On August 5, Johnson put forward a resolution asking Congress for authorization "to take all necessary measures to repel any armed attack against the forces of the United States and to prevent further aggression." It was a blank check. The idea of passing that power to trigger-happy Goldwater scared voters.

Johnson's campaign played up the reckless Eagle side of Goldwater's personality, even though Johnson himself was an over-the-top Eagle. They nailed Johnson with the most famous attack ad in U.S. presidential history.

The ad played just once, on September 7, 1964, and was immediately pulled from the air. Even so, the news stations continued to play and discuss it on their shows because it became news.

The ad shows an adorable little girl with bangs, counting "1…2…3…" as she pulls petals off a daisy. Then, a man's soldierly voice begins to count down from ten. The little girl looks up from her daisy in fear. Footage of a nuclear mushroom cloud fills the screen.

"These are the stakes," says the narrator. "We must love each other, or we must die."

The screen turns black. "Vote for President Johnson on November 3," a new voice says. "The stakes are too high for you to stay home."

As we'll see with George Wallace and Donald Trump, Eagle candidates who lack Dove and Parrot energy often focus on fear rather than hope. They want voters to feel that the world is too dangerous to trust anyone but a tough, protective Eagle.

As if the Daisy ad weren't bad enough, *Fact* magazine's September-October issue read, "1,189 PSYCHIATRISTS SAY GOLDWATER IS PSYCHOLOGICALLY UNFIT TO BE PRESIDENT!"

The article included outlandish, extreme characterizations of Goldwater's personality. One said, "He is a mass-murderer at heart and...a dangerous lunatic.... Any psychiatrist who does not agree with the above is himself psychologically unfit to be a psychiatrist."

Ultimately, Goldwater sued for libel and won. The American Psychological Association (APA) would create the Goldwater Rule, which banned its members from giving their professional opinions on the mental health of public figures.

By this point, you might be thinking, "Hmmmm...Donald Trump sounds like a combination of Johnson and Goldwater." You're on the right track.

LBJ beat Goldwater *badly*, taking 61.1 percent of the popular vote and all but six states. If Goldwater was a Parrot-Eagle—meaning that he was just as electable as Johnson but more likable—why didn't he do better?

Here's a clue from Harry Stein, contributing editor to *City Journal*, who wrote an enlightening article called "The Goldwater Takedown": "Insisting that the campaign be about ideas and not personality, [Goldwater] adamantly refused to present himself as the likable and multifaceted human being that he was. He looked so forbiddingly grim in his own literature that he indeed seemed ready to launch World War III."

By flexing away from his winning personality and refusing to be himself, Goldwater gave up control of his public image. Johnson's campaign was happy to take over for him. In fact, Johnson set up a secret committee tasked with smearing Goldwater. It was called the 5 O'Clock Club because of its after-hours nature. They carried out LBJ's cutthroat Eagle strategy in secrecy.

The 5 O'Clockers wrote letters to newspapers impersonating Americans afraid of Goldwater. They stole advance text of speeches from Goldwater headquarters. They developed anti-Goldwater books, including a kid's coloring book with Goldwater dressed up as a Ku Klux Klansman.

Goldwater's slogan was, "In your heart, you know he's right."

The Democrats had a counter-slogan: "In your guts, you know he's nuts."

Painting Goldwater as mentally unstable worked, even if it was untrue. The Democrats used the same tactic against Trump in 2020, and some psychiatrists were willing to flout the Goldwater Rule, claiming that their "moral and civic 'duty to warn' America supersedes professional neutrality."

On October 27, one Republican tried to stand up for Goldwater. Ronald Reagan delivered a nationwide telecast. The audiences remembered Reagan's mashup of FDR and Roosevelt quotes, delivered with action-star toughness: "You and I have a rendezvous with destiny. We can preserve for our children this, the last best hope of man on earth, or we can take the first step into a thousand years of darkness."

Just as Barack Obama's speech for John Kerry at the 2004 Democratic National Convention catapulted him into the national spotlight, Reagan's 1964 speech on behalf of Goldwater turned the former actor into a rising star for the conservative wing of the Republican Party.

Goldwater had a winning personality, but Johnson was equally electable, maintained a high approval rating during his first term, and ran a cutthroat campaign to halt Goldwater's rendezvous with destiny.

The Eagle Who Couldn't Lose

In 1965, with a renewed mandate to lead, Lyndon B. Johnson signed the 1965 Voting Rights Act, which outlawed some of the nefarious tactics that racists used to keep African Americans from the voting booths. That same year, he signed Medicare and Medicaid into existence.

Johnson's domestic agenda created landmark programs that continue to receive bipartisan support. But the war in Vietnam would stain his legacy and collapse his presidency.

The Vietnam War was a poor match for a pure Eagle. Think about World War II under FDR for comparison. Japan launched an unprovoked surprise attack against the United States. The brutality of the Japanese and Nazi forces was well known to the world. FDR, an Eagle-Parrot, rallied Americans into what was obviously a battle between good and evil. He inspired people to fight for the cause and he reassured them along the way.

President Truman, an Eagle-Owl, ultimately subdued Japan by dropping two atomic bombs on the country. *That* was a war suited to Eagles who don't know anything besides outright winning or losing.

Vietnam was unlike other U.S. wars. Rather than take, occupy, and control land until the enemy had nowhere to hide, the strategy was to kill the enemy. The path to victory was unclear. Eagles struggle with ambiguity, and they *really* do not like to lose.

Thanks to French colonization in Southeast Asia, short-sighted negotiations, and Cold War calculations, the U.S. had become the reluctant benefactor of South Vietnam's authoritarian, anti-communist regime. Johnson did *not* want to be the president who "lost" South Vietnam to the North Vietnamese Communists, who had the upper hand. Like Truman, he was an Eagle who refused to be seen as weak.

In 1964, advisers warned Johnson against getting more involved in Vietnam. As Johnson admitted to his national security adviser in May 1964, "…the more I think of it…it looks like to me we're getting into another Korea…I don't think it's worth fighting for and I don't think we can get out. And it's just the biggest damn mess."

Johnson added, "It's damn easy to get in a war, but it's going to be awfully hard to ever extricate yourself if you get in."

In other words, Johnson knew he was getting the U.S. into a mess, but driven by Eagle pride and grandiosity, he went forward anyway. Essentially, he thought he could use the "Johnson Treatment" on North Vietnam. Only, instead of towering over his colleagues personally, he would tower over North Vietnam with American bombers and firepower. He underestimated how much the North Vietnamese were willing to suffer for their cause.

Johnson had to know that a full-scale war would absorb the resources and political capital he needed to achieve The Great Society. He was caught between losing in Congress or losing in the Cold War.

His execution of the war was disturbing. When LBJ held briefings on Vietnam, he hated that some staff were long-winded—a very Eagle complaint. It's as if he didn't want to hear anything that could challenge his assumption or change his plans. He brought an alarm clock to the meetings and set it for five minutes when someone started presenting. When the alarm went off, the speaker had to stop talking and sit down.

By the end of 1965, Johnson had sent 175,000 American troops to Vietnam. By 1968, there were 535,000 Americans stationed in the country. All total, 58,220 Americans and millions of Vietnamese died. The war divided the U.S., sparking protests and riots.

An Eagle personality ramped into overuse mode can compromise its own judgment. Johnson knew that Vietnam was a trap yet sent American soldiers in anyway. When Eagles are free to fight an all-out war, they are effective. When the objectives are unclear, they struggle to define what victory means and fail to explore all their options.

So, what did the Eagle LBJ do when he knew he couldn't win the war—or the presidential nomination of his own party? He took his toys and went home. Recall that Truman, also an Eagle, chose not to run for another term.

On March 31, 1968, Johnson announced that he would not seek reelection:

> With America's sons in the fields far away, with America's future under challenge right here at home, with our hopes and the world's hopes for peace in the balance every day, I do not believe that I should devote an hour or a day of my time to any personal partisan causes or to any duties other than the awesome duties of this office—the Presidency of your country.
>
> Accordingly, I shall not seek, and I will not accept, the nomination of my party for another term as your President.

It's a confusing end to an Eagle's presidency. Johnson knew the public did not want him in power, yet he wanted to take responsibility— to maybe, just maybe, bring home the troops he knowingly sent into a quagmire. An Eagle can't stomach quitting, even after losing.

In the final days of his presidency, Johnson had a chance to bring the Vietnam War to end. But as you'll see in the next chapter, his efforts were thwarted by an Owl who had been pushed to the brink of paranoia and would do anything to take the White House.

1968, 1972:
Tricky Dick

"Never forget, the press is the enemy. The establishment is the enemy. The professors are the enemy. Professors are the enemy. Write that on a blackboard 100 times and never forget it."

\- Richard M. Nixon

America in Turmoil

The 1968 presidential election was unlike any before it or any since. The three-party race threw wrenches—a treasonous Nixonian wrench, a racist Eagle wrench, and a carefree Parrot wrench—into the pattern of personality.

To understand the personalities in this race, we have to put ourselves in their world.

In 1968, the U.S. death toll in Vietnam hit 1,000 Americans per month. As tragedy visited American families and the illusion of American superiority waned, public sentiment turned against the war. Protests erupted at college campuses, the United Nations, and the Pentagon.

The counterculture movement—hippies, flowers, love, and so on—fed on the seemingly pointless violence. Modern environmentalism and feminism incubated in the heat of cultural tension. Meanwhile, hundreds of race riots broke out in major cities. The National Guard had to restore order in several cases. Civil rights had been enshrined in law, but not in practice.

Conservative and moderate Americans panicked at the pace and intensity of change. Yet 1968 only grew more tumultuous. Martin Luther King Jr.'s assassination led to more rioting. The assassination of Robert Kennedy, JFK's brother and the presumed Democratic nominee for president, weakened an already demoralized and fractured party.

These intersecting forces produced the 1968 Democratic Convention in Chicago. The event was on lockdown because of the threat posed by protesters. Under Mayor Richard Daley's direction, the Chicago Police beat and arrested protestors as they chanted, "The whole world is watching."

The Democrats, divided by the war, the counterculture, and civil rights, could no longer count on their historical base. Former Alabama Governor George Wallace split from the Democratic Party and ran as an independent, pulling Deep South segregationists into his camp.

Vice President Hubert Humphry won the Democratic nomination, but Minnesota Senator Eugen McCarthy, the runner-up, refused to endorse him until the end of the campaign. It was ugly.

By comparison, Richard Nixon, who had left electoral politics for several years to work in a Manhattan law firm, returned triumphantly. He won the Republican nomination on the first ballot.

Nixon, an Owl, faced two competitors with personalities that could have beaten him under normal circumstances. These were anything but normal circumstances.

The Happy Warrior

To understand the difference between Nixon and his Democratic challenger, Hubert Humphrey, look no further than their nicknames.

In one corner there's Gloomy Gus, the perpetual worrier who thought everyone was out to get him. In the other corner, the Happy Warrior, a man who exuded optimism and joy. Can you guess his personality?

Humphrey was born in South Dakota in 1911. He worked his way into the Democratic Party by serving in New Deal agencies and became mayor of Minneapolis in 1945. At the 1948 Democratic Convention, he asked his colleagues to "get out of the shadow of states' rights and to walk forthrightly into the bright sunshine of human rights."

It was so Parrot to use imagery of walking into the bright sunshine. That speech in favor of civil rights earned him notoriety and angered segregationist Dixiecrats to no end. Humphrey won a Senate seat in 1948, lost the 1960 Democratic primary to JFK, and joined LBJ as vice president in 1965.

Like Johnson, smooth-talking Humphrey knew how to rally Congressional votes. But Humphrey urged LBJ to withdraw from Vietnam just after their victory against Goldwater. Johnson was livid and effectively banned Humphrey from the Oval Office. The bullying and alienation eventually got to Humphrey.

A year later Humphrey, reversed his position on Vietnam. Before choosing Humphrey as his VP, Johnson had asked for "unswerving loyalty." Does that remind you of a former Eagle president? To Johnson, loyalty meant unconditional agreement on policies. Humphrey somehow convinced himself that the war was a good idea and promoted it to the public.

Parrots have the ability to fluidly change their perspective then enthusiastically promote their new position. Humphrey may have flipped on Vietnam just to reingratiate himself to LBJ. Parrots like Humphrey have a hard time being disliked and bullied by anyone, let alone their boss.

MERRICK ROSENBERG

Humphrey's speech at the 1968 Democratic Convention in Chicago was bold and demonstrated skilled inflection and timing. *But it just dragged on and on.*

We'll see this Parrot verbosity again in 1994, when Bill Clinton spoke at the Democratic National Convention. He went on for nearly fifty minutes, adding about 2,300 words to a speech that started with 3,200 words of prepared text in the teleprompter.

Like Kennedy, Humphrey's Parrot personality offered an inspirational vision for the country. It was Kennedy's New Frontier in less compelling words:

> Yes, my fellow Democrats, we have recognized and indeed we must recognize the end of an era and the beginning of a new day. And that new day—and that new day belongs to the people—to all the people, everywhere in this land of the people, to every man, woman and child that is a citizen of this Republic.

His speech was political filler linking one famous quote to another, one platitude to the next, without saying much at all. Humphrey constantly repeated words and phrases. Hey, he was a Parrot after all. For example:

> "This moment—this moment is one of personal pride and gratification…"

> "And in the space, and in the space of five years since that tragic moment…"

"And now we must take new initiative, new initiative with prudence and caution"

"These men, these men have given us inspiration and direction…"

"The American Presidency, the American Presidency is a great and powerful office…"

While Humphrey was a Parrot, he was not the rock star type like Kennedy. He was the kind of Parrot who made audiences think, "Okay, already. WE GET IT!!!"

Remember how Johnson asked Humphrey if he could "shut up" for four years? Humphrey was the Joe Biden of his day—unscripted, long-winded, and likely to make a cringe-worthy statement if you left him unsupervised with a microphone for too long.

His famous gaffe during the 1968 campaign was to say in a televised address that "No sane person in the country likes the war in Vietnam, and neither does President Johnson."

Oops. Speaking for an Eagle boss is not the wisest thing to do.

And Then There Were Three

George Wallace was the antithesis of Hubert Humphrey. If Humphrey was the Happy Warrior, Wallace was a hateful warrior. Born in Alabama, Wallace studied law and climbed the ladder of state politics. He ultimately won the race for governor in 1962 and is remembered best for his discriminatory 1963 inauguration speech:

In the name of the greatest people that have ever trod this earth, I draw the line in the dust and toss the gauntlet before the feet of tyranny…and I say, segregation today… segregation tomorrow…segregation forever!

One day, Wallace would recant and apologize for his bigotry—but not in 1968. His Eagle personality stoked the fire of his racist values with the slogan, "Stand Up For America," which captured his vitriol against Vietnam protestors, communists, and people of color.

Wallace is an Eagle who overused his strengths. Recall that when an Eagle overuses assertiveness, it becomes aggressive. When an Eagle pushes directness too far, it becomes blunt insensitivity. When vision is aimed at enemies, it devolves into fearmongering. An Eagle in overuse paints a terrifying future and presents himself as the one and only savior who can stop it.

Wallace's loud, angry campaign attracted poor southern whites who felt threatened by civil rights, the counterculture, and rioting. Wallace's demagogic style has drawn comparison to Donald Trump, who would attract a similar base but direct its fear towards immigrants. Wallace also made inroads in the industrial Midwest, which had begun to rust. Factories were closing and moving to the "right to work" South.

Wallace tried to reframe his segregationist stance as a matter of "law and order," a euphemism for suppressing black people who continued to fight for justice. He warned Americans, "Our system is under attack: the property system, the free enterprise system, and local government. Anarchy prevails today in the streets of the large cities of our country."

Hubert Humphrey never took the challenge from Wallace seriously enough. To a Parrot, how could someone who spews such negativity pose a serious threat to his candidacy?

Lessons Learned

Nixon was a more politically astute Owl candidate in 1968. His campaign choreographed every appearance to gain maximum TV exposure and press coverage. He refused to debate Humphrey or Wallace, lest he screw up or appear less likable on camera, as he did next to Kennedy. His TV appearances consisted of scripted panel shows with everyday Americans (i.e., supporters) lobbing beachball questions. These were perfect for an Owl who didn't like surprises.

Having learned from JFK's example, Nixon mastered the sound bite. Instead of offering specific policies and plans, he made vague appeals. Compared to in 1960, he looked more energetic and stage-trained, waving fingers in his signature "V" for victory sign. This Owl was attempting to tap into some Parrot charisma.

"Tonight, I again proudly accept that nomination for President of the United States," said Nixon at the 1968 Republican National Convention. "But I have news for you. This time there is a difference. This time we are going to win."

He promised to end the Vietnam War, end all crime, and end nuclear brinkmanship with the USSR. He called for an era of negotiation and peace with the Communist powers. He targeted moderate Americans who were overwhelmed by all the chaos:

> It is the voice of the great majority of Americans, the forgotten Americans—the non-shouters; the non-demonstrators…

> …They are not racists or sick; they are not guilty of the crime that plagues the land…

…They provide most of the soldiers who died to keep us free…

…They give steel to the backbone of America. They are good people, they are decent people; they work, and they save, and they pay their taxes, and they care.

Nixon would call these people "The Silent Majority" in a 1969 speech. He related to them in a way no other candidate did. Evan Thomas, one of Nixon's biographers, made this case:

"Hope and fear waged a constant battle in Nixon. At the end of his presidency, fear won out. Nixon was often driven by fear. He was, he believed, surrounded by enemies. At the same time, he understood the hopes and fears of others. The insecurities of the people he memorably named, The Silent Majority."

The 1960 Kennedy campaign taught Nixon not to take any chances in a presidential election. With hope and a connection to The Silent Majority, 1968 Nixon was more likable than 1960 Nixon. However, fear made 1968 Nixon treacherous.

The Extreme Owl

After his loss to Kennedy, Nixon lost faith in humanity and saw himself surrounded by shadowy opponents. Feeling cheated, he became angry, paranoid, and passive aggressive. He believed that winning the 1968 election would justify any means he took to get there.

And why not? The Kennedys taught him that the world is corrupt and unfair, so why should he be held to a different standard? Nixon assumed the worst in his political opponents and did what he believed they would do in his shoes. It was The Big Assumption run amok.

To better understand Nixon's paranoia and how it demonstrates Owl overuse, we have to dig deeper into his psyche. Let's go back to the personality model introduced by Dr. William Moulton Marston in his book, *The Emotions of Normal People.*

Marston explained that there are four kinds of people. Sound familiar?

To simplify this, we'll use the birds instead of Marston's original names for the styles. To start, people view the world as either "favorable" or "antagonistic." Parrots and Doves are on the favorable or friendly side of the continuum, so they inherently trust people. And why not? People mean well. By contrast, Owls and Eagles view the world as antagonistic or hostile. How can you trust people if they are combative and only care about themselves?

In addition, people either feel power over their environment or feel powerless in their environment. Eagle and Parrots believe they are the masters of their environment, so if something goes wrong, they can fix it. On the other hand, Owls and Doves believe they lack control over their environment. If something goes wrong, they are powerless to fix it.

Since **Eagles** perceive the world as hostile but feel capable of dominating their environment, they seek roles of authority in which they can control their destiny.

Since **Parrots** perceive the world as friendly and believe in their ability to change it, life is good! People are nice, and everything will work out for the best because it always does. Or at least that's how Parrots reframe everything that happens.

Doves perceive the world as friendly but believe they have little control over it. This drives Doves to align themselves with others, as there is power in numbers. They seek consensus and avoid conflict to preserve the harmony of their empowering group.

Now let's consider **Owls** like Nixon. Owls perceive the world as hostile *and* believe they lack the power to change their environment. This means that they must try to control everything around them. If they plan everything carefully and do everything perfectly, they will be safe. This also means that they don't trust anyone naturally. Trust has to be earned. And once broken, Owls may never trust that person (or process) again.

After the 1960 race against Kennedy, Nixon lost trust in the fairness of the electoral process. And by God, he wasn't going to be cheated out of another election. Righting a wrong became an all-consuming motivation, and dirty tricks were now fair game.

Nixon's Owl style kicked into overdrive and didn't back down.

Tricky Dick Lives Up to His Name

There *was* a point in October 1968 when Humphrey pulled ahead of Nixon in the polls. Just six days before Election Day, Johnson announced that Hanoi had agreed to hold peace talks in Paris in exchange for a halt to the bombing of North Vietnam. Nixon interpreted the announcement as a ploy to make him lose the election. Of course he did. His over-the-top Owl was now paranoid.

Johnson obviously wanted peace. He was blamed for a controversial war that was killing 1,000 Americans per month and tarnishing his otherwise respected political career. Eagles care a lot about their legacy.

The USSR, North Vietnam's main benefactor, was pressuring Hanoi to reach a settlement so that Johnson would get the credit and Nixon would lose the election. In fact, the Soviets hated the anti-communist Nixon so much that their ambassador to the U.S. offered Humphrey all the help they could provide—financial and otherwise—over lunch. Humphrey rejected their help.

Meanwhile, President Thieu of South Vietnam didn't trust LBJ and feared that he would sell him out to the Communists. Nixon ordered H.R. Haldeman, his campaign chief of staff, to sabotage the negotiations by connecting secretly with Thieu.

The ensuing intrigue became known as the Chennault Affair because Nixon's backchannel to Thieu was Anna Chennault, a China Lobby (i.e., pro-Taiwan, anti-communist) activist. Chennault, acting on Haldeman and Nixon's direction, told Thieu to hold off on negotiations. The message was clear: if you abandon the talks, Nixon will ensure that you get a better deal once he's in office.

Johnson discovered the ploy because he ordered illegal surveillance of Chennault, the South Vietnamese Embassy in Washington, and Thieu's offices in Saigon. However, Johnson and his aides didn't think they had conclusive enough evidence to pin Nixon. So, they kept quiet. Plus, LBJ couldn't publicize the affair without revealing that he spied on political opponents and an ally. Let that sink in for a moment: *Johnson's team illegally spied on Nixon during an election.* Nixon's paranoia wasn't entirely baseless.

South Vietnam boycotted the talks just days before voting began, and Humphrey's momentum tanked.

Keep in mind how treasonous Nixon's actions were. He conspired to keep America in a war that had already claimed 30,000 American lives—and would claim another 28,000—*just to win a presidential election.* Nixon forever denied his involvement in the scheme, but years later, biographer John A. Farrell proved that he was calling the shots.

Remember Nixon's lesson from losing to Kennedy: "I vowed that I would never again enter an election at a disadvantage by being vulnerable to them—or anyone—on the level of political tactics."

The Upset

How did Nixon, an Owl, defeat an Eagle and a Parrot? One could argue that he breaks the Personality Wins Model. In reality, he is the essence of it.

Having Humphrey and Wallace in the same race was like having two country singers on *American Idol.* They split the personality vote and both lost as a result.

Check out the vote totals:

Richard Nixon: 31.7 million popular votes
Hubert Humphrey: 30.9 million popular votes
George Wallace: 9.9 million votes

In many states, Humphrey could have won the electoral votes had Wallace not run. In California, Illinois, Missouri, Virginia, Florida, Ohio, Kentucky, Wisconsin, New Jersey, North Carolina, South Carolina,

Oklahoma, Oregon, and Alaska, Wallace earned enough votes to cost Humphrey a victory.

How close was the race? Political columnist Michael Cohen calculates that if just 42,000 votes had been cast differently in three states—Alaska, Missouri and New Jersey—Humphrey would have tied Nixon for electoral votes.

Combined, the Eagle and Parrot took 9 million more votes than Owl Nixon. Only 43 percent of Americans voted for Tricky Dick.

The Democrats retained control of both the House and the Senate. Not since the 1800s had a president won the election yet failed to gain majorities in either the House or Senate. The power of a third-party candidate should *not* be underestimated.

The Calculating Diplomat

When Nixon took the oath of office in 1969, he was ready to let his peacemaking Dove side fly. Undisputedly anti-communist, Nixon had an advantage in Cold War diplomacy. He could make peace without fearing that opponents would call him "soft" on Communism.

Nixon and his assistant for national security affairs, Henry Kissinger, realized that the road to peace in Vietnam started in Moscow and Beijing, North Vietnam's financiers and arms suppliers.

The USSR and China now had more to fear from each other than the United States. In the 1960s, their relationship began to deteriorate over differences in communist ideology, U.S. relations, and eventually, their shared border, where violence erupted in 1969.

Nixon's Owlish strategy was to play these hostile neighbors against each other. But unlike an Eagle or Parrot who might have done this in the public spotlight, Nixon worked behind the scenes. He and Kissinger went to great lengths to keep their negotiations secret—even from aides and cabinet members—until their work could be packaged and sold to the public.

It started with overtures to Beijing. Mao Zedong, getting the signal, invited U.S. ping-pong players to China in 1971. After more diplomatic work, Nixon became the first U.S. president to visit Communist China and meet with Mao. The Soviet Premier Leonid Brezhnev, worried about letting China and the U.S. become too close, invited Nixon to visit as well. Tricky Dick became the first U.S. president to visit Soviet Moscow. Rapprochement with China and détente, a cold peace with the Soviet Union, were under way.

Nixon always seemed to be playing two hands at once. While withdrawing troops and publicly advocating that South Vietnam take over its own security, Nixon spread the war to Cambodia, where the U.S. aggressively bombed the Ho Chi Minh Trail, the key Communist supply line from North to South Vietnam.

The Owl was calculating. Nixon needed to show Americans that he was ending the war, but he couldn't pull troops out too quickly, otherwise the Communists might take advantage of the power vacuum.

As the 1972 election approached, Nixon had a good story to tell about the wind-down of Vietnam and reconciliation with China and the USSR. But the economy was hurting from inflation and unemployment, and maybe that scared Nixon. He was determined to win again.

Good Heart, Rough Campaign

The Nixon campaign went into 1972 with a mission: make the Democrats pick the candidate with the worst odds of winning. The one person they worried about was Humphrey's former running mate, Senator Edmund Muskie of Maine, a Parrot.

The group that took down Muskie was the Committee to Re-Elect the President (CREEP). It lived up to the name and the acronym. CREEP borrowed tactics that Lyndon Johnson's 5 O'Clock Club used against Barry Goldwater—and went further.

CREEP first struck during the Democratic primaries by tapping into racial tensions. They hired black people to pretend they were campaigning for Muskie in New Hampshire during the primaries when, in truth, they were asked to make rude phone calls to residents. For the Florida primary, they sent fake letters and placed fake ads on behalf of Muskie. One said, "Help Muskie in Busing More Children Now," a ploy to terrify Democrats afraid of desegregation in American schools. As the 2020 exchange between Kamala Harris and Joe Biden would show, busing was a highly controversial issue.

Muskie had some meltdowns and did poorly in the primaries. With the electable and likable Parrot out of the way, the Democratic nomination went to Senator George McGovern of South Dakota.

McGovern was easy to like but hard to elect. He was an idealist Dove-Owl with heartfelt values. The son of a minister, McGovern became a World War II fighter pilot who earned a Distinguished Flying Cross for his bravery in Italy and North Africa.

After the war, he became a history and political science professor and ran successfully for Congress in 1956. He was the first Democrat to win in South Dakota for twenty years. After joining the Kennedy administration to run the Food for Peace program (so Dove), McGovern won election to the Senate in 1962. He championed civil rights, food stamps, and programs to combat hunger abroad while becoming one of the first Democrats to stand against the Vietnam War. To do that during LBJ's prime took guts and an unwavering adherence to his values.

Did McGovern stand a chance against incumbent Nixon? He did. In an Owl versus Dove-Owl matchup, both candidates have a shot.

McGovern campaigned like a Dove: grassroots style. His plan was to start early and win primaries. McGovern announced his candidacy ridiculously early, in January 18, 1971. For a Dove-Owl, slow and steady wins the race.

As a senator, McGovern had been instrumental in reforming the nomination process to ensure that the candidate with the best primary score would run for president. This change helped make ordinary, diverse Americans more important than party bosses and delegates. Fairness is something Doves fight for.

He was a play-by-the-books candidate whose "only prayer was to build a crack political organization," wrote Timothy Crouse from *Rolling Stone*. Crouse went to Wisconsin to interview some of the young, liberal, diverse volunteers who had traveled far to campaign for McGovern. The volunteer corps even included Bill and Hillary Clinton, who served the campaign in Texas.

One McGovern staffer was Ben W. Heineman Jr., now a Harvard fellow who has held various government positions. He admired McGovern's idealism values, "But we knew that he lacked essential qualities of the Robert Kennedy of 1968: charisma and the ability to inspire," Heineman wrote in *The Atlantic* years later. "The much-discussed flat, 'reedy' mid-Western accent would not excite crowds…We could feel that he wasn't connecting with the electorate."

McGovern was innovative in one respect. He was the first presidential candidate to use mass direct-mail marketing to raise money from voters, similar to how Barack Obama, Bernie Sanders, and Elizabeth Warren would raise money—a little bit from a lot of people.

McGovern's campaign was methodical and well structured, playing off of his secondary Owl style. The campaign spent its money carefully, gathered data from potential voters in the field, and gradually raised McGovern from polling at five percent in 1971 to earning the nomination. It's hard to say whether he would have succeeded had CREEP not destroyed Muskie's campaign. Either way, the Democrats had a Dove-Owl at the top of the ticket.

In his acceptance speech at the 1972 Democratic Convention, McGovern was kind, smiley, and so genuinely appreciative of his colleagues in the room. His slogan, "Come Home, America," had a comforting, down-home Dove flavor.

"I accept your nomination with a full and grateful heart," he said. And his vision for America reflected his personality:

> It is the time for this land to become again a witness to the world for what is noble and just in human affairs. It is the time to live more with faith and less with fear—with an abiding confidence that can sweep away the strongest barriers between us and teach us that we truly are brothers and sisters."

McGovern's Dove message of unity and dedication to end the Vietnam War backfired, as he reflected years later. "I don't think the American people had a clear picture of either Nixon or me," said McGovern in a 2005 interview. "I think they thought that Nixon was a strong, decisive, tough-minded guy, and that I was an idealist and antiwar guy who might not attach enough significance to the security of the country."

In truth, McGovern's greatest blunder was to name Missouri Senator Thomas Eagleton as his running mate. Word broke that Eagleton had been treated for depression three times and had undergone electro-shock therapy. This sparked a debate: should someone with a history of mental illness be in a position to inherit the nuclear launch codes? Keep in mind, there was much less understanding and acceptance of mental illness in the 1970s.

At first, McGovern said he was with Eagleton "1000 percent." Then, under pressure, he dropped Eagleton and took on Sargent Shriver as his VP. It was an easy narrative for the GOP: McGovern had poor judgment, he was indecisive, and he backstabbed a friend. Essentially, they conveyed that McGovern was a weak Eagle and a disloyal Dove.

Maybe he could have presented himself better. But he could not have known what Nixon was up to.

Trickier Dick

The 1972 Republican Convention was a victory lap for the popular Richard Nixon. His outreach to China and the USSR was well received. The draft was over, and troops were returning home as Kissinger's negotiations with North Vietnam made progress.

Nixon even displayed some Dove during his speech accepting the Republican nomination. Perhaps no presidential speech in history used the word "peace" so many times—thirty-six to be exact. Peace at home. Peace in Vietnam. Peace with the Soviets and Chinese. The speech covered almost no other theme.

"Let us build a peace that our children and all the children of the world can enjoy for generations to come," Nixon concluded.

Nixon should have felt confident going into the campaign against McGovern, who was further left than most Americans. But Nixon, haunted by his race against Kennedy, wouldn't leave anything to chance. Trust had been broken for this Owl, and he planned to win at any cost.

Nixon's caddy style of villainy made him seem like a character deleted from early drafts of *Mean Girls*. His staff compiled an "Enemies List" that grew to 200 people. Each entry included a name, location, a reason for being on the list, and comments like, "first class S.O.B." and "a scandal would be most helpful here."

CREEP also had company this time. In 1971, military analyst Daniel Ellsberg leaked the Pentagon Papers, which unveiled the shocking level of misinformation and poor decision-making in Vietnam. In response, Nixon formed the Special Investigations Unit, members of which called themselves "The Plumbers" because their job was to fix leaks. They worked to discredit Ellsberg and even broke into his psychiatrist's office looking for damaging information.

Nixon felt he needed The Plumbers because his severe Owl paranoia sensed a plot against him (as evidenced by the Pentagon Papers leak). He couldn't convince FBI Director J. Edgar Hoover to search for conspiracies in the government or the press, so Nixon illegally formed The Plumbers to do the job. They committed a flood of crimes.

On June 17, 1972, five Plumbers were caught breaking into the Democratic National Committee headquarters located at the Watergate complex in Washington, D.C. They wanted to replace an audio surveillance device that had stopped working and conduct additional espionage while they were at it. The Plumbers were found with microphones disguised as ChapSticks, cameras and film, and $3,500 in consecutively numbered Benjamins. Their mistake was to tape the spring locks on the doors horizontally rather than vertically, and a night guard noticed.

When the story hit the papers, Nixon denied any involvement and kept it out of the campaign, even as *Washington Post* journalists Bob

Woodward and Carl Bernstein sounded the alarm. In 1972, Nixon won every state except Massachusetts (and Washington D.C.).

To this day, no one knows the full extent of CREEP and The Plumbers' operations. Nixon, who felt surrounded by enemies, went so far to win an election that he ultimately lost the presidency.

The Crook

Ever since Watergate, numerous scandals have earned their own "gate" nickname. In presidential politics, there has been Iran/Contragate with Ronald Reagan, Troopergate with Sarah Palin, and Whitewatergate with Bill Clinton.

However, future presidents, including Reagan and Clinton, have demonstrated that crime and misconduct don't necessarily sink a presidency. It depends on how the president handles the situation—and personality certainly shapes the response. You probably know that Nixon didn't handle his scandal well.

To see Watergate through Nixon's eyes, rather than the public's, is a chilling experience.

Nixon knew exactly what CREEP and the Plumbers were doing. On June 23, 1972, just six days after the Watergate break-in, Nixon and Chief of Staff H.R. Haldeman held the so-called "smoking gun" conversation. It was captured on the Oval Office's secret audio recording system.

The tape depicts an Owl's mind trying to plot his way out of a trap. The FBI was tracing the source of the $3,500 in cash caught with the Plumbers. Nixon and Haldeman knew it would eventually lead investigators to CREEP and the White House.

Nixon went back and forth with Haldeman trying to anticipate how his operatives would lie and who, if anyone, could challenge them. He was in chess mode, planning where to move the pieces to block the investigation from reaching him. Nixon and Haldeman decided to manipulate the CIA Director into stopping the investigation by claiming (falsely) that Watergate was a sensitive national security matter.

Between June 23, 1972, and August 8, 1974, the day of his resignation from office, Nixon shamelessly lied. In April 30, 1973, he gave a televised address announcing the resignations of key officials who were implicated in the scandal. Just listen to Nixon:

> Last June 17, while I was in Florida trying to get a few days rest after my visit to Moscow, I first learned from news reports of the Watergate break-in. I was appalled at this senseless, illegal action, and I was shocked to learn that employees of the Re-Election Committee were apparently among those guilty.

Nixon didn't just lie in yes-no format; he concocted an alternate reality to protect himself. He tried to convince the public that *he was lied to as well* and insisted that all CREEP members cooperate with the FBI. This from the guy who plotted to sabotage that same FBI investigation.

As the circle tightened around Nixon, he invented more lies and stories to protect himself. Based on the smoking gun tape, it's fair to assume that Nixon planned his lies carefully. He employed all of his intelligence and twisted Owl logic to save himself and no one else.

On November 17, 1973, Nixon participated in a Q&A at the Annual Convention of the Associated Press Managing Editors Association. They hammered him with questions about Watergate, but he brushed away each question with a lie or excuse. Nixon grew short-tempered and defensive as the talk went on. He spoke the words everyone remembers:

> Let me just say this, and I want to say this to the television audience: I made my mistakes, but in all of my years of public life, I have never profited, never profited from public service—I have earned every cent.
>
> And in all of my years of public life, I have never obstructed justice. And I think, too, that I could say that in my years of public life, that I welcome this kind of examination, because people have got to know whether or not their President is a crook. Well, I am not a crook. I have earned everything I have got.

Notice that connection between two disparate things. Nixon is being questioned about whether he lied and obstructed justice, yet part of his defense is that, "I have earned everything I have got."

In that moment, Nixon defended his entire political career and rise to the presidency. No matter what he did on his road to the White House, he earned it—because that is what anyone would have to do to earn it. JFK cheated and earned it. Johnson ran unethical smear campaigns and earned it. Why should Nixon be held to different standards? This is Owl logic mixed with paranoia and a lack of integrity.

On August 5, 1974, out came the smoking gun tape, which left no doubts about Nixon's role in the Watergate cover-up. Nixon announced his resignation on August 8, and Gerald Ford became the thirty-eighth president of the United States the following day. Today, Nixon is a model of how personality can turn a political fiasco into the undoing of a presidency.

1976:
Mr. Nice Guy and The Peanut Farmer

"If compassion and mercy are not compatible with
politics then something is the matter with politics."
- Gerald Ford

"I'd like to be remembered as someone who was
a champion of peace and human rights."
– Jimmy Carter

When A Nation Needs Healing

On October 10, 1973, Vice President Spiro Agnew resigned in disgrace. The U.S. Department of Justice had surfaced his long record of corruption. The crows were circling Nixon's presidency.

Nixon needed a replacement VP, and Congressional leaders gave him one option: Gerald Ford, the House Minority Leader from Michigan. Ford was sworn in as vice president on December 6, 1973.

As the Watergate scandal broke, Ford initially defended Nixon. But by the summer of 1974, the abuses of power had become indefensible.

149

Nixon resigned on August 8. The next day, Ford became the thirty-eighth president of the United States, and a month later, he pardoned Nixon.

Washington Post journalist Bob Woodward, who broke the Watergate story, fondly recalls the middle-of-the-night phone call from his partner, Carl Bernstein: "The son of a bitch pardoned the son of a bitch."

But why did Ford do it?

Twenty-five years later, Woodward finally interviewed former President Gerald Ford about the pardon. For years, Woodward (like most people) assumed that Nixon and Ford traded the presidency for a pardon.

The truth was far from it.

Woodward conducted six interviews with Ford before he would open up about the pardon. Ford *was* offered a deal but refused it. He knew it was wrong and illegal.

Ford ultimately pardoned Nixon so that the nation could heal and move forward. At this point, you can probably guess which personality prioritizes healing over power.

The trial of Nixon would have become a media sensation, another three years of Watergate. Ford knew the pardon would be unpopular, but he needed to redirect America's focus towards its priorities: a struggling economy, the wind-down of Vietnam, and the ongoing Cold War. It was "an act of courage," Woodward believes.

What kind of politician hides a story of integrity, righteousness, and bravery—a story that would have made him look good—for the sake of national healing and unity? A Dove.

Ford didn't want credit for his choice, nor did he attack Nixon when it would have been politically convenient. "This is an hour of history that troubles our minds and hurts our hearts," said Ford in his first address as president. "I am acutely aware that you have not elected me as your President by your ballots, and so I ask you to confirm me as your President with your prayers."

He sounded like a kind doctor concerned about the patient's welfare yet optimistic about the chances of recovery. He said, "As we bind up the internal wounds of Watergate, more painful and more poisonous than those of foreign wars, let us restore the golden rule to our political process, and let brotherly love purge our hearts of suspicion and of hate."

Prayers, heart, and brotherly love are Dove words. On September 8, the day Ford pardoned Nixon, he framed his decision as a Dove would:

> My conscience tells me clearly and certainly that I cannot prolong the bad dreams that continue to reopen a chapter that is closed. My conscience tells me that only I, as President, have the constitutional power to firmly shut and seal this book. My conscience tells me it is my duty, not merely to proclaim domestic tranquility but to use every means that I have to insure it.

Ford ended Watergate because he believed that America needed closure and "tranquility," as he put it. And Ford took the brunt of America's anger.

The slumping economy and ongoing détente—a gradual reconciliation with the Soviets—earned Ford enemies on all sides. Confidence in the U.S. plummeted further when, in the spring of 1975, cameras showed the Vietnamese Communists conquering Saigon as U.S. embassy personnel fled by helicopter, leaving South Vietnamese colleagues to a vengeful enemy.

It seemed like Ford's popularity couldn't drop any lower, then unemployment hit 9.2 percent in June of 1975, the highest rate since the Great Depression. Regardless, Ford announced his candidacy for the 1976 presidential election.

His primary challenger was none other than California Governor Ronald Reagan. Despite being far more dynamic and charismatic than Ford, Reagan narrowly lost the nomination at the Republican National Convention in Kansas City, Missouri. Remember, Parrots beat Owls in general elections, not primaries. Reagan would have his chance soon enough.

The Republican convention was notoriously Machiavellian. There was violence, drunkenness, and efforts to woo delegates that bordered on bribery. Phones were ripped out of the walls to throttle communications between the delegates and campaigns. Ford's team prevented Reagan from speaking before the voting because they knew that would give him the edge. One delegate broke her leg but was prevented from going to the hospital because the Ford campaign thought her substitute might vote for Reagan. Moreover, someone from the Republican National Committee housed the Reagan delegates at hotels seventy miles from the convention to make their lives difficult.

Just because Ford was a Dove, that didn't mean he stopped his campaign or his allies in the RNC from using dirty tricks. This was politics, after all.

Ford won, and his speech accepting the nomination was a Dove's checklist of everything that had gone right since 1974, and everything he would do next. Ford had no vision for the presidency. He just had two years on the job. "My record is one of progress, not platitudes," he said. "My record is one of specifics, not smiles. My record is one of performance, not promises."

Too bad for Ford, the "record" doesn't matter much in presidential elections. His image as a Dove-ish president was sealed. And so was his image as a clumsy, bumbling leader. Cameras caught him falling down and up the steps of Air Force One, and Chevy Chase reenacted the president's klutziness on *Saturday Night Live* week after week.

Jimmy Who?

He was an "oratorical mortician," said Senator Eugene McCarthy, a candidate who had the disposition of sugar-free, lukewarm oatmeal. He was a peanut farmer, a nuclear engineer, and born-again Christian who would give *Playboy* magazine one of the most awkward interviews in its history.

"I'm Jimmy Carter and I'm running for president," he said over and over and *over* again in his Georgia drawl. "I will never lie to you."

Carter was a foil to the corrupt, unethical Nixon. Similar to Bill Clinton and Donald Trump, he was a D.C. outsider who tapped into America's frustration with the political establishment. As a Dove-Owl, Carter was very different from those two candidates.

Unassuming, plain-spoken, and moralistic, Carter ran as a conscientious candidate who would rise above the dirtiness of politics as usual. Carter grew up in Plains, Georgia, under the strict regime of his father, a farmer who employed 200 black tenant farmers, and his mother, a Peace Corps veteran who served as a community nurse. Carter entered the U.S. Naval Academy in Annapolis in 1943, earned top marks in engineering, and spent seven years as a naval officer.

He returned to Georgia in 1953 to take over the family peanut farm from his dying father. Feeling called to public service, he earned a seat on the state legislature in 1962 and ran for Governor in 1966 but failed. Taking the loss quite hard, Carter went through his born-again experience and became a devout evangelical Christian. He won the race for governor in 1970.

Carter gave uninspiring public addresses but excelled at connecting with people in personal settings. There's the Dove. An introvert, Carter spent long hours reading documents alone and often communicated with his staff in writing rather than through conversation. And there's the Owl.

When the peanut farmer from Georgia announced his campaign, the *Atlanta Constitution* wrote a painful headline: "Jimmy Who Is Running For What!?" Keep in mind, Carter was the governor of Georgia at the time!

Carter's campaign strategists carefully analyzed the Democratic Party's new primary voting rules and figured out that Carter could gain delegates based on his percentage of votes in any state—he didn't have to win each state outright.

So, they put Carter on primary ballots in all fifty states and had him campaign all over the country and especially in Iowa because the caucus took place earlier there than in New Hampshire, where candidates traditionally focused. The result was that Carter had stacked up delegates so early and widely that none of his contenders could catch up.

Essentially, Carter won the nomination because he and his staff were the best at reading and applying the rules. That's what Owls do. Accepting the nomination in July 1976, Carter set a new tone: "1976 will not be a year of politics as usual. It can be a year of inspiration and hope, and it will be a year of concern, of quiet and sober reassessment of our nation's character and purpose."

Those are the *fighting* words of a Dove who approached the Oval Office with idealism. When we think of rousing campaign promises, we don't think of "quiet and sober reassessment." Carter smiled like someone who felt happy to be accepted, not someone who felt enlivened by attention and power. He had the demeanor of someone applying to be the next Mr. Rogers, not the next president.

"We need a Democratic President and a Congress to work in harmony for a change, with mutual respect for a change," said Carter. Could that be any more Dove?

Carter thought U.S. politics *should* be better than it was and *could* be better than it had ever been. His Dove idealism sat well with a public who couldn't believe how slimy politics had become under Nixon.

Debates Without Conflict

On September 21, two days before the first of three presidential debates, *Playboy* released excerpts of an interview they conducted with Jimmy Carter. It was *not* what you'd expect from the God-fearing Georgian:

> And Christ set some almost impossible standards for us. Christ said, "I tell you that anyone who looks on a woman with lust has in his heart already committed adultery." I've looked on a lot of women with lust. I've committed adultery in my heart many times.

> This is something that God recognizes I will do—and I have done it—and God forgives me for it. But that doesn't mean that I condemn someone who not only looks at a woman with lust but who leaves his wife and shacks up with somebody out of wedlock.

Christ says, Don't consider yourself better than someone else because one guy screws a whole bunch of women
while the other guy is loyal to his wife.

Most American men probably thought, "Wait, does that mean
I've committed adultery?" And more pious, undecided Americans were
unnerved by Carter's irreverent use of the terms "shacks up" and "screws."
It seemed so out of character, which somehow made it more offensive.
Perhaps Lyndon Johnson could have gotten away with saying that, but
imagine Vice President Mike Pence using the phrase "screws a whole
bunch of women" in a sentence. It just feels wrong.

That slip-up gave Ford some hope. He'd been trailing in the polls,
and Carter's strange confession contradicted everything Americans
thought of the man. Ford had a chance to throw Carter's mistake in his
face. But that's not what a Dove does.

The New York Times described their first encounter as a "genteel
debate" in which the candidates cited "an often bewildering series of statistics and details." While they were both Doves, each had a bit of Owl as
well. The sound went out for twenty-seven minutes while the two candidates stood patiently behind their lecterns. Carter gave his sermon on
"compassion" and "brotherhood" while Ford recounted his record. Again.

"With both Mr. Carter and Mr. Ford exercising obvious efforts
to treat the other respectfully, the debate generated little conflict," *The
Times* concluded. When you get two Doves on stage, that's how it goes.
Neither Ford nor Carter attacked, but Ford was considered the winner.

At the second debate, Ford blew it. Max Frankel, associate editor of *The New York Times*, asked Ford about his handling of Soviet
relations with a roundabout question implying that Ford was being too
weak. Ford's gave an equally roundabout answer that confirmed Frankel's

suspicion: "…there is no Soviet domination of Eastern Europe and there never will be under a Ford administration," he said.

A perplexed Frankel jumped in before Carter could respond: "… did I understand you to say, sir, that the Russians are not using Eastern Europe as their own sphere of influence in occupying most of the countries there…?"

In fact, that's exactly what the Russians were doing.

Ford tried to explain his reasoning: "I don't believe, Mr. Frankel, that the Yugoslavians consider themselves dominated by the Soviet Union. I don't believe that the Romanians consider themselves dominated by the Soviet Union. I don't believe that the Poles consider themselves dominated by the Soviet Union."

Ford sounded out of touch with reality. Somewhere in his rambling response, Carter finally found some Eagle and hammered a nail into Ford's coffin: "And I would like to see Mr. Ford convince the Polish-Americans and the Czech-Americans and the Hungarian-Americans in this country that those countries don't live under the domination and supervision of the Soviet Union behind the Iron Curtain."

Ford never recovered from this error. In debates with so few memorable moments, that one stuck. The public already saw Ford as the clumsy president who couldn't get on or off Air Force One without tumbling. Ford wasn't prepared for the threat posed by staircases—and he sure as hell wasn't ready to deal with the Soviets if he thought Eastern Europe was free and independent.

The third debate was considered a draw for the candidates. Carter kept his lead in the polls, thanks in part to Ford's Eastern Europe gaffe. Carter won the election with 50.1 percent of the popular vote.

A Dove's Rough Four Years

He took the oath of office as "Jimmy Carter" rather than "James Earl Carter" and walked from the Capitol to the White House instead of taking a fancy limousine. He wanted to show solidarity with struggling Americans by not wasting taxpayer money during a recession. His poll numbers suggested that Americans respected this gesture.

His Dove-Owl ways soon backfired. Carter was determined to prevent any activity that seemed wasteful or corrupt. It was classic Dove high-mindedness compounded with Owl stubbornness. His efforts to cut "pork" from bills alienated Congressional Democrats, and his unwillingness to engage in "backroom dealing" derailed the relationship further. Apparently, Carter was too upstanding for Washington.

Even when Carter succeeded, *it didn't look that way to the public.*

It didn't help that Carter alienated the media. As Professor of Politics Robert A. Strong put it, "They chafed at his moralistic, 'eat your peas' attitudes, and portrayed him either as a cynical and manipulative politician or an amateurish incompetent." Carter gave the media his unvarnished Dove feelings, but emotions don't make good stories. So, the media dragged Carter into their more interesting though less flattering narratives.

If you have a Dove in your family, they're probably a peacemaker. And when a Dove is the president, the same is likely true. The high point of Carter's presidency was at Camp David in 1978, where he brokered a lasting peace between Egypt and Israel. The two countries had been in hot or cold war since Israel's founding in 1948. Carter worked for twelve days straight to reach a peace deal wherein Israel would withdraw from the Sinai Peninsula (which it took from Egypt in 1967), and Egypt would recognize Israel's government.

When the talks almost broke down, Carter had choice words to keep Egyptian Prime Minister Anwar el-Sadat from leaving:

> Our friendship is over. You promised me that you would stay at Camp David as long as I was willing to negotiate, and here you have made your plans to leave without even consulting me, and I consider this a serious blow to our personal friendship and to the relationship between Egypt and the United States.

Jimmy shamed a prime minister into continuing peace talks by threatening to end their friendship. *So Dove.*

In 1979, Iranians overthrew Shah Mohammad Reza Pahlavi, their authoritarian leader who was seen as a U.S. puppet. Ayatollah Khomeini, a religious figurehead in exile, returned to Iran and became Supreme Leader. Carter decided to harbor the Shah in the U.S. In response, Iranian college students overran the U.S. embassy and took sixty-six people hostage.

Carter froze Iranian assets and tried to negotiate the release of the Americans, but without any success. The public lost faith in Carter, who seemed too timid or indecisive to end the crisis. As pressure mounted, Carter approved a covert rescue mission, which failed when one of the eight helicopters crashed in the desert, killing all eight servicemen aboard. The hostages were dispersed around Iran so that no further rescue attempts could be made. The bungling of the crisis reinforced the impression that Carter was weak and inept.

No one doubted Carter's honesty and desire to do the right thing. They doubted his effectiveness. Carter was a Dove who showed his hand to everyone yet didn't want or take anyone's help. By comparison, Eisenhower was a Dove who led others to do what he could never accomplish alone. Carter wore his values and his emotions on his sleeve. Eisenhower kept close guard over his image and never let the public see him as anything but a kind, fatherly figure.

Note that Dove-Parrot Joe Biden's disastrous exit from Afghanistan has been framed, by some, as a failure of Carter-ish proportions. How Biden handles that episode—and how his opponent addresses it—could decide the 2024 election.

Thanks to those rough four years, Jimmy Carter has the unique distinction of being considered a better ex-president than president. His work since leaving office has demonstrated Dove compassion at the highest level.

Carter has volunteered his time to improve quality of life and alleviate suffering for people around the world. He has spoken with heads of states on behalf of victims of human rights abuses. He has monitored elections, mediated conflicts between warring states, and worked tirelessly on a campaign to eradicate Guinea worm and other diseases.

In 2002, Carter received the Nobel Peace Prize for his efforts "to find peaceful solutions to international conflicts, to advance democracy and human rights, and to promote economic and social development."

Carter may be a cautionary tale for future presidents. But he is, without doubt, a role model for former presidents who seek to use their experience and power for good.

1980, 1984:
The Great Communicator

*"The most terrifying words in the English language are:
I'm from the government and I'm here to help."*

- Ronald Reagan

Just Kidding

On August 11, 1984, human civilization almost came to an end—thanks to a joke.

During a sound check for his weekly radio address, President Ronald Reagan said, "My fellow Americans. I'm pleased to tell you today that I've signed legislation that will outlaw Russia forever. We begin bombing in five minutes."

By August 14, the story played on Moscow news stations, where it was not treated as a laughing matter. The Soviets went on "Red Alert" the next day, and their military headquarters sent a coded message that said, "We now embark on military action against the U.S. forces."

As a Soviet unit went on wartime alert, so did Japanese units allied with the U.S. Meanwhile, the U.S. and Japan quickly broke the code and went on the lookout for an imminent Soviet attack. Within thirty minutes, the alert was cancelled, and U.S. officials believed this was the Soviet's way of sending a message back to Reagan.

European newspapers considered Reagan's joke "irresponsible" and "unbecoming" of a leader. The Soviets, who thankfully didn't take Reagan seriously, called it "unprece-dentedly hostile."

Oops.

A Reagan associate tried to downplay the situation to *The New York Times*: "He uses his humor to show that he's sensitive to the issues. He'll make statements that he knows will jangle people and would horrify his aides if they were made in public. He uses it to pull people's legs."

What kind of personality jokes about nuclear holocaust? Only a Parrot.

The president who took humor far enough to nearly start a war arguably did more than any other president to *end* the threat of a nuclear war. Reagan was too imaginative, spontaneous, and confident to play by the established rules of politics. His unconventional ways took the White House, popularized trickle-down economics, and rusted the Iron Curtain.

Reagan was born in 1911 in Tampico, Illinois, just southwest of Chicago. The son of an alcoholic salesman, Reagan developed a killer sense of humor, possibly as a coping mechanism for his stressful childhood (the next Parrot president to follow Reagan also had an alcoholic father).

Reagan's years at Eureka College in Illinois put today's resume-padding to shame. He was there on a football scholarship, joined the swim team, performed in plays, debated, reported for the school newspaper, joined a fraternity, worked as a lifeguard and swimming coach, and became the student council president. His interests and energy were inexhaustible.

After graduating with a gentleman's C average, Reagan took a job as a sportscaster in 1931. It was an ideal job for a Parrot. He learned to communicate with a crowd he couldn't see, which would be invaluable in his political career. He spiced up baseball games and commercials with dramatic improvisations. In 1937, Warner Brothers signed Reagan to perform in movies, and by 1954, he'd appeared in fifty-two films. Like Dwight Eisenhower and Donald Trump, Reagan was a public figure before he entered politics.

And like Trump, Reagan was originally a Democrat. In fact, Reagan modeled his political style after FDR—a good pick given their similarities. In the 1950s, Reagan's film career dwindled, so he reinvented himself as a spokesman for General Electric.

His political transition happened during his tenure with GE. One biographer suggests that Reagan's million-dollar contract and exposure to other highly-paid businesspeople soured him on high taxes. Whatever the real motivation, he joined the Democrats-for-Eisenhower campaigns in the 1950s. In 1962, he registered as a Republican for the first time.

In 1966, with businesspeople and Republican operatives pushing his candidacy, Reagan ran for governor of California on a low tax, small government platform. He easily defeated the two-term incumbent. He was becoming famous for his Parrot one-liners. When a reporter asked what kind of governor he'd be, Reagan joked, "I don't know, I've never played a governor."

The truth was that Reagan did play a politician. A reporter asked during the 1980 campaign how an actor could run for president. Reagan replied, "How can a president *not* be an actor?"

Reagan was also keenly aware of his limitations. When he took the helm as governor in 1966, he had no clue how to run a state, so he let aides handle the details while he focused on radio, TV, and rallies. Reagan brilliantly staffed for his weaknesses and played to his strengths.

Although Reagan ran as Parrot, he often flexed his personality to fit the situation. He was able to play an Eagle and Dove and, if necessary, he could pull off a B-movie Owl.

Reagan shared a lot of statistics while on the campaign trail, but they didn't always match up with reality...or his previous iterations of the same statistics. Nevertheless, he projected all four styles and appealed to everyone. We refer to folks who can flex to all four birds as chameleons. We'll meet a few other chameleons in the chapters ahead.

By 1976, Reagan had the resume to challenge Gerald Ford for the Republican presidential nomination. It didn't work out, but he began plotting for 1980. And of all the people who worked hard to make Reagan president, no one worked harder than Jimmy Carter.

The Malaise in the White House

Jimmy Carter was unlucky. He inherited a stagnating economy from Gerald Ford and a train of international crises he was powerless to stop. Still, Carter came across as a self-righteous Mary Poppins insistent on giving America its medicine, but without a spoonful of sugar.

In July 1979, he signed a prescription that reporter John Dickerson once introduced as "the most tone-deaf speech in modern American history." Carter was a Dove who overused his strengths.

On live TV, Carter explained to Americans why *they* as a nation—not his administration—hadn't overcome the energy crisis and accompanying recession "It's clear," said Carter, "that the true problems of our Nation are much deeper—deeper than gasoline lines or energy shortages, deeper even than inflation or recession."

He argued that criticisms of his leadership didn't demonstrate his ineptness as president, but rather a "fundamental threat to American democracy." Carter laid out his thesis:

> It is a crisis of confidence. It is a crisis that strikes at the very heart and soul and spirit of our national will. We can see this crisis in the growing doubt about the meaning of our own lives and in the loss of a unity of purpose for our nation.

> The erosion of our confidence in the future is threatening to destroy the social and the political fabric of America.

Carter made The Big Assumption: if it's important to me, it's important to everyone. You can hear the logic swirling around in his brain: I'm feeling demoralized, so everyone else must be feeling demoralized too. If I validate their emotions, everyone will feel heard and understood.

Some Americans probably felt as spiritually crushed as he did, but they *never* want to hear that from the person who's supposed to revitalize and lead the country. This was a moment for Parrot optimism, not Dove introspection.

President Obama's so-called "apology tour" in 2008 would draw critique for similar reasons: the biggest *faux pas* an American president can make is to say negative things about America, even if they're true. Yes, Obama has some Dove in his personality.

Carter's speech became a checklist of *everything going wrong in America*. It seemed like Carter was campaigning against himself. He even impugned America's material prosperity, which was one of its most effective weapons against Communism: "We have learned that piling up material goods cannot fill the emptiness of lives which have no confidence or purpose."

Doves internalize their issues and can have a loud internal critic. But when they share that critic with the country, it doesn't send a message of hope for the future.

"This is not a message of happiness or reassurance, but it is the truth and it is a warning," Carter assured his audience. He knew the speech was pessimistic, but he couldn't contain himself.

Carter acted like a stressed, rejected Dove. Just as Carter had become despondent after losing his first race for governor of Georgia, he had fallen into another black hole. The last time, Carter climbed out through a born-again experience. This time, Carter projected his "malaise" (a general feeling of discomfort or uneasiness) onto the nation. Although he never used that word, his address was remembered as "the malaise speech."

Carter wrapped up with his six-point plan to fix the energy crisis, but no one remembered it. Voters remembered how their president, who was supposed to lead the nation, blamed an energy crisis on America's spiritual void.

After *that* speech, Republicans were lining up to run against Carter. The president had put the Oval Office on a platter and served it to his hungry Republican guests.

The Opposite of That

Ronald Reagan had the good fortune to be governor of California between 1967 and 1975. He wasn't in Washington during the Vietnam War or Watergate. When Ford lost to Carter in 1976, the GOP knew that

Reagan was on deck. He had a clean slate, and now he had a Democratic opponent doing everything possible to lose the race.

In November 1979, Reagan announced his run for president from the New York Hilton. The dark wood, leather-backed chair, and American flag in the background resembled a presidential office. The Great Communicator spoke in a high-spirited, persuasive Parrot style that was easy to understand and trust.

Reagan's campaign announcement was a Parrot takedown of Carter's malaise speech. First, Reagan framed Americans as a hopeful people—the opposite of what Carter claimed: "Someone once said that the difference between an American and any other kind of person is that an American lives in anticipation of the future because he knows it will be a great place."

Next, he referenced Carter's malaise speech without saying the president's name. Reagan was known for avoiding blunt conflict (though as you'll see, he could bring out the Eagle). As a Parrot, he liked to be liked, even by his enemies. He characterized Carter as a doom-and-gloom leader who believed that America had peaked:

> There are those in our land today, however, who would have us believe that the United States, like other great civilizations of the past, has reached the zenith of its power; that we are weak and fearful, reduced to bickering with each other and no longer possessed of the will to cope with our problems.

> Much of this talk has come from leaders who claim that our problems are too difficult to handle. We are supposed to meekly accept their failures as the most which humanly can be done.

And then, Reagan brilliantly positioned himself as the hero with his cape blowing in the wind, the *real* voice of Americans: "I don't believe that. And, I don't believe you do either. That is why I am seeking the presidency. I cannot and will not stand by and see this great country destroy itself."

Reagan knew better than to make jokes without a live audience. He played the optimistic, upbeat politician, a foil to the pessimistic, dejected Carter. He was determined to hold America to its own highest standards—to be the "city upon a hill" John Winthrop promised in 1630:

> A troubled and afflicted mankind looks to us, pleading for us to keep our rendezvous with destiny; that we will uphold the principles of self-reliance, self-discipline, morality, and--above all--responsible liberty for every individual that we will become that shining city on a hill.
>
> I believe that you and I together can keep this rendezvous with destiny.

After a strong start in the primaries, Reagan had to deal with George H.W. Bush who, like Carter, read the primary rules closely and gained a lead by focusing on Iowa. He famously called Reagan's low-tax ideas "voodoo economics." But Reagan managed to defeat Bush in a made-for-TV moment.

In February 1980, Reagan and Bush wanted to have a debate, but ironically, they couldn't agree on how to format it or pay for it. First, the *Nashua Telegraph*, a New Hampshire newspaper, offered to sponsor the event. The Federal Election Commission wouldn't allow it, so Reagan offered to split the cost with Bush's campaign. They said no, thanks.

Reagan paid in full *and* invited the four other candidates to attend. Bush didn't want the others in the debate—he wanted to narrow the race to himself and Reagan.

Here was the scene at the debate: Bush and Reagan are standing on stage in a high school. The four other candidates are waiting awkwardly off to the side of the stage, wondering if they'll be allowed to participate. Reagan began arguing with Jon Breen, the editor of the *Telegraph* and debate moderator, to include the others before starting. Over the microphone, Breen told the sound engineer to turn off Reagan's mic.

Bush look confused and unsure of what to do. Reagan got fierce. He picked up the mic and went from a funny Parrot to take-charge Eagle: "I'm paying for this microphone, Mr. Green!"

He got the moderator's name wrong, but it didn't matter. Details. The crowd erupted in cheers. Even the four other candidates on stage clapped for Reagan. Bush got the one-on-one debate he wanted, but the content was forgotten. Reagan had already won. He played the Eagle at the top of the food chain. He went on to receive the Republican nomination and made Bush his running mate.

Slaughter Rule

In Little League baseball, sometimes coaches invoke the "slaughter rule." If one team is up by an insurmountable number of runs, it's game over. There's no point in embarrassing the losing team any further.

Unfortunately for Carter, there was no slaughter rule in politics. Although polls occasionally placed Carter within the margin of error, *no* other indicator was encouraging. In a Dove-Owl versus Parrot race in the TV era, Reagan was unstoppable.

However, Reagan had two vulnerabilities that Democrats would try to exploit. First, Reagan and facts didn't get along well. He knew what he wanted to say, but he tended to botch details and statistics. Very Parrot. Carter, oppositely, was obsessed with getting the facts and details right. Very Dove-Owl.

Second, Reagan was considered a warmonger and loose cannon. As we've learned again and again though, American voters don't seem to mind inaccuracy or aggression. This line of attack was bound to fail.

Carter, who four years prior touted his honesty, compassion, and "brotherly love," made vicious attacks against Reagan. He suggested, for instance, that under Reagan's rule, "Americans might be separated black from white, Jew from Christian, North from South." Carter's two most redeeming qualities—telling the truth and being thoughtful—were receding along with the economy.

Reagan, on the other hand, was clever in his attacks: "Recession is when your neighbor loses his job. Depression is when you lose yours. And recovery is when Jimmy Carter loses his."

On another occasion, he told a crowd that Jimmy Carter was supposed to go on *60 Minutes* to talk about his accomplishments, but "that would have left fifty-nine minutes to fill."

The witty Parrot strikes again.

The candidates agreed to just one debate, which took place on October 28, 1980. Carter came armed with facts. Whether they were true or false, Reagan grinned and dismissed them with the same line: "There you go again." His clear language and self-assured smile washed away whatever Carter tried to smear on him.

The clincher, delivered in Reagan's closing statement, became famous: "Next Tuesday is Election Day. Next Tuesday all of you will go to the polls, will stand there in the polling place and make a decision. I think when you make that decision, it might be well if you would ask yourself, are you better off than you were four years ago?"

Carter's last hope was to pull off a so-called "October surprise" by successfully releasing the hostages who had been captured at the U.S. Embassy in Iran. It didn't happen. Reagan won with 489 electoral votes to Carter's 59. Iran released the hostages on Reagan's inauguration day.

America was fed up with Carter's personality, and Reagan, like FDR decades earlier, brought optimism Americans desperately missed. He was likable and electable.

Parrot-in-Chief

Maybe the most revealing moment of Reagan's first term was his near assassination. On March 30, 1981, a deranged assailant named John Hinckley Jr. shot at President Reagan as he was leaving a speaking engagement at the Washington Hilton Hotel. One bullet caught Reagan in the chest. The Secret Service rushed him to the hospital.

Most people don't find humor in an assassination attempt, especially when they're the target. But most people aren't a Parrot on Ronald Reagan's level.

When Nancy Reagan arrived at the hospital, Reagan said, "Honey, I forgot to duck" (a famous line borrowed from the boxer Jack Dempsey). The bullet had narrowly missed Reagan's heart. The odds of survival weren't good. He needed immediate surgery to stop the bleeding.

In the operating room, Reagan didn't miss the chance to perform for the doctors and nurses. "I just hope you're Republicans." he joked. One doctor replied, "Today, Mr. President, we're all Republicans."

Reagan recovered and won widespread praise for his cheerfulness during such a terrifying ordeal.

As a Parrot, Reagan brought emotion, charm, and theatrics to every appearance. But he didn't bother to understand the nuances of his economic policies. His goal was simple: lower taxes and build up defense spending. Reagan left the math to his cabinet and did what he did best: television.

Behind the scenes, Reagan negotiated well with legislators, lobbyists, and various powerbrokers he needed to advance his policies. With one-liners like, "government is not the solution to our problem; government is the problem," Reagan sold the public on downsizing the federal bureaucracy.

Parrots are great at building momentum for their ideas, but generally they're less talented at predicting the consequences. The tax cuts eventually created a massive deficit, which conveniently prevented new spending on federal programs (For better or worse? We'll leave that to partisans).

In 1983, the economy began to boom, so Reagan and his supporters of course credited the president's economic policies. Was it his tax cuts, tax increases, or the Federal Reserve's interest rate policies? If you're a Parrot president, you take credit and don't worry about things like cause and effect.

As for the Cold War, Reagan's instincts and tactics fit the times. As a candidate, Reagan argued that the U.S. should stop trying to ease tensions with the Soviet Union and start building up the military so significantly that the Soviet economy wouldn't be able to keep up (hence, his reputation as a warmonger).

In March 1983, Reagan spoke at the National Association of Evangelicals in Orlando, Florida. He painted the U.S.-Soviet rivalry the way this community liked it: in black and white. He called the Soviet Union "an evil empire." It was Parrot branding delivered with Eagle dominance.

Several weeks later, Reagan proposed the space-based Strategic Defense Initiative (SDI)—a.k.a., "Star Wars"—a system to shoot down Soviet missiles from space. It spooked the Kremlin.

As planned, Reagan lured the Soviets into spending money they didn't have. They were already hemorrhaging lives and rubles in Afghanistan, which they had invaded in 1979. The combination of weakening economy and heavier spending would become unsustainable for the USSR.

The Lap Dog

1984 was the wrong year to be running against President Ronald Reagan as *any* personality. The economy was thriving again; Reagan's legendary response to the assassination attempt earned sympathy and praise; and there was no questioning Reagan's patriotism given his tough stance against the Soviets. America seemed safer and more prosperous than it had been under Carter. All the Democrats had going for them was Reagan's age and forgetfulness. At seventy-three years old, Reagan had already set the record for oldest-serving president.

Carter's former vice president, Walter Mondale, took the lead in the Democratic primaries, and the personality judging began—first by his opponents. One said, "Mondale is mush." Another compared Mondale to a "good lap dog–he'll give them everything they want. He'll lick every hand."

Clearly not an Eagle.

Rolling Stone writer William Greider remarked on his "creaky voice and bland manner." Said Greider, "He seems so old-shoe and predictable when America needs a leader willing to make bold departures." He was the safe, comfortable choice.

Not a Parrot either. His personality stood in stark contrast to the inspirational Great Communicator.

As with many would-be presidents, there was a discrepancy between Mondale's public persona and private demeanor. As Greider noted, "In person, up close in a small group or at a friendly luncheon table, Mondale becomes a sparkling personality, a man of genuine wit and charm. This is notable because so little of that spontaneity is displayed when Mondale appears before large public forums."

Writing for *The New York Times Magazine*, David Harris noted that Mondale did not like to talk about himself or his history. He was guarded about being a minister's son and the way he used to get bullied for it. "He instinctively shies away from any talk that might sound too much like bragging on himself," said Harris. In fact, Mondale was punished as a child for braggery (George H.W. Bush shared that experience with Mondale...hmmm...).

Harris seemed frustrated to be covering Mondale: "He provokes little heat either pro or con and consequently makes bland copy. It is one of the reasons analysts describe his support in the polls as 'shallow.'"

That's a journalist's way of saying that no one was taken by Mondale's personality. He was perceived as cautious and aloof. He looked uncomfortable and sluggish on TV. He rose in the Democratic Party the same way that Ford rose in the Republican Party: by not making mistakes or enemies. He was so nonthreatening that no one bothered to stop him from accumulating power. Mondale was a Minnesotan with Norwegian roots, but he didn't get the Viking Eagle gene. He got the Dove gene.

In the personality melee, Mondale's assets were often overlooked. He was respected for his intelligence, diligence, organizational abilities, and quiet strength. He valued and upheld the institutions of American democracy. But that wouldn't change the fact that he was Jimmy Carter's vice president and too Dove to diss his former running mate.

A Chance He Never Had

Mondale didn't have much going for him, but he captured headlines by picking New York Representative Geraldine Ferraro as his running mate. She was the first female vice presidential candidate in U.S. history. But she couldn't change the momentum of the race.

Mondale's team chose "Gonna Fly Now," the theme song from *Rocky*, for the campaign. They played it before Mondale's acceptance speech at the Democratic Convention. It didn't fit with his warm, Dove smile and timid demeanor.

In his speech, he tried to swing at Reagan, but slipped on The Big Assumption. "I challenge Mr. Reagan to put his plan on the table next to mine and debate it with me on national television."

Oooh. Plans. Yes. That'll knock out The Gipper.

Throughout the campaign, Mondale used attack lines that Democrats have been repeating ever since. The tax cuts only benefit the wealthy. The Republicans are a threat to women's rights. Reagan will take away your Medicare and Social Security. And so on.

Reagan largely avoided the press. Like Parrots such as Goldwater and Biden, all he could do was gaffe and jeopardize his sizable lead.

Since taking office, Reagan's team had carefully choreographed TV appearances, delivered a "line of the day," and kept the reporters at a distance so they couldn't ask pesky questions. Journalists still had to file their reports, so they were filled only with the message and images Reagan's team selected. This strategy served the campaign well.

So did Reagan's famous TV ads. One opened with, "It's morning in America again." It showed Americans doing what they do when the economy is strong: going to work, buying houses, getting married, and raising flags.

His other effective ad was about a bear in the woods, a metaphor for the Soviets. It was a logical take on Reagan's defense spending: "Some people say the bear is tame. Others say it's vicious and dangerous. Since no one can really be sure who's right, isn't it smart to be as strong as the bear?"

Mondale's ads were weak in comparison. One threatened that each American family would be $18,000 in debt because of Reagan's budgetary policy (not quite how that works…). Another took swipes at Reagan tax cuts for the rich.

Reagan's message was that his policies had worked to achieve his vision. Just look around! Mondale had nothing positive to offer. He was just anti-Reagan.

Mondale not only lacked a big-picture vision but seemed unaware of his Dove strengths and weaknesses. While on the campaign trail, Mondale responded to a reporter's question about public perceptions of his personality: "Maybe I am boring," he says, "I don't know. I read about it but I don't think my audiences are bored. You've seen them; are they bored?'"

If you have to ask…

At the first debate on October 7, 1984, Reagan bombed. He played defense and looked tired. He stumbled and seemed to forget his positions. It gave credence to the Democratic argument that Reagan was too old to be president.

Years later, Jim Lehrer asked whether Reagan was tired. His response: "No, it wasn't tired. I was overtrained...I just had more facts and figures poured at me for weeks before than anyone could possibly sort out and use, and I call it overtraining."

Who gets depleted by remembering facts? A Parrot.

Emboldened, the Democrats raised more questions about Reagan's age and made it a central issue in the second debate. One of the debate panelists, Henry Trewhitt from *The Baltimore Sun*, brought up the age issue. It probably made the Mondale campaign very, very pleased:

> You already are the oldest President in history, and some of your staff say you were tired after your most recent encounter with Mr. Mondale. I recall, yes, that President Kennedy, who had to go for days on end with very little sleep during the Cuba missile crisis. Is there any doubt in your mind that you would be able to function in such circumstances?

Try to imagine some other candidates in Reagan's place. You could see an Eagle like Truman or LBJ belittling the dumb question. What the hell does age have to do with it!? A modern Owl, like Hillary Clinton, might have recited average life expectancy statistics. A Dove like Carter might have thanked Trewhitt for asking that important question and then talked about the wisdom of age.

And Reagan? He did what a tai chi master would do: he redirected the momentum of the attack into a counter that sealed the 1984 campaign: "Not at all, Mr. Trewhitt and I want you to know that also I will not make age an issue of this campaign. I am not going to exploit for political purposes my opponent's youth and inexperience."

Everyone roared with laughter. The camera panned to Mondale, who couldn't help but laugh too. Reagan had defused the age issue with humor and won the second debate with one line.

On November 6, the slaughter rule would have been merciful. Reagan won the electoral votes of every state except Minnesota, Mondale's home turf, and Washington D.C. Mondale lost the presidential election 525 electoral votes to 13.

Viral Optimism

"When people say President Reagan brought back our spirit and our sense of optimism," writes his former speechwriter Peggy Noonan, "I think what they are saying in part is, the whole country caught his courage."

Noonan understood the essence of the Reagan years and the power of Parrot leadership. Even the people who hated Reagan's policies would be hard-pressed to deny his impact. He lifted America out of Carter's "malaise" and back to its national promise—one of enduring progress and exceptionalism. Reagan also showed Americans that they didn't have to accept the status quo, which he once defined as "Latin for 'the mess we're in.'"

Nowhere was this transformational attitude more apparent than in Reagan's relationship with General Secretary Mikhail Gorbachev, the last leader of the Soviet Union. In January 1986, Gorbachev (also a Parrot) wrote Reagan proposing they eliminate *all* nuclear weapons by 2000. Most Cold War presidents would have viewed this as a Communist plot. Reagan wondered, why not sooner?

Aides on both sides were appalled! Imagine the Eagles who eyed the deal with suspicion, and the Owls who found all the reasons that it could not be done.

Reagan and Gorbachev ignored their unimaginative detractors. In October 1986 at the Reykjavík Summit, they agreed in principle *to eliminate all their nuclear weapons within ten years.* The only sticking point was "Star Wars," Reagan's space-based missile defense program that was overhyped and still in the laboratory.

Had Reagan and Gorbachev reached an agreement on Star Wars, which Reagan refused to abandon, the U.S. and Soviet Union might have disarmed. That is Parrot leadership: to propose and pursue ideas that everyone else thinks are impossible.

Beyond Reagan's Parrot personality, he had a key trait that made him shine like few before him. He could flex his personality to any situation.

On January 28, 1986, the Challenger Space Shuttle exploded seventy-three seconds after takeoff, killing the seven crew members. It was a national tragedy, watched live by many schoolchildren. Reagan was supposed to give the State of the Union address that evening. He postponed it and instead comforted the nation in a TV address.

Reagan showed the sincere empathy and heartfelt emotion of a Dove. His closing words moved every American who heard them:

> The crew of the space shuttle Challenger honored us by the manner in which they lived their lives. We will never forget them, nor the last time we saw them, this morning, as they prepared for their journey and waved goodbye and slipped the surly bonds of earth to touch the face of God.

Reagan comforted the nation. His speech renewed faith in America's space exploration and immortalized the astronauts as American heroes.

The Great Communicator knew when to be an Eagle too. There's a long list of Reagan tough-guy moments, and none is more famous than, "Mr. Gorbachev, tear down this wall!" It was remembered not for its impact (it had almost none), but for the way history fulfilled Reagan's demand. He spoke those words against the objections of the State Department and his aides.

Even so, the Reagan presidency was not one long, inspirational party. News leaked that the Reagan administration had sold arms to Iran in violation of federal law and then diverted the revenues to the Nicaraguan contras, who were trying to overthrow their country's communist regime.

In March 1987, Reagan took responsibility for authorizing the weapon sales to Iran but denied knowledge of the contra payments with a little too much Parrot: "A few months ago I told the American people I did not trade arms for hostages. My heart and my best intentions still tell me that's true, but the facts and the evidence tell me it is not."

The scandal and that speech hurt his approval ratings for some time, but he bounced back. He was, as a democratic opponent once charged, a "Teflon-coated" president. Nothing sticks to Parrots because they're likable and smooth communicators. Voters forgive them. The next Parrot president would be forgiven for his scandals too.

Reagan, like FDR, JFK, and future President Bill Clinton, understood the power of personality in the White House. And Reagan, more than most presidents, didn't put leadership on a pedestal. The job was a performance. He enjoyed the spotlight, as most Parrots do, but he didn't relish politics the way many Eagles and Owls do.

"Politics is supposed to be the second oldest profession," Reagan said. "I have come to realize that it bears a very close resemblance to the first."

Amen, Gipper.

1988:
George Herbert Walker Bush

"Don't confuse being 'soft' with seeing the other guy's point of view."

- George H.W. Bush

The Bush Dynasty Begins

In May 1988, Vice President George H.W. Bush was on stage in Twin Falls, Idaho, discussing his relationship with President Ronald Reagan. Bush was campaigning to become the Republican nominee for president and wanted to milk his partnership with the Gipper.

"For seven and a half years I have worked alongside him," said Bush, "and I am proud to be his partner. We have had triumphs, we have made mistakes, we have had sex."

Bush froze. "Uh, setbacks," he meant.

The funniest, most human comment of Bush's entire campaign was a slip of the tongue. And not a surprising one. This same politician once told reporters that "I hope I stand for anti-bigotry, anti-Semitism, anti-racism." The Great Communicator Bush was not.

His campaign is remembered as one of the most vicious in presidential history, thanks largely to his Eagle staff members. It set a precedent of mudslinging that would long outlast 1988.

Bush, like FDR and JFK, was groomed for public service. He was the son of Prescott Sheldon Bush, a Wall Street investment banker who became a senator, and Dorothy Walker Bush, daughter of a banker who founded the Walker Cup golf tournament. Bush grew up in Greenwich, Connecticut, and attended the prestigious Philips Academy in Andover, Massachusetts.

Six months after Japan struck Pearl Harbor, eighteen-year-old Bush enlisted in the Navy and became its youngest combat pilot, flying fifty-eight missions in the Pacific.

During wartime, people often earn a cool nickname. In the TV show *M*A*S*H*, set during the Korean War, a character named Margaret Hoolihan was referred to as Hot Lips. Another character was Major Charles Emerson Winchester III. His nickname? Charles Emerson Winchester III.

During WWII, Bush, hoping to be a regular Joe despite hailing from a privileged background, tried to make friends with everyone—so Dove. His good-natured friends stuck it to him with the formal Owl-sounding nickname, George Herbert Walker Bush. That's right, like Charles, his nickname was the name on his birth certificate.

On one mission, Bush's plane was hit by Japanese anti-aircraft batteries and caught fire. Ever the Owl, Bush had a plan and stuck to it. He continued towards the target and dropped his bombs before bailing out of the plane. After being rescued by a submarine and recuperating, Bush *asked* to be put back in combat. The Secretary of the Navy awarded Bush the Flying Cross for his heroism.

After attending Yale University, Bush earned his wealth as an oilman in Texas and then launched his political career. He may have been a determined competitor, but he wasn't much of a campaigner. He struggled with the unpredictability and improvisation inherent to being a public figure—something an Eagle or Parrot would have reveled in. As Robert Strauss, Chairman of the Democratic Party, would say during the 1988 campaign, "George is a damn good guy but he doesn't come through well. It's a case of choking. It takes eleven hours to get George ready for an off-the-cuff remark."

After an unsuccessful Senate run in 1964, Bush won a seat in the House of Representatives and then made another unsuccessful Senate bid in 1970. He ultimately moved up the chain of command through appointments. Bush served as Ambassador to the United Nations, Chairman of the Republican National Committee, Chief of the U.S. Liaison Office in China, and Director of the CIA. He was a highly effective bureaucrat, but he was invisible.

Throughout these years, Bush built what one historian calls a "legendary rolodex" of contacts that included U.S. and foreign officials. In private, face-to-face settings, he had a knack for connecting with people.

In 1980, Bush ran for president but lost the Republican nomination to Ronald Reagan, who invited Bush to be his running mate. Eight years later, Vice President Bush launched his campaign for president, promising the equivalent of Reagan's third term. In policy, maybe. In personality, not even close.

In 1987, *Newsweek* reporter Margaret Garrard Warner kicked off the tradition of judging the candidates' personalities. She asserted that Bush "...is, in a single mean word, a wimp." Media, cartoonists, and Democratic strategists all reinforced this image of Bush. His background as a brave fighter pilot didn't seem to shake that impression.

Lacking Parrot charisma and failing to project Eagle self-assurance, Bush was characterized in a familiar way. Wrote Warner, "He does not project self-confidence, wit or warmth to television viewers. He comes across instead to many of them as stiff or silly. Even his most devout backers can sense his unease on the tube."

Of course, Bush was said to be charming, funny, and personable in private. Like prior Owls—Hoover, Landon, and Dewey—Bush was uncomfortable in the spotlight. But unlike some these Owls, Bush had a softer side.

He was raised by a strict WASP mother to be humble. As Warner reports, Dorothy called her son during the campaign to say, "You're talking about yourself too much, George." He seemed to find comfort in being a member of his college baseball team, a crewmate in war, and a party man in politics.

Devoid of what he called "the vision thing," which bigger person-alities have in abundance, Bush pragmatically adopted the policies that would raise his profile in the Republican Party. That led to a major mis-take: standing against John F. Kennedy's 1964 Civil Rights Act. Bush later recanted that choice, but it sealed his reputation as someone who put partisan unity over firm beliefs. He had the calculating manner of an Owl and go-with-the-flow style of a Dove.

In his speech accepting the Republican nomination, he said, "I want a kinder, gentler nation." He embraced what his public image had become. "I am a quiet man," he said, "but I hear the quiet people others don't."

That's about as Dove as it gets. Bush was a listener, not a speaker. We value that in our personal relationships, but in presidential elections, not so much.

Bush's speech ended with an image that comedians would merci-lessly lampoon: "I will keep America moving forward, always forward—for a better America, for an endless enduring dream and a thousand points of light. That is my mission. And I will complete it." It sounded so corny and awkward coming from Bush, but he meant it.

In most years, the Owl-Dove Bush would have been easy prey for an Eagle or Parrot. However, he had the luck to run against former Massachusetts Governor Michael Dukakis.

The Boy Scout

Dukakis was another "cerebral technocrat, a man without passion," wrote journalist Fox Butterfield, whose advisers urged him to "leaven his appearances with more humor and emotion." His campaign was "well-organized and efficient." He was an Eagle Scout as a kid and seemed to run for president as one.

Throughout his life, Dukakis was a rule-follower, a do-gooder, a by-the-books type. More than a few commentators called him "straight laced" or a "straight arrow." He was the 1988 version of Dewey, the little man on the wedding cake.

His former Lieutenant Governor Thomas P. O'Neill III tried to make excuses for Dukakis's lack of emotion and flat communication style: "...I don't think that comes from lack of passion. He just articulates it in other ways. He does it by implementing a program for welfare or housing."

Who exhibits "passion" by implementing a governmental program? Only an Owl.

Dukakis was the son of Greek immigrants who achieved the American dream. He studied at Swarthmore College, served two years in the Korean War, and then attended Harvard Law School. After taking the Governorship of Massachusetts in 1974, Dukakis managed to alienate everyone in the state. He was renowned for not accepting anyone else's advice.

So, he lost reelection in 1978 but won his 1982 comeback campaign. Massachusetts was in poor financial shape, and Dukakis balanced the budget by cracking down on tax evasion. His well-regarded employment retraining programs, infrastructural projects, and business loan initiatives created an economic renaissance. He promised to recreate the "Massachusetts Miracle" throughout America.

On July 21, Dukakis accepted the Democratic nomination for president. His forced, stiff smiles betrayed a discomfort with the spotlight. When he promised to take the nation to "the next American frontier," it wasn't believable. When he said, "We're going to win this race. We're going to win this race," he sounded as excited as the teacher calling Ferris Bueller's name while taking attendance.

Behind the scenes, Dukakis was micromanaging the campaign. Reports would surface that he ignored his strategists and insisted on reviewing *every* ad, brochure, and message the campaign put out. His relationships with advisors would deteriorate throughout the race as Dukakis locked into Owl mode and refused to stray. In a few years, we'll see this happen again with Mitt Romney.

Two Species of Owls

The 1988 campaign was a toss-up between an Owl and an Owl-Dove, but they ran drastically different campaigns. Dukakis insisted on a straight-shooting, policy-focused campaign. Bush, more willing to take his strategists' advice, let *them* go into aggressive Eagle mode for him. This allowed him to be himself while adding electable Eagle energy to his campaign.

Lee Atwater, Bush's campaign manager, made the race all about America's rising drug and crime problems. The lynchpin in this strategy was Willie Horton.

Horton was convicted of first-degree murder in 1974 for stabbing a man to death. In 1986, he was released temporarily for a weekend through Massachusetts's prison furlough program. Horton didn't return to prison and, the following year, committed a brutal assault, rape, and kidnapping in Maryland.

An infamous attack ad put out by Bush supporters used Horton to make it seem like Dukakis was soft on crime and endangering Americans. They characterized the furlough program as giving "weekend passes" to murderers and squarely blamed Dukakis for allowing Horton to roam free. Whether Dukakis deserves blame remains contested—he didn't start the furlough program, but he did veto a bill that would have excluded first-degree murderers from temporary release.

Another TV ad depicted Dukakis's furlough program with a line of convicts walking into a revolving door and right back out. Local Republican groups sent out Monopoly-styled cards that said, "Get out of jail free—Compliments of Michael Dukakis" on one side and, "Michael Dukakis is the killer's best friend and the decent, honest citizen's worst enemy" on the other.

Dukakis was too much of a do-gooder to fire back with attack ads. It goes to show that two Owls can express themselves quite differently. Dukakis stubbornly focused on policy and stuck to the "rules" of presidential politics. Bush allowed his campaign team and political action committees (PACs) to do the dirty work while he maintained his diplomatic stance.

George H.W. Bush and Michael Dukakis faced off in two debates. The first took place on September 25, 1988, and reflected the personalities of the candidates. It was a wonk fest of statistics.

As usual, Bush butchered the English language. "Those are two hyporhetorical questions," Bush said, after trying to stick it to Dukakis with *rhetorical* questions about how he'd stop the Soviets.

Boy Scout Dukakis reminded the audience that he was more principled than his opponent: "Mr. Bush, I don't question your patriotism. When you were attacked for your military record, I immediately said that it was inappropriate, it had no place in this campaign, and I rejected it."

Neither candidate won. Nor did the audience and TV members who endured it. However, Dukakis blew the second debate. Moderator Bernard Shaw asked, "Governor, if Kitty Dukakis were raped and murdered, would you favor an irrevocable death penalty for the murderer?"

Everyone was *stunned*. Who would ask something like that about a candidate's wife?!

Surely Dukakis would stand up to the inappropriate question. Instead, he gave a calm, issue-based answer about how he opposed the death penalty and said, "There are better and more effective ways to deal with violent crime."

A Parrot or Eagle would have shamed the moderator for asking such a question. Even a conflict-averse Dove would have come to his wife's defense. But logical Dukakis played into the Republican message that he was too lenient on crime and too out of touch to be president.

Years later in an interview with Jim Lehrer, Dukakis acknowledged that he'd made a mistake yet doubled down: "I didn't think it was that bad."

But the public did. Bush won the 1998 election with 54 percent of the popular vote and 426 electoral votes to 111.

At His Best

George H.W. Bush's presidency was a success by many accounts. Rather than tangle with a Democrat-controlled Congress, Bush focused on foreign affairs. He was the deliberate, pragmatic, careful president you'd expect.

Bush demonstrated how Owl-Doves, despite being poor campaigners, can be highly effective in office. He always built a strong case for his actions and thought through unintended consequences. By comparison, Eagle presidents like Truman and FDR acted first and worried about public perceptions later. Parrots like JFK and Reagan often made choices that were popular in the short-term but bad for Americans in the long-term.

For example, in 1989, after Beijing killed hundreds of peaceful protestors in Tiananmen Square, Bush used light sanctions to censure their behavior while restraining hawks in Congress who wanted a harsher response. His tact left the door open for renewed relations with China, which were essential to maintaining peace and security in East Asia.

In Panama, Bush successfully toppled Manuel Noriega, a CIA informant-turned-dictator, with widespread support from the Panamanian public and Americans. After the Berlin Wall crumbled in November of 1989, Bush didn't claim it as a victory or rub it in the Soviet's faces. Rather, he worked with the Soviets to reunify the country and negotiated to make Germany a NATO ally without spooking the Warsaw Pact countries.

Bush's pragmatism and restraint shined when Iraq under Saddam Hussein invaded Kuwait on August 2, 1990. Bush again reacted as a poised, rational Owl would. Saddam's violation of international law needed to be countered, so Bush first demanded that the Iraqis withdraw using a United Nations Security Council resolution—*with* Soviet support. To build consensus that way was a Dove move.

Bush exhausted all diplomatic solutions to Iraq's invasion and meanwhile built a military coalition of NATO states and Arab governments. The UN gave Saddam a deadline by which to end the occupation. When he failed to comply, Bush approved Operation Desert Storm, which liberated Kuwait in two months but left Saddam in power (the wisdom of that decision remains up for debate).

At the end of the Gulf War, Bush didn't boast, "We won!" with Parrot enthusiasm or Eagle hubris. Instead, he said, "This is not a time of euphoria. Certainly not a time to gloat…This is a victory for the rule of law and for what is right." Owl-Dove to the core.

As the Soviet Union finally crumbled in 1991, Bush's relationship with General Secretary Mikhail Gorbachev helped keep the peace. Gorbachev let the world's largest empire separate into independent countries with minimal violence (that would come later).

Owls are careful not to goof anything up, and between 1988 and 1992, there were so many chances for a U.S. president to make world-shifting, needless mistakes. Yet the U.S. became the world's undisputed superpower during those years. Bush's personality was ripe for the moment.

With sky-high approval ratings, Bush was in prime election shape for 1992. His one glaring error was to break his promise about never raising taxes ("Read my lips: no new taxes"), which was unavoidable given the deficits the Reagan tax cuts had created.

Then the economy slowed, and Bush did little about it. Just as Herbert Hoover's inaction paved the way for FDR's election, Bush's timidity would do the same for another big personality.

1992, 1996:
The Comeback Kid

"If one candidate is appealing to your fears, and the other one's appealing to your hopes, you'd better vote for the person who wants you to think and hope!"

- Bill Clinton

Slick Willie

Of all the guests that David Letterman hosted on *The Late Show* during his twenty-two-year run, he says that only two made him anxious. One was the rock musician Warren Zevon, who was terminally ill during the interview. The other was former President Bill Clinton, Letterman's guest on September 11, 2002.

Letterman had made ruthless Clinton jokes on primetime TV for almost a decade and, like every comedian, showed no mercy during the Monica Lewinsky affair.

"I guess he's never seen the show," Letterman joked during his opening monologue that evening in 2002. Letterman and Clinton talked for nearly forty minutes about the 9/11 attacks.

"What I learned about Bill," said Letterman, "was that you don't even need to be in the studio for that interview. He'll take care of it."

As a social and adaptable Parrot, Clinton knew what to say, how to say it, and when to say it. Lucky for Letterman, Clinton had shrugged off a decades' worth of grueling jokes, which Parrots easily do. They let things go and live in the present moment. The public, similarly, shrugged off everything Clinton had done to burn their trust. Clinton left office in 2000 with a record-high approval rating.

Born William Jefferson Blythe in Hope, Arkansas, the future president lived a volatile childhood. His father, a traveling salesman, died in a car accident three months before Bill was born. So, he was raised in his grandmother's home while his mother, Virginia, traveled back and forth to New Orleans for nursing classes. Bill moved from one unstable situation to another when Virginia married Roger Clinton, an abusive, alcoholic car dealer.

Bill became his parents' mediator and hid the family's dysfunction behind academic achievement, his saxophone skills, and an intense need to meet and be liked by people. He ultimately took on his stepfather's last name to show solidarity with the family.

Life in an alcoholic home taught Clinton to avoid conflict, maintain the peace, and leave no trace for outsiders. A result of this upbringing, Clinton told *New York Times Magazine* in 1992, was empathy:

> I can feel other people's pain a lot more than some people
> can. I think that is important for a politician. I think you
> literally have to be able to sit in the quiet of a room and
> accurately imagine what life must be like for people grow-
> ing up on mean streets, people living their lives behind
> bars, people about to face death's door.

Clinton's personable, charming personality was a megaphone for that empathy. He seemed to connect with everyone, though he would occasionally overuse his persuasive skills to manipulate others, as you'll see.

After graduating from Georgetown University's School of Foreign Service in 1968, Clinton won a Rhodes Scholarship to study at Oxford University. An objector to the Vietnam War, Clinton took steps to avoid being shipped overseas. Ultimately, he submitted to the draft and pulled a fortunate number in the lottery.

In 1970, Clinton entered Yale Law School, where he met Hillary Rodham. The two married in 1975 and soon became Arkansas's youngest political power couple. In 1978, Bill won the race for governor at the age of thirty-two, making him America's youngest governor in four decades. He ran a disorganized administration that pushed far-reaching, impractical policies—a classic Parrot mistake. He lost his reelection bid, only to run again as a more seasoned, well-groomed moderate in 1982.

Clinton adjusted his politics to what would win in Arkansas. He adapted this way throughout his career. He didn't seem to have a deep attachment to platforms—he was willing to advocate for whatever voters and his allies preferred.

Clinton retook the governorship but hurt his chances of running for president by giving one of the longest, most boring speeches ever heard at the 1988 Democratic National Convention. Very Parrot of him to be long-winded. Not very Parrot to be boring. He went on *The Tonight Show* with Johnny Carson to do damage control, mainly by making fun of himself—a Parrot strategy to deflect criticism.

In January 1992, Americans hadn't forgotten the speech. "Aren't you the guy who gave that awful speech for Dukakis at the 1988 Democratic Convention?" asked a newspaper editor.

"You want to hear the rest of it?" Bill Clinton joked.

America did. It had to be more interesting than whatever President George H.W. Bush had to say. There was just one problem. Or several. There weren't enough luggage tags in America for all of Clinton's baggage. But if there's any personality style that can deal with baggage, it's the Parrot.

Teflon Parrot

After Clinton's campaign launched in October 1991, rumors of affairs and sexual misconduct proliferated. On January 23, 1992, the supermarket tabloid *Star* reported that Arkansas state employee, model, and cabaret singer Gennifer Flowers had a twelve-year affair with Bill. Flowers had sold her story and tapes of her conversations with Bill to the tabloid. During a press conference, Flowers played tapes of her and Clinton calling each other "honey."

Clinton couldn't just brush off this rumor. On January 26, immediately after the Super Bowl screening on CBS, Bill and Hillary Clinton went on *60 Minutes* to address the allegations. Their timing was calculated to reach the biggest audience possible.

Bill denied the Flowers affair. At first, he sounded stilted and unconvincing. "She was an acquaintance. A friendly acquaintance." He added, "It was only when money came out...that she changed her story."

Hillary blamed everything on the "media war" going on. In fact, both Clintons disparaged the media's handling of these rumors. Which forty-fifth president does *that* sound like?

Clinton dialed up his Parrot oratorical skills with smooth, heartfelt delivery: "I have acknowledged wrongdoing. I have acknowledged causing pain in my marriage. I have said things to you tonight and to the American people from the beginning that no American politician ever has."

When journalist Steve Kroft made the mistake of referring to the Clintons' marriage as an "arrangement," Bill went on offense.

"Wait a minute. Wait a minute. Wait a minute. You're looking at two people who love each other. This is not an arrangement or an understanding. This is a marriage. That's a very different thing."

Unlike Dukakis who failed to stand up for his wife, Hillary stood up for Bill: "I'm sitting here because I love him and I respect him and I honor what he's been through and what we've been through together, and, you know, if that's not enough for people, then heck, don't vote for him." She was tough and direct like an Eagle (which would have served her well during her own presidential runs).

The performance worked. Clinton made a turnaround in the New Hampshire primary, nicknaming himself "The Comeback Kid." A few weeks later, he successfully fended off allegations that he'd dodged the Vietnam War draft. Bill made it through the primaries having already addressed his vulnerabilities.

Clinton, never shy about taking the spotlight, supercharged his campaign on June 3, 1992, when he appeared on *The Arsenio Hall Show*. Up to this point, presidential candidates spent their time on news shows discussing the issues. Clinton, a Parrot unafraid to break the norm, had a different idea.

Arsenio and the campaign staff dressed Clinton up in a loud yellow tie and a pair of Ray-Ban Wayfarers sunglasses that quickly became famous. The show opened with Clinton on his tenor saxophone jamming to "Heartbreak Hotel" as Arsenio made his entrance. It won over youth and minority voters who, until that moment, expected politicians to give dull policy talks. The "cool" impression and resulting news coverage helped Clinton secure the Democratic nomination.

Clinton went from a scandalous candidate to leading the polls. Nothing sticks to Parrots like Clinton and Reagan. Parrots, and often Eagles, get away with behaviors that crush Owls and Doves. Big personalities are just good at redirecting attention.

In this case, Clinton denied the allegations head-on, built sympathy by painting the media as disrespectful of his privacy, and then changed the dialogue by going on Arsenio Hall. Clinton was, in fact, lying about the Flowers affair, as the public would find out in 1998, when he testified under oath during the Lewinsky affair.

In November 2016, Donald Trump would use similar tactics when news broke that the *National Enquirer* had purchased and killed a story about Playboy model Karen McDougall's extramarital affair with him. He'd spent months attacking the media's credibility, so his campaign simply denied the affair.

Hoover Reincarnate

As Clinton defused his affairs and remade his public image, George H.W. Bush, forty-first president of the United States, seemed annoyingly unbusy. The economy slid into a recession, and unemployment climbed from just over 5 percent to a peak of 7.8 percent in June 1992. Like an Owl before him, Bush repeated Herbert Hoover's mistake during the Great Depression by failing to respond decisively. He seemed coldly indifferent.

As the economy sank, Bush gave a campaign speech in Exeter, New Hampshire, in January 1992. He reassured voters that his administration had "programs" in place and was trying to do better. Then, he accidentally read a stage direction out loud: "Message: I care."

He was such an Owl that speechwriters needed to coach him in what emotion to express.

In February, he fumbled again. A famous TV clip shows Bush at a meeting of the National Grocers Association. He looked confused in front of a modern checkout line and was "amazed" to see that a scanner could read prices. This was not new technology anymore. It seemed like Bush was so insulated and privileged, first as vice president then as president, that he hadn't gone shopping in at least a decade.

To be fair, Bush was shown a new, high-tech scanner that could weigh groceries and read torn barcodes, but *The New York Times*, which first broke the story, insisted that he'd been amazed by a basic scanner. Whatever the truth of the matter, the damage was done. He seemed out of touch, especially compared to his saxophone playing opponent.

Bush's moderateness and lack of likability spurred a Republican challenge from Pat Buchannan, the far-right TV commentator and culture warrior, who did surprisingly well in the New Hampshire primary. It was embarrassing for a sitting president to face such a tough challenge from within his own party.

After this strong performance, Buchanan was tapped to give a speech at the Republican National Convention. He railed against abortion, homosexuality, and women in combat, asserting that Republicans were in "cultural war" for "the soul of America." It alienated moderates and made Bush seem like he was on the fringe of his own party.

A second challenge came from the Owl billionaire Ross Perot, who self-financed an independent campaign. In half-hour infomercials, he explained America's problems, often holding up bar charts and circle graphs. He bashed Bush's handling of the economy and put forward his own budget-balancing platform. Perot attracted surprisingly large TV audiences. Although his supporters spanned the political spectrum, his attacks focused on the incumbent Bush.

Yet another problem confronted Bush's campaign: no one liked his bland running mate, Vice President Dan Quayle. Dropping Quayle would have strengthened the campaign, but Bush was unwilling to do that.

After the Republic National Convention in August 1992, Quayle promised to be "a pit bull" during the race. Bill Clinton was asked for comment.

"That's got every fire hydrant in America worried," jested Clinton. Face to Face

It wasn't clear in 1992 that Bush was campaigning for anyone, let alone himself. He seemed incapable of touting his achievements in foreign affairs. Lacking in charisma and energy, he could not get Americans excited about his reelection. Next to Clinton, his Owl-Dove personality was too dry and uninviting.

Meanwhile, Clinton ran a single-issue campaign. The words "The economy, stupid," cooked up by campaign strategist James Carville, were posted up at Clinton campaign headquarters and became an unofficial slogan.

Bill's acceptance speech at the Democratic National Convention in Madison Square Garden was masterful. It had Parrot charm, Eagle toughness, Dove empathy, and Owl statistics. He looked so natural on stage. He knew when to keep his hands steady, when to point them for emphasis, and how to time every sentence for maximum impact. "It's time for change in America," Clinton said convincingly. Clinton rubbed the economy in Bush's face as only a Parrot could:

Tonight, 10 million of our fellow Americans are out of work. Tens of millions more work harder for lower pay. The incumbent President says unemployment always goes up a little before a recovery begins. But unemployment only has to go up by one more person before a real recovery can begin—and Mr. President, you are that man.

Notice the similarity to Reagan's joke about Carter ("...recovery is when Jimmy Carter loses his [job]"). When these two Parrots attack, they don't get mean—they get clever.

George H.W. Bush's acceptance speech could have tranquilized a horse. In smile-free monotone, Bush delivered the same kind of speech we've heard from decades of Owls: heavy on facts, light on inspiration. It focused "on the stark choice" Americans had in this election.

Of course, Bush's speech operated on The Big Assumption: that everyone cared about what he cared about. "I know," said Bush, "that Americans have many questions—about our economy, about our country's future, even questions about me. And I'll answer them tonight."

Only an Owl attempts to rile up a crowd by promising to answer their questions about the economy. He delivered some decent jokes, but they didn't connect. It was clear that speechwriters had supplied them. Bush didn't know when to smile or how to time the delivery when he said, "I'm heartened, by the polls, the ones that say that I look better in my jogging shorts than the Governor of Arkansas."

In the first debate, the three candidates—Clinton, Bush, and Perot—faced the TV cameras. There was no definitive winner or loser.

Then, the personality gap widened. On October 18, 1992, the three candidates participated in the first town hall debate ever held during a presidential election. They fielded questions from undecided voters instead of professional moderators. A woman stood up and asked, "How has the national debt personally affected each of your lives? And if it hasn't, how can you honestly find a cure for the economic problems of the common people if you have no experience in what's ailing them?"

As she began the question, Bush looked down to check his watch, as if he didn't have time to listen to an American's struggles. It signaled yet again that Bush was out of touch and indifferent. Standing awkwardly by his stool, he gave an evasive answer that led the asker to press him. In response, Bush said, "I'm not sure I get it. Help me with the question and I'll try and answer it." Can you say, Owl?

Bush missed a chance to express his humanity. Clinton didn't. He stood up from his stool, walked confidently to the woman, looked her right in the eyes, and asked, "You know people who've lost their jobs and lost their homes?"

"Well, yeah, uh-huh," she replied.

"Well, I've been governor of a small state for 12 years. I'll tell you how it's affected me." He went on, "I have seen what's happened in this last four years when—in my state, when people lose their jobs, there's a good chance I'll know them by their names. When a factory closes, I know the people who ran it. When the businesses go bankrupt, I know them."

The Town Hall format magnified Clinton's talent for connecting with people and feeling their pain. The Owlish Bush and Perot both flopped.

By the third debate, all Bush could do was attack Clinton's character, record in Arkansas, and intent to spend heavily. If Bush had a positive vision to share with America, he was long past talking about it. His debate performance was the work of a critical Owl flustered by pressure. Clinton's charisma continued to widen his lead in the polls.

There was no way for Bush to shake the image of elite indifference. Clinton's Parrot ways won the election. Experts still disagree on whether Perot hurt Bush or not.

The Comeback Kid Comes Back Again

Clinton's first two years in office left a trail of scandals but few victories. In 1993, an Arkansas banker alleged that Bill had pressured him into making a fraudulent loan to the Clinton's partners in the Whitewater Development Corporation, a real estate venture. The attorney general brought on independent counsel Kenneth Starr to investigate.

Starr was to Clinton what Robert Mueller would be to Donald Trump: a threat looming behind the scenes, due to drop bombshells. Things got worse. Paula Jones, an Arkansas state employee, accused Clinton of sexual harassment. That, too, became subject to Starr's investigation.

In 1994, the Republicans took control of Congress for the first time in forty years. They hadn't swept Congress like that since Harry Truman's first term.

Thankfully for Clinton, the economy had rebounded and was thriving. He could point to some wins: a bill to reconcile the budget, a face-to-face agreement between the Israeli government and the Palestinian Liberation Organization, and the North American Free Trade Agreement (NAFTA). Still, Clinton suffered in the approval polls.

The momentum changed on April 19, 1995, when a bomb exploded inside the Alfred P. Murrah Federal Building in Oklahoma City, killing 168 people and injuring 500. First, Clinton responded in Eagle form, declaring what his administration would do to find the perpetrators and protect employees in other federal facilities. "Justice will be swift, certain, and severe," he promised, and it was. Timothy McVeigh and his accomplice, Terry Nichols, were soon apprehended.

Four days after the bombing, Clinton attended the memorial prayer service in Oklahoma City to address the nation. "I am honored to be here today to represent the American people," said Clinton, "But I have to tell you that Hillary and I also come as parents, as husband and wife, as people who were your neighbors for some of the best years of our lives."

He convincingly wore two hats—that of a leader and that of a fellow human being who could feel their pain.

"Today, our nation joins with you in grief. We mourn with you. We share your hope against hope that some may still survive," he added. He deeply touched the men, women, and children who lost loved ones in the attack.

The Oklahoma City speech "...was a real turning point in his administration," said Clinton's media advisor Frank Greer. "I thought that from that point forward...Clinton found his voice.... It was really the first time, I thought, that he had been a national leader."

It was a testament to Clinton that he, like Reagan after the Challenger explosion, flexed his personality to offer comfort. It was not the smiley, Parrot Clinton on stage. It was a Parrot being an Eagle and then a Dove because that was what America needed. His approval rating soared.

Clinton soon found the courage to stand up to the Republican Congress. When Speaker of the House Newt Gingrich tried to ram through cuts to education, environmental protection, and Medicare, Clinton vetoed the bills. It triggered a standoff and two government shutdowns, which deprived Americans of vital services. Gingrich was blamed, and Clinton entered the 1996 election cycle having made yet another comeback.

Bob Dole, Allegedly Human

On April 10, 1995, Senator Bob Dole announced his candidacy for president of the United States. His voice was stern, deep, and flatter than Kansas, where he delivered the speech. He cracked jokes—he was in fact legendary for his wit and wrote books on political humor—but they were too deadpan to score points on TV. He smiled for his jokes and then regressed to dour Dole.

Bob Dole seemed to have a secondary Parrot style that shined in private with small groups of people. On stage, however, Dole's Owl took over. Either way, his personality became the subject du jour for political journalists. Columnist Scott Harris wrote an entire piece in third person to mock the way Bob Dole spoke.

"Scott Harris has read enough campaign stories to know that, in interviews, Bob Dole says 'I' fairly often," wrote Harris. "In addition, he has difficulty delivering simple sound bites because he knows the world is not a simple place. It's on the podium, speechifying in front of TV cameras, that he becomes that other Bob Dole."

Public Bob Dole spoke in third person, as if to distance himself from the physical Dole standing before the cameras and crowds. Dole was yet another Owl who, from day one, would struggle in a modern presidential election.

Dole had depth, though. As a twenty-two-year-old fighting in Italy during World War II, he was hit by an exploding shell that left his right shoulder, arm, and hand limp. He learned to cope with his disability but lived a private life, choosing to mostly eat at home. He didn't want people to see that he could not cut his own food.

Dole's experience led him to advocate for the rights of the disabled long before it became a mainstream civil rights issue. And while his personal challenges earned respect, it seems that Dole was *very* hard on himself, as Owls often are. Katherine Seelye of *The New York Times* noted that when Dole wrote his signature for fans left-handed, "The result is often primitive, and Mr. Dole frequently mutters that he has not done a good job."

Dole's campaign strategists tried to humanize Dole with news stories about his disability. Still, *Washington Post* journalist Laura Blumfeld cynically viewed it as "Dole's way to break Clinton's lock on empathy."

Many commentators made the link between FDR's polio and Dole's disability, but their personalities could not have been more different. Dole was considered a grouch, called "Darth Vader, and a vampire, and the Aya-Dole-ah" by various commentators. At seventy-two years old, he also was considered old to be running for president.

The Dole campaign's humanization strategy didn't work. No matter what stories were told about Bob Dole, he came across stiff and sullen in his August speech accepting the nomination.

Like Bush, Dole initially leveled his attacks at Clinton's character, which, polling showed, voters weren't concerned about. And he ran on a message that will sound *very* familiar: "To those who say...that America has not been better, I say, you're wrong, and I know, because I was there. And I have seen it. And I remember."

Dole did a 1996 Owl's version of "Make America Great Again," but it came across as, "I'm old, so I have experience. Vote for me."

Another Parrot and Owl Contest

In August 1996, Bill Clinton accepted the Democratic nomination for president. The crowd was lit up and buying every word. Clinton had come into his own as a chameleon politician. Like Reagan, he had something for the Eagles, Parrots, Doves, and Owls in the audience.

He made a promise to voters that had an important impact on the race. "I believe that Bob Dole and Jack Kemp and Ross Perot love our country," he said. "But I will not attack; I will not attack them personally, or permit others to do it in this party if I can prevent it. My fellow Americans, this must be a campaign of ideas, not a campaign of insults. The American people deserve it."

His theme was to "build a bridge to the 21st century." It was the opposite message of Dole, who harkened back to supposedly better times. It was a fight between a forward-looking Parrot and backward-looking Owl.

Lucky for Dole, Ross Perot was excluded from the 1996 debates. Dole's team hinted that the Senator would break out his secret weapon: humor.

Why hadn't he already? One reporter speculated that "Mr. Dole's jokes—biting, bone dry and often uttered as an aside—do not translate very well into television sound bites." Plus, "there is Mr. Dole's deadpan delivery. He does not give cues that prompt people to laugh."

That is Owl humor. You have to be there for it, because without the context and full set up, you just won't get it.

Clinton flexed his Owl, and Dole attempted to flex his Parrot.

Dole had tried to exercise his wit as Gerald Ford's running mate in 1976. While debating Walter Mondale, Jimmy Carter's running mate, Dole's one-liners vacillated between funny and out of line (for the time).

He quipped about the role of vice president being "indoor work and no heavy lifting." He offended the host, the League of Women Voters, when he said "they tend to be a little bit liberal."

One dark comment tainted Dole's entire performance: "I figured up the other day," said Dole, "if we added up the killed and wounded in Democrat wars in this century, would be about 1.6 million Americans, enough to fill the city of Detroit."

Twenty years later, Dole's reputation as a "hatchet man," as Mondale called him, hadn't been forgotten. So, Dole left his wit at home for the two debates. The difference between the charismatic, charming Clinton and formal, stifled Dole could not have been clearer.

Clinton kept his promise not to insult Dole and, in fact, opened by praising his public record. It was a Dove's anti-conflict move by a Parrot, and it set a congenial tone for the first debate. Dole the Owl wasn't about to pick a fight either. Intentionally or not, Clinton's olive branch strategy led Americans to see the common ground between Clinton and Dole. They were both moderates. They both wanted the best for America. Dole passed up obvious opportunities to question Clinton's ethics.

The second and final debate in San Diego was in the town hall format that, once again, brought out Clinton's magic. There was no competition. Clinton lingered at the venue for forty minutes afterwards, continuing to schmooze and win over undecided voters.

After losing the election to Clinton, Bob Dole went on Dave Letterman's show to recap the campaign. He was livelier and funnier than he'd ever been during the race. He had the audience and Letterman cracking up. "Bob, what have you been doing lately?" asked Letterman.

"Apparently not enough," Dole responded.

When asked about his concession call to Clinton, Dole said, "I called him. Collect."

Dole went on to have one of the most unusual careers of any politician who'd lost the presidential campaign—as a TV spokesman for Viagra, Visa, Dunkin' Donuts, and Pepsi.

Slick with Consequences

Bill Clinton's second term in office was, well, eventful. His affair with a twenty-one-year-old White House intern began in 1995, and the details began to leak in 1998.

After lies upon lies—some under oath—Clinton finally admitted to "inappropriate intimate contact" on August 17, 1998. Kenneth Starr was still on his case and had expanded his inquiry to the Lewinsky affair. Whether that was overreaching or justified is up to legal scholars.

Starr's report captured the famous exchange where Clinton is asked how he could be truthful when affirming "there is absolutely no sex of any kind" with Lewinsky. Clinton gave the answer of a Parrot under siege: "It depends on what the meaning of the word 'is' is. If the—if he—if 'is' means is and never has been, that is not—that is one thing. If it means there is none, that was a completely true statement...."

Don't re-read that too many times, especially if you're an Owl. This is textbook Parrot to think out loud before thoughts have fully formed.

On October 8, the House of Representatives voted for impeachment proceedings to begin. The House approved two out of four articles of impeachment, for perjury before a grand jury and for obstruction of justice.

The Senate would take on the trial next. Oddly, Clinton's approval rating rose to a record-high 73 percent in the interim. On February 12,

1999, the Senate acquitted Clinton. The Republicans could not reach the necessary two-thirds majority to remove the president.

Years later, in true Parrot style, Clinton responded to a survey of journalists that ranked the Monica Lewinsky scandal as the fifty-third most significant story of the century. "What's a man got to do to get in the top fifty?" he quipped.

Considering everything that happened, it's incredible that Clinton left office with the highest approval rating of any president since approval polling began in 1937. For eight years, he lived in the spotlight and commanded the world's attention. Along the way, he soaked it in as only a Parrot could. After leaving office, he said, "I may not have been the greatest president, but I've had the most fun eight years."

By the time Letterman anxiously hosted Clinton in 2002, the ordeals of the Clinton presidency had taken a backseat to the budget surplus and thriving economy. He easily could have won a third term had the rules still permitted it. Like a true Parrot, he reinvented himself in a positive light.

2000, 2004:
Dubya

"One of my proudest moments is I didn't sell my soul for the sake of popularity."

- George W. Bush

Captain Frat-tastic

In 1967, President George W. Bush made his first *New York Times* headline for conducting torture with a hot branding iron. Only he wasn't president of the United States—he was president of the Yale fraternity Delta Kappa Epsilon. Allegedly, Bush conceived the idea of branding freshman pledges with the Greek letter Delta using the tool of true artists: a coat hanger.

Bush didn't deny the story. The wound, he insisted, was "only a cigarette burn." Why was everyone having such a hissy fit? The young Bush seemed confident in his choices and shameless about the backlash. This young Eagle didn't equivocate or apologize. It was an inauspicious beginning for "Dubya," son of future President George H.W. Bush.

George Jr. attended the prestigious Phillips Academy Andover, scraped by at Yale, and then served in the National Guard during

Vietnam. After completing his service, Bush earned a Harvard MBA and joined the oil industry in Texas.

As Bush Sr.'s political career took off, so did Jr.'s. After campaigning in his dad's successful run for the White House in 1988, Dubya bought the Texas Rangers baseball team with a group of investors and eventually sold it for a profit. As owner of the Rangers, he built a name for himself in Texas and ran for governor in 1994, defeating the favored incumbent. He won reelection in 1998.

It was hard to see the "real" Bush through the partisan pettiness of the early 2000s. This was the era of Rush Limbaugh and TV shows like *Crossfire*, which turned politics into a gladiatorial sport. Times had changed since FDR first tapped into the power of radio and Eisenhower ran the first TV election ads.

The result: Americans understood less about the candidates' platforms and policies but more about their personalities.

Deep down, was Bush a heavy-drinking, reckless, frat-boy who rode on his daddy's coattails? Liberals pushed that narrative. Or, was he a young man who overcame his demons, found God, and took responsibility as a father and statesman? Conservatives preferred this story of redemption.

Bush had an alcohol problem but connected with religion after meeting the evangelist Billy Graham in 1985. Bush's newfound faith helped him quit drinking the following year.

The Eagle Bush was notoriously good at shrugging off insults and mistakes, never letting the haters bring down his positive, move-forward attitude. Bush was more complex than either side gave him credit for, but simplistic narratives made better TV.

Regardless of what pundits said, the Bush you saw on TV was the Bush you got. He did have a hotheaded, freewheeling, swaggering side. He also had a decisive, responsible, take-action side. Behind closed doors, his charm, humor, and ability to defuse tension earned him political allies. He was an Eagle on public stages but a Parrot in private and personal settings.

As Bill Clinton's second term ended, Bush Jr. was the clear front-runner for taking the White House back from the Democrats. He picked a darn good year for it.

Sheer Goredom

Vice President Al Gore had the immense advantage—and disadvantage—of being associated with the president. Bill Clinton presided over a flourishing economy and budget surplus. Despite the Monica Lewinsky affair, he left office riding a 66 percent approval rating. Would Gore surf that wave or get drowned by it?

The son of a powerful senator, Gore was groomed for politics. He studied at Harvard and then enlisted for service in Vietnam, although Gore Sr. could have pulled some strings to get him out (with political consequences). After working as a journalist and then earning a law degree at Vanderbilt University, Gore served as a Tennessee representative and senator before becoming Bill Clinton's running mate in 1992.

There were stark differences between Clinton and Gore's personalities. A *New York Times Magazine* correspondent thought Gore did a good job of rallying a crowd in Waco, Texas—until there was some contrast: "Standing beside Bill Clinton at an impromptu news conference at a power station outside Waco, Gore looks wooden and startlingly aloof; his arms dangle awkwardly like a department store mannequin, and his demeanor is so icily serious that he could easily pass for a Secret Service agent."

In private, he was supposedly a different character. The same article notes how Gore, laughing with his nineteen-year-old, gave a dramatic reading of a tabloid article about a "gassy granny" who farted in church and then jumped off a cliff in embarrassment.

Unfortunately, Gore's humor and drama skills never materialized on public stages. He sounded condescending and cerebral and often looked detached and uncomfortable. But when he spoke about the near-death of his son, who was hit by a car at nine years old, Gore evoked emotion and humanity that he struggled to convey while talking about his platform.

At the end of party conventions, candidates' spouses traditionally accompany them on stage for hand holding, waving, and a quick peck on the cheek. As scripted, Tipper Gore dutifully joined her husband for a moment that is permanently etched on anyone's brain who saw it… *the kiss.*

Tipper and Al looked longingly into each other's eyes with the same anticipation of Jennifer Grey's character at the end of *Dirty Dancing*, looking at Patrick Swayze in the distance. Like Swayze, Gore gave Tipper a look that said, "Are you ready?" He pulled Tipper in and their lips locked, and remain locked, and remain locked, and remain locked.

It felt like the audience should have turned away. The moment held all the romance of two high school students forced to perform their first kiss on a theater stage in front of their friends and family. It was awkward. It was meant to humanize Gore. It did not.

However, Gore showed passion in one arena: policy. His prowess as a technology and environmental wonk had a heartfelt dimension. No politician knew the facts about climate change like Gore, and no politician felt such a deep, spiritual responsibility to do something about it.

In 1999, Gore dominated the Democratic primaries. But pundits thought Gore, who felt lied to by Clinton during the Lewinsky debacle, was in a tough position. Could he claim the Clinton administration's record of governance without seeming like he'd condoned the president's infidelity and lies?

That was the wrong question. The real question should have been, how was this dull Owl-Dove, completely outshined by his Parrot-Eagle boss, going to deal with George W. Bush?

The *SNL* Treatment

The 2000 election was supposed to be a contest between Republican Bush and Democratic Gore, but we all know who really won: comedians.

The contrast between the seemingly dimwitted Bush and the yawn-fest Gore was the fresh meat comedians craved after gorging on the Lewinsky affair. Nothing cemented America's perception of the candidates quite like Will Farrell and Darryl Hammond's impressions on *Saturday Night Live*.

It started in October 1999 with Hammond playing both Al Gore and Clinton in a TV address from the Oval Office.

"Hey...I'm Al Gore.... Oh darn it, I can't do this."

"Sure you can, Al!" says Clinton, standing nearby. "Make it sexy!"

Gore carries on, "Now, I'd like to be your president..." and he catches Clinton yawning.

"No, you're doing good!" Clinton assures him.

After giving his take on America's "malaise," he says, "I don't think it needs to be that way. Because I'm here to fire you up…Al Gore style…."

He announces his new campaign slogan meant to "raise the roof." It is "Cautious Optimism with Hesitant Guarded Hope."

SNL *nailed* the Owl-Dove personality. And what about Bush?

Will Farrell swaggers Eagle-style into the office holding a can of Budweiser with three pledges from his Yale fraternity (presumably he branded them too). Gore gets testy and talks about how he'll crush and snort Bush….

"Hey, bring it on, robot boy!" says Bush.

As they discuss the issues, they realize that, well, their positions are all the same. Bush, the "compassionate conservative," and Gore, a southern Democrat, were both moderates.

"How are we different?" asks Bush. "I have no idea," said Gore.

The difference was their personalities.

SNL rehashed these Eagle-Parrot v. Owl-Dove encounters into some of the best political comedy sketches of all time. *SNL* exaggerated the substance, but as for the personalities, they nailed it.

Fuzzy Math

In Gallup polls taken between June 1999 and August 2000, Americans rated Bush and Gore on a variety of dimensions. Bush was considered the "strong and decisive leader" with 20+ point margins over Gore. Of course, he's an Eagle. Bush was also seen as the candidate more able to "manage government effectively." Again, Eagle. Meanwhile, Gore's Dove shined through as he polled higher on "shares your values" and "cares about the needs of people like you."

In May 2000, with Bush leading the polls, *The New York Times* reported that "The vice president's lagging ratings appear to have more to do with personality than policy." No kidding! The public viewed Bush as "more of a leader," but respondents to the poll just couldn't explain *why* they felt this way.

America's mind was made. The debates affirmed what voters already thought because neither candidate attempted to flex his personality. Instead, Gore and Bush played their *SNL* personalities to a tee.

At the first debate, Gore, in his sloth-paced, monotone voice, sounded like Siri's grandfather reading policies and statistics out loud. His answer to the first question felt like it would never, ever end. Bush came out as his Texan cowboy persona.

As the debate touched on Medicare, Gore tried to claim that under Bush's plan, 95 percent of seniors wouldn't get benefits for the first four or five years. Bush wasn't having it: "I guess my answer to that is the man's running on Medi-scare, trying to frighten people in the voting booth."

Gore didn't know how to handle this. He went back to impersonating a speech synthesizer.

Eagle Bush, not at all interested in getting numbery, took digs at Gore as if they were kids in junior high. Bush said, "Look, this is a man that's got great numbers. He talks about numbers. I'm beginning to think that not only did he invent the internet, but he invented the calculator. It's fuzzy math."

Again, Gore didn't know how to counter an opponent who engaged the audience with down-home humor. His eye-rolling, sneers, and sighs made it seem like he was too much of a know-it-all intellectual to engage with Bush. As moderator Jim Lehrer wrote, "Gore was judged the clear loser in the debate, based almost entirely on his body language and not on what he actually said."

Remember the impact of television on the Kennedy-Nixon debates? Yet again, TV magnified personalities while minimizing the substance of what the candidates said. This is why Eagles and Parrots have been beating Owls and Doves

One of Gore's answers was so—darn—long and over the time limit that Bush forgot what Lehrer had asked: "Well, I've been standing up to big Hollywood, big trial lawyers. What was the question? It was about emergencies, wasn't it?"

Bush kept digging at Gore's personality and character, questioning how the VP *didn't* know that an infamous luncheon at a California Buddhist temple was actually a fundraiser (and that the monks were laundering campaign contributions).

Gore said, "Governor Bush, you have attacked my character and credibility, and I am not going to respond in kind. I think we ought to focus on the problems and not attack each other."

There's Gore's Dove again: take offense rather than counterpunch. His closing argument admitted what everyone in America was thinking: "If you entrust me with the presidency, I may not be the most exciting politician, but I will work hard for you every day."

Self-aware? Sure. A winning personality? Nope.

The Apologizer

Gore's looks of exasperation and condescension hurt in the first debate. When he turned down the Owl but cranked up the Dove in the second debate, that didn't help either.

Gore tried to build consensus while Bush tried to give him a political wedgie. After Bush spoke, Gore repeatedly would reply, "I agree with that" or "I don't disagree with that."

Even worse, Gore validated Bush's critiques about fuzzy math: "I got some of the details wrong last week in some of the examples that I used. I'm sorry about that, Jim. I'm going to try to do better. One of the reasons that I regret it is that getting a detail wrong interfered several times with the point that I was trying to make."

Gore must have been ruminating on his misstatement for weeks, adding, "I can't promise that I will never get another detail wrong. But I will promise that I will try not to—and hard."

Here's The Big Assumption again. Getting the details right is important to Gore, so it must be important to everyone. Gore thinks the weakness in his performance was *getting a fact wrong*. If he admits to it, America will respect him because he would respect a candidate for correcting himself.

By the way, one of the details that Gore apologized for was citing an example in which a girl had to stand up in her classroom because there weren't enough chairs for the students. *He got wrong the number of days she had to stand.* Such. An. Owl.

Down to Florida

The differences between Bush and Gore on policies were so unclear that *SNL* continued to mock their sameness. The difference between their personalities, however, could not have been clearer.

In the final debate, Dubya laid himself out for the public. "How do you see the differences between you and the Vice President?" asked Jim Lehrer.

"The difference is, I can get it done," said Bush. "That I can get something positive done on behalf of the people. That's what the question of this campaign is about. It's not about what's your philosophy and what's your position on issues. But can you get things done? And I believe I can."

Get what done? For who? How? The details didn't matter for an Eagle. Nor did Bush's philosophy and positions on the issues, which would change *drastically* over the following years (e.g., Bush denounced using the military for nation-building in the second debate).

Five days before the election, news broke that Bush had a drunk driving citation as a younger man. It immediately hurt him in polls. Would it cost him the White House?

No voter could forget what happened on November 7, 2000. Florida was too close to call. At first, the electoral votes were called in favor of Gore, and then Bush. The campaigns dispatched their lawyers to oversee recounts.

After weeks of battling, the Florida Supreme Court ruled in favor of a selective recount. On December 12, the U.S. Supreme Court reversed that decision in *Bush v. Gore*. There would be no recount. Bush's victory would stand.

Gore won the popular vote by about 500,000, but it didn't matter. Bush took the White House. The unbroken trend of Eagles and Parrots beating Owls and Doves continued.

Us Versus Them

George W. Bush charged into office with a vision for how to harness America's economic prosperity and budget surplus for good. The terrorist attacks on September 11, 2001, derailed that vision. A total of 2,977 people lost their lives that day, and the world rallied to America's side.

What does an Eagle leader do when his nation is attacked? Bush declared a war on terror. Similar to the Cold War, this struggle was framed as a conflict between competing ideologies and cultures. Different from the Cold War, the enemy was a stateless network.

Osama Bin Laden, the leader of Al Qaeda who organized the attacks, was being harbored by the Taliban regime in Afghanistan. In a joint session of Congress on September 20, Bush made a simple offer: "The Taliban must act, and act immediately. They will hand over the terrorists, or they will share in their fate."

Bush declared his us-versus-them mentality. It was pure Eagle: "Every nation, in every region, now has a decision to make. Either you are with us, or you are with the terrorists."

The bombing of Afghanistan began on October 7, 2001.

In his 2002 State of the Union address, Bush named the members of a so-called Axis of Evil: North Korea, Iran, and Iraq. Their efforts to develop weapons of mass destruction were considered a threat, as they could hand their WMDs over to terrorists. Bush's Eagle presidency became all about getting revenge, isolating bad guys, and flexing America's military muscle.

Today, the events that led to the invasion of Iraq remain hotly contested. Congresspeople and the public were told that Iraqi dictator Saddam Hussein had stockpiles of biological and chemical weapons. Whether this faulty information resulted from an intelligence failure or a deliberate misinformation campaign will be debated for decades to come.

Regardless, what does an Eagle leader do when his country appears to be in danger? He attacks.

Bush was confident that the invasion, regime change, and democratization of Iraq would be straightforward. Why *wouldn't* Iraqis want freedom too? He applied The Big Assumption to a country of 25 million people with a radically different history and culture than America's.

Compared to Owls and Doves, Eagles and Parrots tend not to worry about the downstream consequences of their decisions. They're quick to act and even quicker to dismiss people who point out flaws in their plan.

The Walking Tree

On February 23, 2004, the *Dallas Morning News* introduced Massachusetts Senator John Kerry as a hero who once did CPR on Licorice, the family hamster. Did he do mouth to mouth? Or just chest compressions? His daughters disagreed.

And, oh yes, he was a decorated Vietnam War veteran who served as a swift boat captain and once rescued a Green Beret from a river. After serving valiantly, he built a reputation as a leader of Vietnam Veterans Against the War.

The story of Kerry the hamster savior was supposed to humanize him. Whenever you see the word "humanize" in this book, you know the candidate is in deep trouble. The public already thought of Kerry as "wooden, stuffy, stilted and long-winded," said the *Dallas Morning News*. Can you get a better collection of Owl words in one sentence?

A champion debater at Yale and a member of the secret society Skull and Bones (along with Dubya), Kerry was another Ivy Leaguer like Gore who showed too much brains and too little heart. As policy wonk with a quiz-show vocabulary and high-brow sensibilities, Kerry was yet another fact-loving foil to Bush.

Kerry had voted in favor of invading Iraq but later recanted that decision. Self-reflecting, Kerry considered the pros and cons of his past actions, sometimes out loud. This gave him a reputation for flip-flopping.

Eagle Bush, on the other hand, made decisions and never appeared to question them.

By now, you're familiar with Kerry's personality and why it loses presidential elections. He's supposedly warm and fun when the cameras are off (his daughters swear it), but he thinks and talks like Spock from *Star Trek*.

Nothing Kerry or his campaign did between February and July 2004 seemed to help. *The Economist*—not exactly known for bubbly, sexy writing—wrote that "[h]is stump speeches are eye-crossingly dull. He expresses simple ideas in weird, circumlocutory ways, showing special fondness for multiple negatives."

Owls often speak in the negative. Ask a Parrot how they are doing, and they say, "Great!" Ask an Owl, and they say, "Not bad." During elections, "great" is far more inspirational. Can you imagine a hat that says, "Make America Not Bad Again"?

Perhaps more telling, *The Economist* and YouGov ran a poll asking Americans, "Who would you rather hang out with for an hour over a beer or coffee?" A majority of Americans chose Bush over Kerry (but John Edwards, Kerry's Parrot running mate, beat Dick Cheney by about 20 percentage points).

Kerry, always one to ponder, cloaked his decisions about policies, positions, and even his running mate until he reached a final conclusion. No one understood his campaign strategy or what he stood for. It was shuffled around in his indecisive Owl mind.

In the Senate, Kerry was known for rooting out corruption and scandals, not for drafting new legislation. He was a critical problem-solver. Maybe he was too practical to commit to anything but a case-by-case pragmatism.

America could do wrong, in Kerry's opinion, and needed leaders with the flexibility to rethink decisions. Bush, on the other hand, had an Eagle worldview that went down easier than apple pie and vanilla ice cream: there's good and evil, and America, no matter who it bombs or waterboards, is good.

Owl to the End

On October 1, 2008, Bush and Kerry met on the debate stage at the University of Miami in Coral Gables, Florida to discuss foreign policy. In this debate and all that followed, both politicians clung to The Big Assumption: *If it's important to me, it's important to everyone.*

Kerry opened strong, arguing that "This president has made, I regret to say, a colossal error of judgment." But when moderator Jim Lehrer asked Kerry to elaborate, this digestible point became a ten-course meal about every little thing Bush had done wrong in the wars. Can you hear shades of Al Gore? Kerry meant to reinforce his argument that Bush had poor judgment. You have to back up your viewpoint with a preponderance of evidence and statistics, right? Of course you do—if you're an Owl.

What did Bush do? He attacked Kerry as an unsuitable, flip-flopper: "He voted to authorize the use of force and now says it's the wrong war at the wrong time.... I don't think you can lead if you say wrong war, wrong time, wrong place. What message does that send to our troops?"

To an Eagle like Bush, a leader *cannot* have doubts. And although Kerry was widely considered to have won every debate, he reinforced what people already believed: he was stiff, uninteresting, and too willing to change his positions (in light of new evidence, Kerry would argue). Bush drove that narrative home: "The only thing consistent about my opponent's position is he's been inconsistent."

Interestingly, Bush repeated Gore's mistake from their first debate. Throughout, he looked irritated, impatient, and dismissive of the whole affair. When Eagles and Owls dial up their personalities too high, they come across unlikeable.

The second debate featured questions from the audience that sent Kerry deeper into Owl territory. One person said her friends, co-workers, and family wouldn't vote for Kerry because "you were too wishy-washy. Do you have a reply for them?"

Kerry tried to defend himself with examples that didn't address the concern. He sounded wishy-washy while claiming that he wasn't. Bush piled on. "I don't see how you can lead this country in a time of war, in a time of uncertainty, if you change your mind because of politics."

Again, Kerry had sound Owl reasons for why his positions changed over time. But in a debate, where just a few answers get condensed for the highlight reels and newspapers, none of the nuance survived.

Kerry later told Jim Lehrer just how much he hated the debate format: "I had ninety seconds to talk to America about why I thought what I thought." Herein lies the Achilles heel of the Owl candidate. Kerry thought it was his job to share logic and provide details. Instead, the winning candidates energize the masses by emanating strength and enthusiasm.

Bush's campaign favored the ninety-second response format because they knew that the less Bush had to talk, the better he'd do.

Even when Kerry attempted to speak in sound bites, he restated Bush's critiques. "He's trying to attack me," said Kerry. "He wants you to believe that I can't be president, and he's trying to make you believe it because he wants you to think I changed my mind."

A classically trained debater, Kerry identified the president's criticisms and then tried to defeat them with logic. All he did was give those impressions more airtime. Conversely, Bush starved Kerry's arguments of oxygen by never addressing them directly or rationally. Again and again, Bush showed complete confidence and faith in every single decision he'd made. His Eagle defense was impenetrable against Owl attacks.

The third debate was more of the same. Kerry performed Owl-style debate for the kinds of judges he learned to impress in high school and college. He never gave America a simple, inspiring vision of what his presidency would look like.

As former *Daily Show* correspondent Samantha Bee joked on November 2, the night of the election, "Kerry's people say that with all the focus on election results, tonight is the perfect night for their man to lay out his vision of America to the voters."

A confused Jon Stewart asked, "It's a little bit late for that, is it not?"

It was. Bush won.

The Decider

George Bush's approval rating hit its high point of 90 percent ten days after 9/11, when he stood up to terrorism. By the time he left office in 2009, his approval rating was at 34 percent.

Bush's second term was a rough one—for the whole country. The wars in Iraq and Afghanistan continued to take American lives without achieving durable victories or building stable democracies. The Great Recession, which began in December 2007, forced the Bush administration to take extremely controversial actions, especially after the Dow Jones suffered its worst loss in history on September 5.

Depending on who you ask, Bush's decision to bail out banks and car companies might have averted a full-blown depression. Or, it favored rich Wall Streeters and car executives at the expense of middle-class Americans who had no relief from foreclosures and the loss of their retirement funds. Either way, the economy would become the next president's problem.

Bush never tempered his Eagle ways or moderated his approach to foreign policy. When speculation arose that Bush would fire Secretary of Defense Donald H. Rumsfeld in 2006, the president doubled down.

"I hear the voices and I read the front page and I know the speculation," said Bush, "but I'm the decider, and I decide what's best. And what's best is for Don Rumsfeld to remain as the secretary of defense."

Nothing quite captured Bush's Eagle personality like "the decider." He didn't give a damn what people thought. He believed Rumsfeld was doing a good job and defended him. It was an admirable act of loyalty in the eyes of the president's supporters. It was foolish and stubborn to his detractors. Like most Eagles, Bush was at ease with making polarizing decisions.

Bush never publicly questioned the invasion of Iraq. As he wrote in his book *Decision Points*, "Every American who served in Iraq helped to make our nation safer, gave twenty-five million people the chance to live in freedom, and changed the direction of the Middle East for generations to come. There are things we got wrong in Iraq, but that cause is eternally right."

Bushisms, Dubya's famous made-up words, mis-pronunciations, and ridiculous phrasings, became so legendary that they inspired entire books and poems. Other presidents misspoke too, but something about Dubya's Texan, Eagle voice and scrunched up, serious face added to the hilarity.

"They misunderestimated me," and "nucular" never got old. Neither did, "Rarely is the question asked: Is our children learning?"

Perhaps one Bushism was a moment of honesty rather than a slip up: "I'm also not very analytical. You know I don't spend a lot of time thinking about myself, about why I do things."

Perhaps a little more Owl would have been helpful.

2008, 2012:
No Drama Obama

"Change will not come if we wait for some other person or some other time. We are the ones we've been waiting for. We are the change that we seek."

– Barack Obama

MLK's Successor

It was a simpler time when Senator Barack Obama announced his presidential campaign in Springfield, Illinois, on February 10, 2007. The cellphone videos of his speech were grainy. Americans had ten more months until the Great Recession. Obama's hair was still black.

"I recognize there is a certain presumptuousness—a certain audacity—to this announcement," said Obama, expressing a humility that seems endangered thirteen years later. "I know I haven't spent a lot of time learning the ways of Washington. But I've been there long enough to know that the ways of Washington must change."

He laid down one-liners that sounded original yet familiar, compelling yet restrained, fierce yet loving. His personality was hard to place.

Obama was an orator unlike any America had heard in a generation. His tempo and style were reminiscent of Martin Luther King Jr.

MERRICK ROSENBERG

It felt like Obama was calling Americans to a higher mission, preaching to a nation in desperate need of hope and change amidst two wars and soon a recession.

Obama, in fact, shares the same rare personality as MLK—that of an Eagle and a Dove, both in equal measure. We'll denote that as Eagle/Dove rather than Eagle-Dove, which implies the Dove's secondary nature. This is the most misunderstood combination of all the bird styles. How does the take-charge, confident Eagle blend with the empathetic, compassionate Dove?

It's like mixing two reactive substances together. A change occurs, and a new substance is created. The chemical reaction of combining the Eagle and Dove creates an entirely new personality that contains elements of both styles. The combination is so uncommon, it is difficult to understand the seemingly contradictory behaviors. This combination personality is described as someone who will "fight for justice and equality" in *Taking Flight!*, this author's book that introduced the birds to the world.

Let's take a few examples from history to see this personality in action. In addition to Martin Luther King Jr., let's add two other Eagle/Doves to the list: Mahatma Gandhi and Nelson Mandela. They all preached "non-violent resistance." Non-violent comes from the Dove. Resistance comes from the Eagle. We will fight (Eagle) for people (Dove). And make no mistake, we will win (Eagle). Not through violence, but through patience (Dove).

Recall that before Obama was in Congress, the civil rights movement inspired him to become a community organizer for underserved communities on Chicago's South Side. From 1985 to 1988, he mobilized community members to stand up for water safety, asbestos testing in the housing projects, job training, and other needs. It was the perfect job for an Eagle/Dove.

Like the three other Eagle/Doves mentioned above, Obama was an eloquent orator. People often mistook this ability for a Parrot trait because it looked like verbal agility. In actuality, Obama's Eagle side gave his calm and deliberate Dove tone more self-assurance. The result was a poised speaker who could stir emotions and move millions.

Critics derisively called Obama "silver tongued," which is defined by Merriam-Webster as, "able to speak in a way that makes other people do or believe what you want them to do or believe." His eloquence propelled him onto the national scene when he gave the keynote speech at the Democratic National Convention in 2004. He never looked back.

Still, the senator from Illinois was an enigma. Comedian Jon Stewart, America's political conscience in the 2000s, couldn't find the words: "The effect that you have on a crowd…it's unusual for a politician. There is a certain inspirational quality. My question to you: is that something America is really going to go for?"

The laughter and applause from the audience said it all: Yes We Can.

Decoding Obama

Obama outwardly seemed like a Dove. He was humble about his experience, calm about America's challenges, and respectful of rivals. Yet the crowds didn't respond to him like a Dove.

Obama had the body and paint of a Dove, but the engine of an Eagle. He was in this race to win. He energized crowds and inspired passion. Like his Eagle/Dove forbearers, he led a movement, not a campaign.

Unlike a pure Eagle, Obama didn't lace his speeches with aggressive overtones. His Dove softened his approach. He spoke of hope and optimism. It was rare to see Obama lose his cool—Doves rarely do. It was also rare to see him back down—a core Eagle trait. "Look," Obama's favorite interjection, commanded others to see his perspective. It was fit for an Eagle, not a Dove who would rather make suggestions.

Obama was not without detractors, of course. To many voters, he seemed like an arrogant Ivy League elitist. His famous look-in-the-distance pose could strike you as visionary or haughty depending on your ideology. His coolness could come across as aloof, which frustrated people drawn to more passionate leaders. As Obama said in his book *The Audacity of Hope*, "By nature, I'm not somebody who gets real worked up about things." And there's the Dove.

Obama didn't apologize for being himself. "He doesn't strive for an Everyman quality," wrote Larissa MacFarquhar in *The New Yorker*. He "is relaxed but never chummy, gracious rather than familiar. His surface is so smooth, his movements so easy and fluid, his voice so consistent and well-pitched that he can seem like an actor playing a politician, too implausibly effortless to be doing it for real."

"Smooth" is not a word you'd ever associate with Obama's first opponent.

Not Miss Congeniality

On October 26, 1967, Lieut. Commander John S. McCain III was shot down over Hanoi, Vietnam during a bombing run and subsequently captured. POWs released in 1969 said that McCain was seriously injured and had spent at least a year in solitary confinement.

During his captivity, McCain was tortured, beaten, and starved. The North Vietnamese knew McCain was the son of a famous admiral and, by offering him early release, hoped to score propaganda points and stir resentment towards the young pilot.

He refused to play along. McCain insisted that POWs be released in the order they were captured. The North Vietnamese punished McCain with extra torture and time in solitary for foiling their plot. He languished for five and a half years in prison for refusing special treatment.

McCain entered the 2008 campaign like the man who had been to war, seen the dark side of humanity, and vowed to defend his country from "violent extremists who despise us, our values and modernity itself." He was an Eagle in combat mode, setting high expectations and goals for our "good nation upon whom all mankind depends."

As he scrolled through America's problems, he repeated the same refrain for dramatic effect: "That's not good enough for America. And when I'm President, it won't be good enough for me."

Unlike Obama, McCain was *not* out to cultivate hope. He was a Hollywood gunslinger who'd arrived to kill the bad guys, free the captives, and ride out on the sunset.

Said McCain, "We face formidable challenges, but I'm not afraid of them.... I know how the world works. I know the good and the evil in it.... I know who I am and what I want to do."

To doubters, McCain had a message: "Don't tell me what we can't do."

There's not a tinge of Dove, Parrot, or Owl in this speech. He didn't give a damn what you thought of him. As McCain would say during the first debate with Obama, "I didn't win Miss Congeniality in the United States Senate."

Likability? Who needs likability when you have courage, resilience, and grit. He was direct, bold, and unshakably committed to his values. He was known as a "maverick" for standing up to his party. That is as Eagle of a nickname as you can get.

Even his book titles—*Why Courage Matters, The Restless Wave, Hard Call*, and *Worth the Fighting For*—were Eagle through and through. One of his prior campaign slogans, The Straight Talk Express, was perfect for a blunt, pull-no-punches Eagle.

McCain talked about what *he* wanted to talk about on the campaign trail. He didn't care what his advisers suggested. He was as spontaneous and unscripted as possible. His renown as a war hero, foreign policy leader, and alpha Senator made him a serious contender.

When two foreign wars are going poorly, McCain is the kind of leader you might want in the Oval Office. But if you're looking for inspiration or empathy, maybe not.

Bush's Third Term

A 2008 political cartoon by Gary Varvel shows Obama and McCain pointing at each other. Obama's bubble says, "Don't vote for Bush's 3rd term." McCain's bubble says, "Don't vote for Jimmy Carter's 2nd term."

McCain's cartoon was right. He was another Eagle in the George W. Bush tradition. Obama's was half right. He shared Dove characteristics with Carter, but as the debates would demonstrate, Obama's Eagle made him far more forceful than Carter.

The first debate was about foreign policy. Obama was out to make McCain seem impetuous and poor tempered in light of the Eagle aggression that had led the U.S. into two intractable wars. He pushed the narrative of McCain being Bush's third term.

"John, you like to pretend like the war started in 2007 [the year of The Surge]…you said it was going to be quick and easy. You said we knew where the weapons of mass destruction were. You were wrong. You said that we were going to be greeted as liberators. You were wrong."

McCain didn't attempt to defend his record. He took the arch-Eagle approach of claiming that Obama didn't think the U.S. was winning the war, as if to doubt America was a crime. Rather than questioning his own beliefs—not something Eagle's enjoying doing—McCain tried to paint Obama as a peace-loving Jimmy Carter who would *lose* America's wars.

Still, America saw a confident, calm Obama laugh off the cranky, domineering rhetoric of McCain, who lost every post-debate poll. He looked like the candidate who was good at starting wars, not ending them.

Obama had Mr. Miyagi'd his opponent into submission, and this continued in the second debate. Americans saw Obama smiling at McCain as if he were listening politely to a grumbling old uncle at Thanksgiving dinner. The more McCain went on his Eagle offensive, the more Obama's soft smiles and even-keeled presence made it look like Obama was in charge. Despite being far more experienced than Obama, McCain looked like a novice being schooled by the master.

By the final debate on October 15, McCain was trailing Obama in the polls, and his campaign had turned negative. McCain no longer seemed to have a positive vision of his presidency, nor hope for Americans suffering from foreclosures and unemployment as a result of the Great Recession. McCain acted like an Eagle expecting a loss.

Obama called it: "100 percent, John, of your ads—100 percent of them have been negative."

The aggressive tone of McCain's campaign shaded his reputation for integrity and honor. By overdoing his Eagle energy, McCain lost touch with qualities that made him one of America's most respected politicians. The more that McCain attacked, the less he looked like America's president. The angrier he got, the angrier his crowds got. They slandered Obama for being a liar, terrorist, Muslim, and Arab.

To his credit, McCain defended Obama against a woman who called him an Arab intending it to be a slur: "He's a decent family man [and] citizen that I just happen to have disagreements with on fundamental issues, and that's what the campaign's all about. He's not [an Arab]."

Obama, the cool Eagle/Dove, seemed like he'd be calm and composed behind the wheel of an America heading into uncertainty. McCain the Eagle seemed like the type who'd flick off drivers, blow through a red light, and get America T-boned.

McCain embodied people's fears about George W. Bush's third term. Obama cast off the Carter comparisons. Despite being understanding and warm, he was tough, even in the ring with America's Maverick.

Voters craved the hopefulness that an Eagle/Dove could uniquely bring. The Dove in Obama's personality softened the rough edges of the Eagle and made him likable. He had the winning personality of 2008.

Obama took 52.9 percent of the vote, and McCain earned 45.7 percent. The electoral votes painted a bigger loss for the war hero with a final tally of 365 to 173. Obama became the first African American president in U.S. history.

Eagle/Dove in Action

When President Barack Hussein Obama took the oath of office on January 20, 2009, America was in crisis. The Iraq and Afghanistan occupations remained costly and precarious. The recession teetered on the brink of a depression, as unemployment surged to 7.6 percent. The U.S. needed a leader who, like FDR in the 1930s, could instill hope once again. As an Eagle/Dove, Obama was well-suited to the job.

His inauguration speech on January 20, 2009, set a different tenor from the Bush's Eagle White House. "My fellow citizens," said Obama, "I stand here today humbled by the task before us, grateful for the trust you have bestowed, mindful of the sacrifices borne by our ancestors."

He opened as a self-effacing Dove and acknowledged "a sapping of confidence across our land." Sounds awfully Carter. Then out came the Eagle: "Today, I say to you that the challenges we face are real, they are serious and they are many. They will not be met easily or in a short span of time. But know this America: They will be met."

And why would Obama succeed? Because he assumed that America had united behind him. "On this day, we gather because we have chosen hope over fear, unity of purpose over conflict and discord," he said.

If only that were so. Making The Big Assumption, this Eagle/Dove underestimated the degree to which political polarization would divide the country and paralyze Congress. His signature cause, the Affordable Care Act (ACA), became a reality check for Obama, sending him into defensive, resentful Dove mode.

In his speech to Congress about the ACA in September 2009, Obama accused opponents of using "scare tactics" and trying "to score short-term political points" at the expense of solving a critical problem: the plight of uninsured Americans.

However, when parrying his critics, Obama explained the proposal in such crippling detail that he made it even easier for opponents to attack and misrepresent the plan. Too much Owl that day. Although Obama signed the ACA in March 2010, he did so through Eagle force, not Dove compromise. Republicans still haven't forgiven it.

President Obama also brought his Eagle/Dove personality to international affairs. On June 4, 2009, he delivered a speech in Cairo to establish "a new beginning between the United States and Muslims around the world; one based upon mutual interest and mutual respect; and one based upon the truth that America and Islam are not exclusive, and need not be in competition."

In Bush's black-and-white mind, anyone who showed sympathy towards terrorists was as evil as the 9/11 hijackers. Obama saw grey, as Dove do.

Diverging even further from the zero-apologies Bush, Obama suggested that America had overreacted: "The fear and anger that it provoked was understandable, but in some cases, it led us to act contrary to our ideals. We are taking concrete actions to change course. I have unequivocally prohibited the use of torture by the United States, and I have ordered the prison at Guantanamo Bay closed by early next year."

The Cairo speech and others like it became known as Obama's "apology tour" in right-leaning media. Later that year, Obama was awarded a Nobel Peace Prize "for his extraordinary efforts to strengthen international diplomacy and cooperation between peoples."

They might have jumped the gun (no pun intended).

Saltines for President

It was a windy day on June 2, 2011, when the former governor of Massachusetts, wearing a businessman's crisp, pinstriped shirt, announced his campaign for president.

He was proper, straitlaced, and precise. It looked as if his arms were controlled by a novice puppeteer who didn't know where to put them. His attempts at sounding emotive earned an "E" for effort. He gave what was supposed to be a casual chili cook-off an air of formality. After a

long-winded lead-in, Mitt Romney finally said the words that made the
highlight reels: "Barack Obama has failed America."

The tough words gave way to a laundry list of facts about America's
battered economy. It was data, data, and more data. Sounds like Dukakis
and Gore, huh?

If you haven't guessed already, Romney is an Owl. And it plagued
his campaign from day one. Romney considered himself his best campaign adviser. Who else could an Owl trust to solve problems and archi-
tect a successful run for president?

So, like Duakakis, he micromanaged his campaign. Afterwards,
insiders revealed that he had created a system that assigned point values
to rallies, speeches, fundraisers, and other events that could occupy his
day. The more effort the event required, the more points it was worth.
900 points was the limit for any day. *That* was Romney's idea of time
management.

The goal of Romney's team was to humanize him. They needed to
make the wealthy, private equity executive relatable to swing voters who
saw Obama as a beacon of hope in tough times.

Humanizing Romney was like trying to make dessert out of saltine
crackers and cottage cheese. No matter how much sugar you added, it
was never going to taste good. Here was a highly accomplished governor
and businessman who could make a five-minute video feel twenty minutes long. Here was a leader who never seemed to know what to do with
his hands. More than a few commentators portrayed him as a robot trying to mimic human behavior. Owls just don't convey emotion naturally.

For Romney, likability did not compute. Maybe he understood
the recession better than Obama and could get America out of it more

efficiently. He had turned around companies, so maybe he could turn around the world's largest economy.

At the 2012 Republican Convention, everyone tried to make Mitt relatable. The absurdity of this effort gave birth to a meme: Relatable Romney.

"I know what it's like to be unemployed," said one, with Romney in rogue hand mode. "I haven't had to work in years."

"Sometimes it's hard to ask for help," said another. "Because they've all gone home for the day."

"I know you want change," said yet another. "But I only have $100 bills."

Obama, a Dove who could read the room, told his donors and aids that "Romney never did seem quite human enough to get elected." He was too Owl to win a general election against an Eagle/Dove.

Mr. Relatable

Romney, already failing to convince anyone that he could relate to the challenges of ordinary Americans, managed to kill off any remaining chance. Normally a calculated and careful Owl, Romney got caught with his pants down by a smartphone videographer.

On September 17, *Mother Jones* received leaked footage of Romney sharing his campaign strategy with wealthy donors in Boca Raton, Florida:

> There are 47 percent of the people who will vote for the president no matter what. All right, there are 47 percent who are with him, who are dependent upon government, who believe that they are victims, who believe the government has a responsibility to care for them, who believe

that they are entitled to health care, to food, to housing, to you-name-it. That that's an entitlement. And the government should give it to them. And they will vote for this president no matter what.

And I mean the president starts out with 48, 49 percent … he starts off with a huge number. These are people who pay no income tax. Forty-seven percent of Americans pay no income tax.

So our message of low taxes doesn't connect. So he'll be out there talking about tax cuts for the rich. I mean, that's what they sell every four years. And so my job is not to worry about those people. I'll never convince them that they should take personal responsibility and care for their lives.

Romney's claim about 47 percent not paying tax was true if he was referring to federal income tax (which fact-checkers assumed he was). *Of course*, Romney had the numbers right. He's an Owl. But saying that his "job is not to worry about" nearly half of the population seem callous and unpresidential.

Struggling, hard-working Americans heard this multimillionaire demean their efforts to support their families. On the heels of the second-worst economic disaster in U.S. history, here was a rich guy saying that low- and middle-income families needed government assistance because they "don't take personal responsibility."

Romney didn't walk back his comments very well, telling reporters, "It's not elegantly stated, let me put it that way. I was speaking off the cuff in response to a question. And I'm sure I could state it more clearly in a more effective way than I did in a setting like that."

Owl Romney ruminated on the fact that he could have said the same thing better. In essence, Romney was saying yes, he still thought that 47 percent of Americans were freeloaders mooching off the government and his donors. As a candidate and president, he wasn't going to focus on them. Subsequent polling found that 57 percent of independents looked negatively upon the comment. It was not a fortuitous start to debate season.

The Relatable Romney memes kept coming: "I know what it's like to live in a crime-ridden community…. 47% of Americans keep trying to take my money."

Declawing an Owl

It's widely agreed that in the first debate, Romney trounced Obama. The president didn't show up prepared. Maybe he needed some Owl energy. He stubbornly refused to practice pre-written attack lines or memorize sound bites. He kept telling his team, "I got this." It was overuse of Eagle confidence. He didn't look like he wanted to be at the debate at Denver University.

Romney had the look of an Owl winning—of someone who felt prepared and far more knowledgeable than his opponent. His smirk said it all. The split-screen view highlighted the difference between the struggling Obama and laser-precise Romney.

Obama came across as defensive and dismissive. Romney surged ahead in the polls temporarily.

In the second debate, Obama showed up armed and dangerous. The phrase he repeated again and again after Romney spoke was variations of,

"Not true." It forced Romney into the Owl task of substantiating everything he said. No one remembered his defense. They remembered Obama calling B.S. on the facts guy. It was reminiscent of Reagan's "There you go again," the line he used to dismiss Carter's facts. This minimalist tactic seems to be a favorite of Eagles, as you'll see in 2016 and 2020.

In the third debate, Obama clinched victory with one-liners that Romney couldn't parry. Romney, fixated on the number of ships in America's Navy, noted that it was smaller than at any time since 1917. Obama, pounced:

> But I think Governor Romney maybe hasn't spent enough time looking at how our military works. You— you mentioned the Navy, for example, and that we have fewer ships than we did in 1916. Well, Governor, we also have fewer horses and bayonets—because the nature of our military's changed. We have these things called aircraft carriers where planes land on them. We have these ships that go underwater, nuclear submarines.

Obama made the Owl look illogical, unknowledgeable, and even childish. When Romney talked about stopping China from taking American jobs, the Eagle landed another blow:

> "Well, Governor Romney's right. You are familiar with jobs being shipped overseas, because you invested in companies that were shipping jobs overseas...
>
> ...But I've made a different bet on American workers. You know, if we had taken your advice, Governor Romney,

about our auto industry, we'd be buying cars from China instead of selling cars to China."

Obama reframed Romney the turn-around agent as Romney the indifferent millionaire who turned companies around by offshoring their jobs. Obama finally used his Eagle to full effect and overwhelmed Romney. Once intent on being America's problem-solver, Romney became the candidate who was *least* in touch with America's problems. It showed on November 6, 2012, when Obama won reelection with 332 electoral votes to Romney's 206.

The Power of Empathy

McCain and Romney were less likeable than Obama. Capable, respected, and competent? Yes. But they just weren't empathetic. Voters didn't feel understood and heard by them. Empathy allowed Obama to think from the perspective of his adversaries. And it made him uniquely able to connect with Americans as a campaigner and president.

Perhaps no instance showed Obama's empathy more heart wrenchingly than the Sandy Hook massacre of December 2012. A mentally ill gunman stormed into Sandy Hook Elementary School in Newtown, Connecticut, with an assault rifle, multiple pistols, and a shotgun. He killed twenty-eight people, including twenty school children.

Addressing the massacre on live TV, Obama tried to stay composed, but grief overwhelmed him. It was not the first such tragedy Obama had addressed. "And each time I learn the news" of a shooting, said Obama, "I react not as a President, but as anybody else would—as a parent." Before the cameras, he thought of his two daughters.

"The majority of those who died today were children—beautiful little kids between the ages of 5 and 10 years old," said Obama. The tears came. His left hand brush one away. He paused and looked down at the lectern. "They had their entire lives ahead of them—birthdays, graduations, weddings, kids of their own."

He struggled to speak without being overcome by emotion. More tears came. More pauses. More tears brushed away.

"This evening, Michelle and I will do what I know every parent in America will do, which is hug our children a little tighter, and we'll tell them that we love them, and we'll remind each other how deeply we love one another," said Obama. "But there are families in Connecticut who cannot do that tonight. And they need all of us right now."

Obama empathized with the families of the fallen. Seeing Obama's tears and hearing his words, one could not help but mourn with him. This is what a president with a strong Dove side looks like in a time of tragedy. Can you picture Trump with tears streaming down his face while addressing the nation?

Today, Obama's legacy remains an open question. The Affordable Care Act was hotly contested throughout his tenure in office, and Republicans still seek to overturn it. His Dove vision to expand healthcare to uninsured Americans now seems moderate compared to the Medicare for All plans that Democrats floated in the 2020 election and continue to espouse.

As for Obama's handling of Iraq, Afghanistan, the Arab Spring, the Syrian Civil War, and the Islamic State, it is too soon to judge. The Middle East remains unstable, the way Obama received it. His decision in 2011 to take out Osama Bin Laden with a Navy SEAL raid in Pakistan seemed rather Eagle. It was a revenge mission as much as it was a strategic move. An Eagle/Dove cannot embrace nonviolence as president of the United States. Obama, unlike MLK, Gandhi, or Mandela, was responsible for global security.

Indeed, Obama authorized 540 unmanned aerial drone strikes against militants in multiple war zones. These missions killed 3,797 people, including 324 civilians. This, too, seems rather Eagle compared to the Dove we saw after Sandy Hook. Whatever the intelligence reports said, they must have overcome his Dove's objections.

Without more years of perspective, we can't say what Obama's presidency means. It still hasn't yet aged from politics to history. Obama was the first Eagle/Dove president we examined in two-and-a-half centuries of U.S. history.

2016: The Donald

"I am attracting the biggest crowds, by far,
and the best poll numbers, also by far."
- Donald Trump

Commander-in-Attention

In a New York building named after himself, Donald Trump announced his candidacy for president of the United States on June 15, 2015. His speech went on for about 55 minutes.

It was a Jackson Pollock painting in words, an Eagle's collage of boasts, warnings, business achievements, net-worth calculations, policy tirades, personal attacks, compliments, prejudices, and suspiciously self-serving stories. Through the chaos came a slogan borrowed from Reagan's 1980 campaign: Let's Make America Great Again.

Trump removed the collaborative Parrot "Let's" and shortened it to the command, "Make America Great Again."

Trump's personality was on 4K display. No one could forget the words, "…they're bringing drugs. They're rapists. And some, I assume, are good people."

He spoke several lines that few bothered to report. They were the closest thing to a campaign strategy that Trump would ever articulate:

So, the reporter said to me the other day, "But Mr. Trump, you're not a nice person. How can you get people to vote for you?"

I said, "I don't know." I said, "I think that number one, I am a nice person. I give a lot of money away to charities and other things. I think I'm actually a very nice person."

But I said, "This is going to be an election that's based on competence, because people are tired of these nice people. And they're tired of being ripped off by everybody in the world."

From day one, Trump intended to win by flexing his Eagle personality. The "nice people"—Doves like Jeb Bush and John Kasich (recall his famous line, "rhymes with 'basic'")—would get steamrolled. And they did.

Trump knew that he wasn't likable. He knew he didn't grasp policy and law like his Republican primary contenders or Hillary Clinton, his eventual Democratic opponent. But Trump understood that *perceived* competence could lead him to victory.

To win, Trump would play up his deal-making abilities, business prowess, and superlatives never before spoken (or tweeted) in the English language (e.g., "I am [the] least racist person there is."). He would go so over-the-top Eagle that voters would see confidence as competence. He would command attention.

No Cherries to Pick

Two days earlier in New York City, Hillary Clinton had launched her campaign with all the charisma of an insurance policy. It was a speech we'd all heard before about creating an economy in which middle-class folks can achieve the American Dream. "I'm running," she said, "to make our economy work for you and for every American."

She analyzed how the economy had gone wrong. "In the coming weeks," she said, "I'll propose specific policies to…" and announced more than 20 distinct policies. They were more specific than anything Trump said during his campaign or would say during his presidency.

Clinton's speech was about problems and logical solutions. It was about plans. It was Owl to the core.

Sometimes, news stations get accused of cherry-picking sound bites. In Clinton's case, it was hard to find any cherries. The best remembered was, "I'm not running for some Americans, but for all Americans."

Did it sound nice and unifying? Sure. Did it arouse any emotions? Not so much.

Clinton sounded prepared and clear. She sounded focused and consistent. She sounded like she had a plan to fix America's problems. Hillary Rodham Clinton sounded like the kind of Owl who loses general elections in the 21st century.

The Unlikables

The 2016 election was a personality contest unlike any prior. "This is unprecedented," said Democratic pollster Mark Mellman in April 2016. "It will be the first time in the history of polling that we'll have both major party candidates disliked by a majority of the American people going into the election."

He was dead on. This was the first election since 1932 in which neither candidate had a secondary Dove or Parrot style. As you've learned, Eagle and Owl candidates are less likable than Parrots and Doves. Both

MERRICK ROSENBERG

Clinton and Trump fall into this category. The result: the most polarizing election in modern history.

Trump was confident, visionary, competitive, blunt, dynamic, nonconformist, and driven by big ideas. In Eagle form, he gave his enemies demeaning nicknames and went to war against them.

Clinton's personality was calculated, careful, nonconfrontational, nuanced, objective, systematic, logical, and fact driven. Clinton expected victory because data from pollsters said it would happen. This was her moment; she'd been preparing for this race since her loss to Obama in the 2008 primaries. Her Owl planning was too good to fail. Or so she thought.

No presidential race has ever been covered in such exhaustive detail. There was (and still is) insatiable curiosity about whatever Trump said. His antics were too profitable for news organizations not to report. No matter how unlikable he was—and no matter how unlikable Clinton was—Trump took the headlines. We didn't get a taste of Trump. We got the all-you-can-eat Trump Casino buffet.

Trump was an Eagle performer aiming to win an attention contest. He was no novice in this arena. On shows like *The Apprentice*, he didn't have to act. "You're fired!" was the tagline of an all-powerful Eagle whose qualification was being a billionaire.

He had accumulated followers and hundreds of on-air hours by playing himself on TV. So Trump produced his campaign as if it were a one-man show starring The Donald.

Trump gloated about his crowd sizes throughout the campaign because that is the metric that mattered to him. It indicated how many people were getting exposed to his personality. As Hannah Hope wrote in *The St. Cloud Times*, Trump's persona "sucks the air from media coverage of his rivals and places him center stage in water-cooler and dinner-table talk from coast to coast."

Knife at a Gunfight

In the 15 months between Trump's campaign launch and his first presidential debate with Clinton on September 26, we learned almost nothing new about his personality. But the differences between Trump and Clinton became glaringly obvious on the debate stage.

Clinton came prepared with facts, policies, and rehearsed jabs. That's what Owls have done since the first televised debate in 1960. Trump came ready to tear Clinton to shreds. None of the highlight reels recalled Clinton's plans for improving America. Instead, they captured the drama of two radically different personalities becoming ever more aggressive. With each debate, Clinton became more Eagle but less likable. Trump was himself throughout.

In the first debate, Clinton, an Owl supremely concerned with rules, tried to make Trump look like a bad boy. "He didn't pay any federal income tax," she said, as if it were a gotcha blow.

"That makes me smart," said Trump.

Clinton jabbed Trump about his tax returns, and it backfired. "I will release my tax returns when she releases her 33,000 emails that have been deleted," he said.

Trump didn't tangle with Clinton's policies, which she came prepared to defend. He reinterpreted her mild, stone-cold Owl demeanor for voters: "She doesn't have the stamina. I said she doesn't have the stamina. And I don't believe she has the stamina."

In a telling moment, Clinton made The Big Assumption. She believed that her preparation for the debate would be respected by voters, even if it wasn't respected by Trump. She believed in the power of specific policies and thought that everyone else would too. Of course, they would. How else could they possibly differentiate between her and Donald Trump?

"I think Donald just criticized me for preparing for this debate," said Clinton. "And, yes, I did. And you know what else I prepared for? I prepared to be president. And I think that's a good thing." Only an Owl brags about preparation.

Clinton's supporters thought she won the first debate because she understood the issues and made sense. Unless you watched the debate end to end, you didn't pick up her policy ideas because the news didn't report them.

Clinton showed up to a gunfight with hundreds of miniature knives called facts and arguments. Trump showed up with a rocket launcher.

"Such a nasty woman"

At the second debate on October 9, two days after Trump's "Grab 'em by the pussy" comment leaked to the media, Clinton still couldn't stick it to Trump. Anderson Cooper of CNN, not Clinton, tried to make Trump admit that he'd sexually assaulted and harassed women.

In Trump's words, "…it was locker room talk." He went on, "Nobody has more respect for women than I do." Trump turned to extreme Eagle grandiosity and hyperbole in a moment where most people would have played defense.

Clinton's response? She shared evidence upon evidence that he didn't respect women. The Owl couldn't settle for sharing one anecdote! She lost the audience's attention.

What didn't lose any attention was Trump's comeback: "If you look at Bill Clinton, far worse. Mine are words, and his was action. His was what he's done to women. There's never been anybody in the history of politics in this nation that's been so abusive to women." Trump accused Hillary of being complicit and attacking the women her husband had abused.

Attack an Eagle and they attack back. Attack an Owl and they pummel you with data.

Thinking she'd nail Trump, Clinton said, "…it's just awfully good that someone with the temperament of Donald Trump is not in charge of the law in our country."

"Because you'd be in jail," Trump said, and the audience exploded into applause.

Trump was Teflon, just like Bill Clinton and Ronald Reagan. He didn't just block Hillary's attacks, he counterattacked every time and blamed her for everything. Whether it was immigration, the Iraq War, the Syrian Civil War, debt, stagnant wages, or rising healthcare costs, Trump pinned it on Clinton. Her logic couldn't defeat such consistent disregard for facts.

The third debate was more of Clinton falling into the same traps and creating more moments for Trump to be an Eagle. Clinton just couldn't score points that would make the newsreels. As she pontificated about Social Security and suggested that Trump would find a way to avoid paying it, he interrupted with words that stuck permanently:

"Such a nasty woman."

Uhhh...Sexism?

Without a doubt, Hillary Clinton faced sexism in the 2016 election. Women candidates face well-documented prejudices that affect how we perceive their personalities. Disturbingly, "such a nasty woman" might have reflected how American men *and* women felt.

In 2010, Yale professors Victoria Brescoll and Tyler Okimoto ran an experiment in which they showed participants fictional biographies of two state senators—one male and one female. The biographies were identical. When they added Eagle words like "ambitious" or "strong will to power" into these biographies, the male senator gained support, while the female senator not only lost support, but also provoked "moral outrage."

For male senators, power-seeking behaviors signaled competence, toughness, and assertiveness. For female senators, seeking power triggered disgust and contempt. Female participants were *just as likely as male participants* to hold this double standard toward female politicians.

The professors concluded that when women are perceived to be seeking power, they defy the stereotype that women should be sensitive, empathetic, and caring.

What is a presidential election if not an attempt to seek power?

In other words, Clinton's choice to run for president was cause for condemnation. She seemed "nasty" because she aspired to break the glass ceiling. Then, add Clinton's Owl personality into the mix, and she faced a real uphill battle.

Why Couldn't People Stop Talking About Him?!

Trump's call to Make America Great Again (on Twitter, #MAGA) was the vision of a romanticized past where today's disenfranchised masses of rural and industrial America were prosperous. Voters were mesmerized by Trump's imagined world, where America could unravel its corrupt layers or, as he put it, "drain the swamp." His confidence made this glorified world sound easily achievable—or at least better than the world we lived in.

Who could bring the United States back to greatness? "Only Donald Trump," he would say, often referring to himself in the third person. He was a fighter who didn't back down; who didn't take crap from anyone; who played offense when rational people would play defense; who doubled down when accused of lying; who realized that all he had to do was be an Eagle on the public stage and never, ever stray.

Voters couldn't look away from Trump's campaign because he said and did things no candidate had ever done before. By being himself, Trump controlled the information diet of every American with a smartphone or TV.

Meanwhile, as Clinton defended charges against her use of a private email server—with facts and logic—she created even more suspicion. Unlike Trump, she did not have a Teflon coating. She couldn't stop being an Owl even when she tried to be an Eagle: "You know, to just be grossly generalistic, you could put half of Trump's supporters into what I call the basket of deplorables. Right? The racist, sexist, homophobic, xenophobic, Islamophobic—you name it."

She had tried to qualify her statement and later defended herself for overgeneralizing. Recall when Al Gore spent valuable minutes in a debate apologizing for a few inaccurate statistics. We're lucky Hillary didn't try to calculate what percentage of Trump supporters were actually deplorable.

Trump ran one of the most unconventional political campaigns in U.S. history. He spent more money on MAGA hats than on pollsters. He traveled to states like Wisconsin and Michigan that pundits said he would lose anyway. Rather than amassing a get-out-the-vote operation to knock on doors, Trump held massive rallies. No one could promote Donald Trump better than Donald Trump.

If you read just a few of Trump's tweets or watched one of the more than 320 rallies he held during the 2016 campaign, you knew this: Trump believed in himself and maybe nothing else. This Eagle self-assurance was enough to capture disenchanted swing voters and even some Democrats.

An estimated 9% of Americans who voted for Obama in 2008 and 2012 cast ballots for Trump in 2016. In presidential elections, 9% is often the difference between victory and defeat. In 2016, 16 states were decided by less than 9% of the electorate. In critical states like Michigan, Wisconsin, and Pennsylvania, Trump won by 0.3%, 1%, and 1.2% respectively.

Swing voters matter, and personality is the driving force behind their decisions. Confidence, self-assurance, and self-reliance—the landmark traits of an Eagle—won over the undecided.

But too much of a good thing is not a good thing. Too much confidence becomes arrogance. Too much directness becomes insensitivity. In our personal relationships, when we turn up the volume on our strengths, we turn people off. Trump's time in office became a case study in Eagle overuse.

King of the Twitterverse

After his inauguration on January 20, 2017, President Donald J. Trump monopolized the world's attention. He set policies, conducted international affairs, commended allies, and attacked enemies on the public stage of Twitter. By tapping on a smartphone, he sent stocks rising or tumbling.

Trump carried on the presidential tradition of adopting new communication technologies to wield political power. Like FDR with radio and Reagan with staged television, Trump honed his command of Twitter.

With over 87 million Twitter followers at his peak, he broadcast himself to all Americans, unmediated by the press. The economics of 24-hour, ad-based news were such that the press couldn't afford to *not* cover Trump's tweets, amplifying their reach even further.

Between opening his account in 2009 and losing access to it in 2021, he tweeted 56,571 times, averaging 18 tweets per day during his presidency. Trump wrote his own narrative—and facts—faster than anyone could challenge them.

History is likely to remember Trump's presidency mostly for its scandals, shenanigans, and ignominious end (which we'll get into). That has everything to do with his Eagle personality and the way he overused it. That same personality did, however, manage to gratify MAGA voters and create almost cult-like reverence for Trump.

Even conservatives who loathed Trump acknowledge some successes. He secured $1.375 billion from Congress to partially build a border wall with Mexico (which didn't pay for it). He named three conservative justices to the Supreme Court: Neil Gorsuch, Brett Kavanaugh, and Amy Coney Barrett.

On the foreign policy front, Trump challenged China's intellectual property theft and one-sided tariffs, and he renegotiated North American free trade to the benefit of domestic manufacturers. Trump also withdrew the U.S. from the Paris Agreement on climate change and the Iran nuclear deal, drawing applause from conservatives. He recognized Jerusalem as Israel's capital and moved the U.S. embassy there. Whether it was an acknowledgement of facts on the ground or a blunder that will delay peace further, only time will tell.

Here's the thing: Trump had a pathological need to "win," which is common among hard-core Eagles. Sometimes, this need even leads to inspiring, powerful results. Just look at basketball legend Michael

Jordan—a hard-core Eagle, as the docuseries *The Last Dance* made clear. If anyone questioned or doubted Jordan, he made sure they regretted it.

Unlike Jordan, Trump didn't have the emotional intelligence to balance out his strong Eagle. Again and again, he made America wonder, "Did he really say that?" and "Is this actually happening?"

Recall, for example, Trump's spat with North Korean dictator Kim Jong Un, whom he nicknamed Little Rocket Man. In response to North Korea's intercontinental ballistic missile (ICBM) program and aggressive but typical rhetoric, Trump threatened Kim with "fire and fury." After another missile test, Trump upped the ante during a middle-schoolish exchange of threats, tweeting "North Korean Leader Kim Jong Un just stated that the 'Nuclear Button is on his desk at all times.' Will someone from his depleted and food-starved regime please inform him that I too have a Nuclear Button, but it is a much bigger & more powerful one than his, and my Button works!"

Can you imagine Truman, Eisenhower, Kennedy, or Nixon telling the Soviets to watch out because we have a bigger and better nuclear button? No.

Ultimately, Trump's bickering with Kim Jong Un morphed into negotiations, a cordial meeting in June 2018, and a second gathering in June 2019, when Trump became the first sitting U.S. president to set foot in North Korea. Trump didn't get any real concessions, and the détente hasn't lasted.

Trump's Eagle need to win spilled into his scandal management too. It was blunt, direct, and remarkably inept yet effective. During the 2016 campaign, Trump and his team were accused of collaborating with Russia to defeat Hillary in 2016. Hell, Trump publicly asked Russia to find Hillary's 30,000 missing emails!

Once in office, President Trump asked FBI Director James Comey to drop charges against campaign advisor Michael Flynn, who had lied about his contacts with Russia. Comey refused, so Trump fired him, triggering accusations that the President had obstructed justice. As an Eagle in the red zone, he demanded loyalty.

So *of course* he fired Comey! How could Trump rely on an FBI Director who was unwilling to pledge his loyalty or follow orders? Ditto with Attorney General Jeff Sessions, who recused himself from the investigation. He was supposed to quash it, not hand it off to special counsel Robert Mueller. While Mueller concluded that Russia had tried to help Trump get elected, he didn't determine whether Trump had or had not obstructed justice.

Then in October 2019, Trump was accused of pressuring Ukrainian President Volodymyr Zelensky to investigate the Biden family by withholding military aid. As with Russiagate, Trump wasn't subtle. Eagles in overuse rarely are. The whole exchange was recorded. That didn't stick either. It led to Trump's first impeachment but no conviction. Trump "won" in the sense he never showed any remorse and never suffered lasting consequences.

Far from hurting Trump, the investigations and impeachment played to his personality. Extreme Eagles thrive on us-versus-them dynamics. An Eagle in overuse mode needs enemies, and there was no shortage during his term. The Democratic Party, the deep state, and "the fake news" had all colluded in a "witch hunt" against him. They all served Trump's need to be in a state of siege with enemies to attack and blame.

Because COVID-19 and January 6 are so integral to the story of the 2020 election, we'll save them for the next chapter. But of all the events that illustrated Trump's personality and foreshadowed his behavior in 2020, one deserves a special mention: Sharpiegate.

It was hurricane season and Trump was trying to be helpful. On September 1, 2019, he tweeted that "In addition to Florida - South Carolina, North Carolina, Georgia, and Alabama, will most likely be hit (much) harder than anticipated. Looking like one of the largest hurricanes ever. Already category 5. BE CAREFUL! GOD BLESS EVERYONE!"

But Hurricane Dorian was never going to hit Alabama, and Trump's tweet caused panic. The National Weather Service (NWS) station in Birmingham announced on Twitter that Alabama was safe from Dorian. Nevertheless, Trump continued to insist that Alabama would get hit.

The media criticized Trump for his misstatement. He lashed out at "the fake news" for fact-checking him and insisted in multiple tweets that in the "original scenarios," Dorian was projected to hit Alabama.

On September 4, in a televised appearance, Trump presented a NOAA forecast that had been altered by a black Sharpie to put Alabama in Hurricane Dorian's path. An anonymous White House official told *The Washington Post* that Trump had altered the map.

On September 6, someone at NOAA released an unsigned statement claiming that the NWS station in Birmingham was wrong. Alabama had been in danger. This contradicted what scientists at NOAA knew and prompted an investigation. Allegedly, Commerce Secretary Wilbur Ross had threatened to fire top NOAA appointees unless they refuted the NWS's claims.

Trump could have tweeted a correction on September 1 and moved along without any drama. But an Eagle in overuse *can't* be wrong. It would be as if Michael Jordan lost a basketball game but shot two more baskets anyway and then claimed victory.

Many Americans chalked Sharpiegate up to "Trump being Trump." We use the phrase forgivingly, but only for Eagles and Parrots. The same was said about baseball player Manny Ramirez for more than a decade. That's just Manny being Manny. He, too, was an Eagle in overuse. He forgot to show up for team pictures, neglected to give tickets to friends whom he'd invited to games, refused to play left field for Boston, and peed on the field mid-inning—but he played damn good ball. As of October 2008, the phrase "Manny being Manny" had appeared in print 1,621 times.

Almost daily during his presidency, you could find someone talking about "Trump being Trump." Classic Trump lines like, "I'm an extremely stable genius," "I am the Chosen One," and "...in my great and unmatched wisdom..." get written off as Trump being Trump.

Lying about a hurricane forecast is genuinely dangerous to people who might be in its path. We would have been shocked if any president before Trump did the same.

Confident Eagles stand up for their views. Even if their position is weak, they may argue for it longer than a Parrot, Dove, or Owl would. Eagles like being right and winning arguments, but ultimately they want the truth because it will help them achieve their goals. If they do lie and spin, it's for strategic reasons.

Not Trump being Trump. There was nothing strategic about doctoring hurricane forecasts. Sharpiegate foreshadowed how he might handle a bigger crisis like, oh, a global pandemic. His inability to be wrong or lose defined his term in office—and his attempt at reelection.

2020:
Amtrak Joe

"Look, I know by now no one ever doubts that I mean what I say; the problem is I sometimes say all that I mean."

\- Joe Biden

The Not Trump

In Joe Biden's telling, his presidential campaign began on August 12, 2017. Protestors had descended on Charlottesville, Virginia to oppose the removal of a statue of Confederate general Robert E. Lee. Bearing Nazi and Confederate regalia and carrying tiki torches, they chanted, "Jews will not replace us," among other hateful things. Clashes between the Unite the Right marchers and counter protestors ensued. Eventually, a neo-Nazi rammed his car into a group of counter protestors, injuring 35 and killing one.

The script for a president in this situation is obvious. But as we know, Eagle Trump was not one to bow to convention—or to condemn *anyone* who showered him with praise, as leaders of Unite the Right had. After Trump's rambling press conference, the public only remembered one thing the President said: There were "…very fine people on both sides."

Days later, former Vice President Biden denounced President Trump in an op-ed for *The Atlantic*. "We are living through a battle for the soul of this nation," Biden wrote. "You, me, and the citizens of this country carry a special burden in 2017. We have to do what our president has not. We have to uphold America's values…We have to show the world America is still a beacon of light."

Notice the verbiage: soul, values, and light. Biden would run almost his entire campaign on those emotive words.

Initially, though, we thought Joe would crank up his Parrot-Dove optimism. His slogan, "Our Best Days Still Lie Ahead," was reminiscent of Kennedy's New Frontier, Reagan's "rendezvous with destiny," and Bill Clinton's "bridge to the 21st century." As Biden's campaign website read, "We are the United States of America. And together, there is not a single thing we cannot do."

Put your aviator sunglasses on, America. Let's do this!

Well, not quite. That Joe never arrived. You know, finger guns Joe. *The Onion* Joe washing his Trans Am shirtless and drinking a cold one. The Uncle Joe who laughed at himself after asking Missouri State Senator Chuck Graham to stand up for a round of applause, forgetting that Graham is paraplegic. The Joe with an irrepressible, toothy smile. The Parrot-Dove Joe America knew since he entered public office in 1972 and who appeared in the 2020 edition of *Personality Wins*.

Although Joe gaffed like a talkative Parrot, his political personality had changed. Words like "decency" and "empathy" and "compassion" and "warmth" showed up in news profiles of Biden and his campaign. He no longer exuded charisma and vision the way he had as a Senate and VP candidate in years past. Rather, Joe's campaign moved like the steady old Amtrak train he took from Delaware to Washington, D.C. some 8,000 times during his career.

Biden's stories didn't feel Parrot either. With COVID-19 claiming so many lives and livelihoods, Joe expressed empathy instead of humor. He'd lost his first wife and daughter in a car accident in 1972, and his son Beau passed of brain cancer in 2015. Throughout the campaign, Joe spoke often of that "deep black hole that opens up in your chest," evoking those losses.

He also recalled the moment his father, unable to find work in their hometown of Scranton, Pennsylvania, told young Joe he was moving the family to Delaware; he could no longer play for his little league team. It was Biden's version of "I feel your pain," the Clinton rhetoric that made George H.W. Bush, an Owl, seem cold by comparison.

Most Americans expect their president to serve as "consoler in chief" during national crises like a pandemic. Whereas Trump rarely flexed his Eagle style to that role, Biden took to it naturally. His personality came across heavy with emotion and genuine concern.

Most tellingly, Biden said, "I view myself as a transition candidate" in April of 2020. *That* is a Dove candidate—one who feels that American has gone so far off the (Amtrak) rails that progress isn't possible without a restoration of stability first. No Eagle or Parrot would ever bill themself as a "transition" anything! They see themselves as too important and historic. Only a Dove can lay such a modest claim to the presidency.

Biden had become more Dove-Parrot than Parrot-Dove since his time as vice president. These personality changes do happen. Major life events can energize sides of our personality while calming others. As an example, Nelson Mandela underwent such a shift. His experience in prison changed him from an Eagle to an Eagle/Dove, like Obama. The passing of Beau, the Unite the Right rally, and the tragedy of COVID-19 seemed to draw out Biden's Dove.

Biden always showed some Dove, as we discussed in the 2020 edition of this book. As a child, Biden had a stutter that he said was "the single most defining thing in my life." It led to bullying and humiliation at his all-boys Catholic school. Even a teacher mockingly called him "Mr. Bu-bu-bu-Biden" on one occasion. Biden overcame his stutter by memorizing and reciting Irish poetry.

Although Biden didn't change his personality intentionally for 2020, he intuited something important about it. When CBS's Ed O'Keefe asked Biden why voters should support him, other than for the reason he's not Trump, Biden said, "Look, I'm running because Trump is the president, and I think our democracy's at stake, for real. And what seems to be the case is many Americans, those who don't like me and those that do, view me as the antithesis of Trump. And I believe that I am."

Biden was correct. A Dove who cherishes venerable institutions and long-standing traditions *is* the antithesis of a hard-core Eagle like Trump. A Pew Research poll released in August 2020 found that 56% of Biden voters supported Amtrak Joe because "he is not Trump."

Since 1932, not a single Dove had beaten an Eagle in a presidential election. Did Biden, a Dove, break the Personality Wins Model by defeating Trump in 2020?

The answer depends on whether voters viewed Biden as a Dove or perceived him to be adapting to the turmoil of COVID-19. Biden had been an elected official for nearly a half-century, so it's possible that voters still viewed him as a Parrot and attributed his Dove behavior in the 2020 election to current events. Or perhaps voters recognized the change in Biden's personality, in which case, yes, a Dove beat an Eagle in 2020.

In our view, the most convincing explanation is that repulsion to Trump, not passion for Biden, shaped the outcome. Remember, Eagles can be less likable as candidates than Doves and Parrots, but they are electable, and since 1928, electability has beaten likability every time.

However, by overusing his Eagle personality, Trump undermined his electability. He showed that when assertiveness devolves into aggressiveness, directness into bluntness, and confidence into arrogance, personality *loses*.

False Assurance

While Biden ran his crusade for the soul of America, Trump faced a different battle. On January 22, 2020, he addressed the coronavirus publicly for the first time. "We have it totally under control. It's one person coming in from China. We have it under control. It's going to be just fine," he said on CNBC.

Trump was at the top of his game. The stock market had reached an all-time high weeks prior, and employment was at a decade low. Trump happily took credit for "the greatest economy in the history of the world," as he often described it. He would soon be acquitted in his first impeachment trial ("the Russian collusion hoax"). An Eagle president with a strong economy is difficult to beat.

Trump initially approached the pandemic with healthy confidence and leadership. He tweeted in praise of his Chinese counterpart, Xi Jinping, for working hard to contain the virus. On March 14, he even gave a rare nod to bipartisanship: "Good teamwork between Republicans & Democrats as the House passes the big CoronaVirus Relief Bill." His administration formulated what would become known as Operation Warp Speed, an ultimately successful effort to develop COVID-19 vaccines quickly. Maybe the crisis was bringing out the best in this Eagle?

Although Eagles tend to be firm and decisive in emergencies, impatience is often their weakness. Trump, eager to declare victory over the coronavirus, began to assert that the pandemic wasn't a big deal. Despite having declared a national emergency, he compared COVID-19 to the flu and pushed Americans to get back to in-person work. Rather than support his public health experts, as he had initially, Trump began to question their expertise and publicly flout their recommended safety measures—classic Eagle overconfidence.

As coronavirus spread rampantly in the U.S., Trump refused responsibility. He lambasted China, liberal news outlets, "Do Nothing Democrats," and others while insisting there were "Great reviews on our handling of Covid 19," as if it were a TV show.

His conflicting messages—it's not that bad, but it's not my fault—were signs of an Eagle in the red zone, overusing a strength and turning it into a weakness. Eagles want credit and acclaim for victories. But when victory demands patience and adaptability, an Eagle in overuse mode will struggle.

In 2016, Trump's assertiveness and perceived competence won him the White House. Now, those Eagle traits would work against him. He would destroy the veneer of electability that defeated Clinton in 2016.

On April 23, 2020, clearly speaking off the cuff, Trump riffed about using ultraviolet light and bleach to cure human beings of COVID-19. To be clear, he never told anyone to drink or inject bleach, but that's what the public heard. Interpreting his statement wasn't exactly easy:

> And then I see the disinfectant, where it knocks it out in one minute. And is there a way we can do something like that, by injection inside or almost a cleaning, because you see it gets in the lungs and it does a tremendous number

on the lungs, so it'd be interesting to check that, so that you're going to have to use medical doctors with, but it sounds interesting to me.

Like many confident Eagles, Trump had gotten away with disguising ignorance as certainty on many occasions. But with roughly 2,000 Americans dying of coronavirus daily, it was poor taste and timing. Makers of disinfectants had to put out statements urging customers not to drink or inject bleach. Trump tried to play his statement off as sarcasm, but not many people bought that excuse.

While Biden remained conspicuously quiet—hiding from COVID-19 in a Delaware basement, as his critics would claim—Trump's Eagle excesses continued to pile up. On August 4, as U.S. coronavirus deaths approached 150,000, Trump interviewed with Axios's Jonathan Swan on HBO. No reporter had ever held the president to account quite like Swan.

Trump insisted everything was under control with COVID-19. "How?" asked Swan. "A thousand Americans are dying a day." Then came Trump's infamous response: "They are dying. That's true. And you—it is what it is."

Your loved ones are dying. *It is what it is.* Trump's lack of empathy was typical of an Eagle overusing their personality. True, people die in a pandemic, but that's not what the public wanted to hear from their president. They expected a consoler-in-chief. They expected recognition that the government could and would do better.

Trump, however, appeared to care more about perceptions of his leadership than its impact on human lives. If Trump indeed believed he was doing an incredible job, then those people *had* to die. There was no saving them. Taken to its extreme, Trump's need as an Eagle to be respected and celebrated made it impossible for him to face reality.

Trump thought he'd go into the election boasting of "the greatest economy in history." Coronavirus and these unforced errors blocked that path. Thus, Trump began to form a Plan B: questioning the integrity of the election system.

He began to tarnish mail-in ballots as early as April 2020. In July, with his disapproval levels at a peak, he sat for a Fox News Sunday interview with Chris Wallace, who probed whether Trump would accept the election results. Trump demurred. Wallace, reminding Trump that the "peaceful transfer of power" is a tradition and that the "loser concedes to the winner," wouldn't relent.

"…can you give a direct answer you will accept the election?" asked Wallace.

"I have to see," said Trump. "Look, you—I have to see. No, I'm not going to just say yes. I'm not going to say no, and I didn't last time either."

Trump gave Wallace the understatement of the century, "I'm not a good loser." Again, this is what an Eagle in the red zone looks like. When Eagle children lose a game, they may not accept defeat. They might say something like, "Not in my book. You cheated." Like Lyndon Johnson, they may bow out before the game ends, so they don't actually lose. Or, anticipating defeat, they may change the rules to benefit themselves. Trump chose the "not in my book" option.

National Humiliation

It was a "shitshow," "national humiliation," "disaster," and "chaos" said the commentators. The first presidential debate between Joe Biden and Donald Trump was a low point in American political decorum.

Undecided voters watched Trump repeatedly interrupt Biden and ignore Chris Wallace, the debate moderator. It was likely a strategy, not a loss of self-control. Recall that in the 2016 debates, Trump belittled Hillary Clinton to throw her off her game. This time, perhaps Trump thought that if he broke the rules—as Eagles often feel entitled to do—and rattled Biden enough, the substance wouldn't matter. Voters would see Trump as the more powerful and therefore electable candidate.

At first, Biden smiled and laughed when he disagreed with Trump, countering aggression with Dove calm and Parrot nonchalance. He turned to the camera and spoke to viewers while Trump yelled at Biden and shook his head in disagreement. Eventually, though, Biden became fed up with the constant interruptions. "Will you shut up, man?" said Biden, exasperated and in disbelief. #turnofftrumpsmic trended on Twitter.

To be fair, Biden interrupted Trump too, but Biden was clearly disappointed in the debate. Doves don't appreciate it when people trample the rules and disrespect people like Wallace, who are supposed to uphold them. If Trump had any reservations or doubts about his behavior, he didn't show it.

At one point, Chris Wallace asked Trump if would condemn the white supremacist and militia groups that had engaged in violence that summer (and in 2017). Biden, chiming in, specifically wanted him to condemn the Proud Boys. "Proud Boys, stand back and stand by," said Trump. Far from feeling condemned, the Proud Boys felt elated. Trump, it seemed, was telling them to be ready.

Opinion polls following the debate captured the public's disappointment with Trump. Although Eagles tend to dominate conversations, Trump went way too far. He bullied rather than debated to the point where neither candidate could claim to have won anything. The Commission on Presidential Debates decided that at the next debate, they would mute microphones to ensure each candidate could speak during their designated time.

Between debates, Trump caught COVID-19. Although Trump was hospitalized at Walter Reed National Military Medical Center—and given experimental drugs normal Americans wouldn't have received—he downplayed the severity of the disease, tweeting, "Don't be afraid of Covid." The Eagle could show no weakness.

Trump's diagnosis led the next debate to be cancelled because he refused to debate virtually. In the second and final debate, the candidates performed a more typical, unmemorable exchange. By then, over 40 million Americans **had already voted**, and polls suggested that few were still persuadable.

Going Loudly

On November 3, 2020, Americans went to the polls. The results would be unclear for another four days. "We're feeling good about where we are," **said** Biden that evening. Like a good, obedient Dove, Biden was willing to wait. "As I've said all along, it's not my place or Donald Trump's place to declare who's won this election."

Meanwhile, Trump insisted that the counting of ballots stop. "This is a fraud on the American public," **said** the president in his election-night speech. "This is an embarrassment to our country. We were getting ready to win this election. Frankly, we did win this election. We did win this election."

On November 7, four days after in-person voting, the Associated Press called the election for Biden, who had done little to win the battle for the soul of the nation. He managed to be likable and to be… not Trump. Meanwhile, Trump, coming off the economic high of 2019, couldn't adapt his personality to the demands of the pandemic. He couldn't flex his personality to the needs of scared, exhausted Americans undergoing the worst pandemic in 100 years. Once his personality lost the election, Trump could not accept it.

Unwillingness to accept defeat is a hallmark of an Eagle who has the dial turned up too high. Sometimes, that personality trait can work for good. We admire Eagle athletes who turn around a game against all odds. We admire Eagle surgeons who refuse to give up on a patient. But there is a difference between a persevering Eagle and a sore loser.

"The simple fact is this election is far from over," said Trump on November 7. He never accepted defeat and hasn't as of this writing.

In the weeks following, state and federal courts dismissed over 50 lawsuits presented by President Trump and his allies alleging election fraud. The Republicans fractured into two camps: those who believed the election was fraudulent, and those who didn't. As of June 2022, about 70% of Republicans don't consider Biden the legitimate winner of the 2020 election.

To be clear, Americans had questioned and denied election results before. In a July 2001 Gallup poll, 17% of Americans believed that George W. Bush had stolen the election from Al Gore. In fact, 26% of Americans did not accept Bush as a legitimate president. The difference is that Al Gore conceded. He accepted the Supreme Court's decision.

On January 2, 2021, running out of options, President Trump called Georgia Secretary of State Brad Raffensperger. Trump insisted he won Georgia. "I mean, you know, and I didn't lose the state, Brad. People have been saying that it was the highest vote ever…As you know, every single state, we won every state."

The rant went on for an hour with brief responses from Raffensperger, who stood his ground. "We don't agree that you have won," said the secretary. Still, Trump insisted on victory, insisted on fraud, and even insisted that Raffensperger was committing a criminal offense by doing nothing about it.

"I'm notifying you that you're letting it happen," said Trump. "So, look. All I want to do is this. I just want to find 11,780 votes, which is one more than we have because we won the state."

Personality doesn't predict if someone will act unethically. However, personality can drive someone to do so. The effort to bully, threaten, and gaslight Raffensperger was Eagle to the extreme. Whereas Nixon, an Owl, tried to be subtle and cover his tracks, Trump did the opposite.

To recap all the events that culminated in the violent occupation of the U.S. Capitol on January 6, 2021, goes beyond the scope of this book. Suffice it to say, Trump expressed neither remorse nor responsibility nor regret for the day's events, which led to five deaths and countless injuries. It was the first unpeaceful transfer of presidential power in U.S. history.

To the extent that Trump's personality won the 2016 election, it also lost the 2020 election. It became a one-on-one personality contest between Trump and himself. All Biden had to do was stay out of the limelight, avoid making unforced errors, shrug off the attacks, and embody empathy for those who were suffering, which are all hallmarks of the Dove style. Biden simply waited for Trump to self-destruct. And he did.

A Tough Position

Since taking office, President Biden has increasingly drawn comparisons to Jimmy Carter. Both are Doves. Both viewed themselves as healers of the nation and restorers of its proper values. Both seem better at attracting flak for their failures than credit for their victories.

As author and Carter researcher Jonathan Alter notes, Americans tend to remember Carter's failure to address inflation and energy costs. We forget that he passed energy policies that would significantly increase domestic energy production and reduce dependence on foreign oil and gas—but not until Reagan's term. Carter seemed to care more about claiming moral victories than touting material, real-world accomplishments.

Can Biden avoid that Dove trap? His key legislative successes—a $1.9 trillion relief package for COVID-19, a $1 trillion infrastructure bill, and $739 billion Inflation Reduction Act (i.e., a watered-down climate bill)—rival Franklin D. Roosevelt's New Deal and Lyndon Johnson's Great Society in their magnitude.

Yet these bills fell trillions short of Biden's original Build Back Better Plan, and the media won't let Americans forget it. Plus, the latter two bills won't show dividends for the average American until after Biden's first term. What these victories say about Biden's personality is probably unclear to the swing voting public.

Conversely, Biden's signature failure has grabbed mass attention. After NATO toppled the Taliban in 2001 for harboring Osama bin Laden, mastermind of the 9/11 terror attacks, the U.S. and its allies installed a democratic government in Afghanistan and kept it afloat. After nearly 20 years of violence, Biden's administration negotiated a conditional peace with the Taliban and committed to remove NATO forces from Afghanistan by September 11, 2021.

As NATO forces wound down operations, the Taliban went on the offensive. The Afghan security forces crumbled, and eventually, the Taliban retook Kabul, the capital, on August 15, 2021.

Americans watched the chaos unfold on TV, as NATO forces and civilians evacuated by air in scenes reminiscent of the fall of Saigon in

1975. Most Afghan interpreters and other local allies were left behind. On August 26, an attack on Kabul International Airport masterminded by ISIS-K claimed the lives of 13 U.S. service members and 150 Afghans.

August 30, the day the last American military plane departed Kabul, was the first time that Biden's aggregated disapproval rating clocked higher than his approval rating. It hasn't recovered.

Toward the end of his first term, will Biden be seen as a brave realist for ending a military operation that had no foreseeable conclusion and no longer served a vital national interest? Or will the public pin Afghanistan on a Dove personality that was weak and naïve in dealing with the Taliban?

Afghanistan may explain why Biden has taken such a firm stance against Russian President Vladimir Putin's invasion of Ukraine, launched on February 24, 2022. Putin perhaps thought America had lost its appetite for foreign intervention after withdrawing from Afghanistan. He misjudged. Now that the U.S. has spent over $100 billion on aid for Ukraine, there is no turning back for Biden. The fate of Ukraine will be a referendum on Biden's Dove-Parrot personality, not his policies.

COVID-19 is now in the rearview mirror for most Americans, which means Biden can't campaign as consoler-in-chief in 2024. He will need to ratchet up the Parrot side of his personality, especially if the Republicans run someone other than Trump. Likability works against a self-destructing Eagle, but a healthy Eagle or Parrot would be a tough opponent for Amtrak Joe.

The 2024 Election
Looking Forward

We began with a question in need of a better answer. How did Donald J. Trump take the White House in 2016 when all the polls and pundits predicted that Hillary Clinton would win in a landslide? After seeing how personality determined the last 22 elections, we ought to reframe the question.

How could Trump *not* have won?

It was a classic Eagle versus Owl race that we've seen many times. Franklin D. Roosevelt, an Eagle-Parrot, beat three Owls: Herbert Hoover, Alfred Landon, and Thomas Dewey.

Harry S. Truman, an Eagle-Owl, beat Thomas Dewey too. George W. Bush defeated Al Gore and John Kerry, both Owls. Barack Obama overcame Owl Mitt Romney.

Why should Hillary Clinton have done any better against Donald Trump than historical Owls did against Eagles?

We now have a model for understanding the role of personality in the last 23 presidential elections. So, what does the Personality Wins Model tell us about the 2024 presidential election?

The Personality Bias

American voters clearly have a personality bias. For 88 years, we elected Eagles and Parrots over Doves and Owls whenever we had the chance.

Yet somehow, Dove-Parrot Biden defeated Eagle Trump in 2020. Trump was the first Eagle since 1932 to lose reelection and the first Eagle to be beaten by a Dove or Owl (excluding the three-way race where George Wallace lost to Richard Nixon).

Does that mean the model is shifting again, as it did in 1932? Probably not. Trump did more than any modern candidate to defeat himself—even more than Barry Goldwater and Michael Dukakis. If Biden finds himself running against a more balanced Eagle or Parrot, his chances of winning will be slim.

The outcome of the 2024 election could be decided the moment Republicans declare their nominee. Our judgment of personality depends on minimal input because our first impressions of the candidates are sticky and surprisingly accurate. If we judge a candidate to be decisive, assertive, charismatic, or visionary, our impression is positive and unlikely to change. If we judge a candidate to be analytical, data-driven, peaceful, or accommodating, that impression is negative and unlikely to change.

Political pundits, late-night television hosts, and political satirists are bound to reaffirm rather than challenge these snap impressions of personality. That said, Biden and his opponent are not held hostage to their personalities. Like Bill Clinton and Ronald Reagan, candidates can invoke all four styles. They can be a commanding Eagle at the convention, a quippy Parrot on the debate stage, a rigorous Owl at private donor events, and an empathetic Dove in vulnerable conversations with struggling Americans.

Personality is going to win in 2024. The only question is, which candidate will prevail?

Section VI:
Conclusion

Nobody Heard You

In 1984, CBS News correspondent Lesley Stahl produced a TV segment about the contradictions between President Reagan's words and actions. In one scene, Reagan spoke at the Special Olympics after cutting funding for children with disabilities. It was so damning that Stahl worried about losing access to the Reagan White House. She expected the segment to drop like a bombshell.

Instead, Stahl received a call from Dick Darman, an aide to the president, *thanking* her for the coverage.

"Way to go, kiddo," Darman said to Stahl. "What a great piece. We loved it."

"Didn't you hear what I said?" asked Stahl.

"Nobody heard what you said."

"Come again?"

Darman continued, "You guys in Televisionland haven't figured it out, have you? When the pictures are powerful and emotional, they override if not completely drown out the sound. I mean it, Lesley. Nobody heard you."

Viewers *saw* Reagan's big personality but did not *hear* his hypocrisy. The substance of the presidency had become secondary to its performance. Watching President Reagan was like watching a movie about a president with a decent plot, memorable lines, and juicy drama.

Entertainer-in-Chief

In the 1980s, Neil Postman, a media theorist and professor at New York University, was pondering how Americans could be so susceptible to spin, hypocrisy, and misinformation in politics. He noticed that American political news had become a series of sound bites, conveyed with colorful images and theatrical music. Even magazines and newspapers were cutting words and adding graphics to compete with TV. Stahl's segment about Reagan exemplified this trend toward infotainment. With pretty pictures to gawk at, few viewers absorbed the content of what Reagan said.

Why had public discourse evolved this way? Postman gave his answer in a book called *Amusing Ourselves to Death* published in 1985: "Our politics, religion, news, athletics, education and commerce have been transformed into congenial adjuncts of show business."

As presidential politics became show business, Eagles and Parrots started to win every audition for the lead role. The moments that determined the outcomes of 23 straight presidential elections from 1932 to 2020—that revealed the personalities of presidential candidates—*were* entertaining. Before long, we expected presidential candidates to amuse and fascinate us.

From FDR to Biden, you read about one-liners and exchanges that lasted tens of seconds in real life. Yet those seconds influenced how millions of voters cast their ballots. Think about that: Mere moments of radio, TV, and social media have determined who leads the United States of America and who does not.

Of course, the presidency wasn't always this way. George Washington loathed the spectacle of high office. He didn't nominate himself or compete for the presidency and only took office reluctantly, with humility, anxiety, and a sense of duty to the nation. For the next 152 years, candidates followed his lead. They acted like they didn't want the presidency and rarely campaigned on their own behalf. Being amusing or self-promotional was not part of the job.

The Owls and Doves that, for the most part, led America for its first 152 years would have a harder time winning the presidency today. Just look at the numbers. Between 1789 and 1928, there were 13 Owl and 12 Dove presidents versus three Eagles and two Parrots. Since 1932, five Eagles and three Parrots have won compared to just two Owls and three Doves (excluding Obama since he is equally Dove/Eagle). The Owls and Doves only won against each other and in two anomalous cases.

The style shift is significant. In percentages, from 1789 to 1928, 17 percent of presidents were Eagles or Parrots. That leaped to 64 percent from 1932 to 2020. During that time, Owl and Dove presidents decreased from 83 percent to 36 percent.

In 88 years, only two Eagles lost an elect ion: John McCain to Barack Obama (an Eagle/Dove) and Donald Trump to Joe Biden (a Dove-Parrot). The only elected, incumbent presidents to lose reelection were Herbert Hoover (Owl), George H.W. Bush (Owl-Dove), and Jimmy Carter (Dove-Owl).

Since 1932, we've been living in an ever more amusing America where Eagles and Parrots draw our attention. Their dynamic, energizing personalities have convinced us that they are more electable and likable than the calm, thoughtful personalities of Doves and Owls. Because Eagles and Parrots are so entertaining, we get more exposure to their personalities, which have nothing to do with how effective they'll be in the White House.

The Personality Wins Model confirms what many Americans have come to accept or fear: Presidential elections are, in fact, personality contests. So what lessons should voters and politicians take away from this book? What does the Personality Wins Model mean for the future of America?

Consider the Whole Person

Our advice to voters is simple in principle but hard in practice: *Consider the whole person.* Just because personality determines elections, that doesn't mean it should be the overriding factor in whom we choose to lead the United States.

Subconsciously, most of us link assertiveness, electability, and charisma to likability. We've all made some snap judgments unaware of having done so. On the web, we inadvertently look for information that validates our favorite candidates. Meanwhile, news aggregators and social media learn to feed us more of that same information. Soon enough, ChatGPT and other generative AIs will serve up articles, images, and videos personalized to our political biases.

We can't help making instinctive judgments about personality, but we can let our impressions evolve throughout the election process. We can pierce the veil of personality and see what candidates truly stand for.

Some websites are designed to help us confront our biases and discover which candidate best represents our beliefs. Try taking the quiz at ISideWith.com. You may be surprised to learn that your favorite candidate does not share your views on key issues. This knowledge can help you navigate beyond the pull of personality.

In addition, beware of getting all your political news from one source or one medium. As Lesley Stahl learned, we take away different information from the visual medium of television versus written news. A TV clip about one candidate may be inspiring, intentionally or not. A news article about the same candidate might be equally disenchanting.

The written word is easier to scrutinize and question than a Hollywoodized news segment. Reading is one of our best tools for overcoming the personality bias. Long-form podcasts also take flashy visuals out of the picture. Just beware that radio and podcasts still convey more personality than AP-style news.

Challenging your opinions about the candidates will take persistence and an open mind. Why do you prefer your candidate over another? What do you want from a president? What do you want for our culture and society? What do you wish for your family, friends, and neighbors? These questions can help you define your political vision before personality distorts it.

Bottom line: Don't let a candidate's engaging personality cause you to vote against your own interests.

Be the Chameleon Candidate

Since 1932, two presidents transcended their innate personalities. Ronald Reagan and Bill Clinton gracefully flexed to the Eagle, Parrot, Dove, and Owl styles. They are chameleons who appeal to all personalities.

Presidential candidates who learn to adapt like a chameleon are almost unstoppable in a general election.

How can politicians cultivate this ability?

As a start, politicians need to become aware of their own personality along with its strengths and weaknesses. The most successful people are the most self-aware people. Which bird(s) are you? How do you naturally attract or repel voters? What drives you to be the way you are and do the things you do?

After exploring those questions, begin to notice when you are acting out The Big Assumption. Are you sharing details because you'd want them if you were a voter or because the electorate needs them? Are you discussing your values because they would help you decide how to select a candidate or because you feel values are important to voters?

To overcome The Big Assumption, offer something to Eagles, Parrots, Doves, and Owls in every speech and appearance. Cover the four styles in your website, messaging, and media.

Doves, are you being too nice? Are you the debate stage mediator? Do you find yourself lamenting how uncivil everyone else is being? We say this with love and your best interest at heart: Mr. or Ms. Nice no longer wins presidential elections. Add some Eagle or Parrot energy to your campaign and devise some clever attack lines.

Owls, are you fighting your opponents with data and plans? Since 1932, not one president has won the White House by captivating the electorate with details and policies. It doesn't work. If you reach a point where staff are strategizing how to "humanize" you, it's all over. Add some humor and subtract some statistics before it's too late.

Flexing your personality *will* push your comfort zone and feel draining at first. Train yourself to handle that discomfort. It will get easier. But remember, first impressions and snap judgments have shaped the outcome of 23 presidential races. Your election will be no different.

We hope that voters begin to look beyond personality, but it will take time. Be the chameleon if you want to win the presidency.

The Cost of Personality Bias

Americans vote based on personality, but that doesn't mean it's the best way to choose a candidate. In surveys that ask presidential scholars to rank presidents, there are Eagles, Parrots, Doves, and Owls (and combos) in the top 10. There are also Eagles, Parrots, Doves, and Owls in the bottom 10! In other words, there's no evidence that Eagles and Parrots are better presidents. They're just more electable than Doves and Owls in our present age. Again, if radio, TV, and social media had existed in the 18th and 19th centuries, George Washington, Thomas Jefferson, and Abraham Lincoln would not have been elected. Three of the four faces on Mt. Rushmore would be gone!

The era of Eagle and Parrot presidents is new in the American experiment. So, what has been the cost of eliminating Owl and Dove presidents from office?

Well, hypotheticals are tricky. What if we'd had the idealist George McGovern for president rather than the scheming Richard Nixon? Would Thomas Dewey have handled the Korean War more prudently than Harry Truman and potentially saved American lives? What if Al Gore had been in charge after 9/11? How would Hillary Clinton have handled COVID-19?

We don't know the answers. However, we do know that Doves and Owls are valuable to American government. Dwight D. Eisenhower reorganized the White House and national security apparatus to protect

Americans during the Cold War. His calm, nonreactive leadership helped prevent nuclear confrontation with the Soviet Union. Gerald Ford's courage helped the nation move forward after Watergate. George H.W. Bush wound down the Cold War gracefully and used American military might wisely.

By sharing the Personality Wins Model, we can hopefully decrease the personality bias in presidential elections.

One Thing Is Certain

Presidents are more than just chief executives. They are role models, cultural icons, and shapers of American character. They define who we are as a nation and set a pathway to the future. After 23 elections, you have a new way to see and predict U.S. presidential elections. We hope the Personality Wins Model serves you well in 2024 and beyond.

We also hope that this book inspires you to learn more about your own personality. Just like the presidents, we all have strengths and challenges. Every one of us is susceptible to The Big Assumption at home and at work. The lessons in this book can be of service far beyond the world of politics.

As for the 2024 election, there's one thing we know for sure: *Personality Wins.*

Bibliography

This book would not have been possible without the scholars, journalists, archivists, and enthusiasts who have written about the presidents before us. We're especially grateful to the Miller Center at the University of Virginia for its extensive effort to document the presidency. Their profiles, audio recordings, and speech transcripts were vital to understanding the personalities of the candidates. The American Presidency Project at the University of California Santa Barbara was another key source of primary research material. *The New York Times*, the most important journalistic source for this book, not only profiled the candidates but transcribed many of their speeches and debates.

A huge thank you to C-SPAN for publishing digital footage of modern presidents and many of their contenders. These videos allowed us to study the body language and facial expressions of the candidates and hear their tone and rhythm as well. We also thank the members of the YouTube community who have uploaded historical footage of the presidents and their campaigns. Without your dedication to preserving history, we could not have seen these personalities in such vivid detail.

Finally, thank you to Brendan Brown, creator of the Trump Twitter Archive. Without your hard work, it would have been impossible to find our way through @realDonaldTrump's 56,571 tweets.

"1932: FDR's First Presidential Campaign." 2014. *See How They Ran!* (blog). December 2, 2014. http://www.roosevelthouse.hunter.cuny.edu/see-howtheyran/portfolios/1932-fdrs-first-presidential-campaign/.

"1960: First Televised Presidential Debate." 2012. 60 Minutes Overtime. October 3, 2012. https://www.cbsnews.com/news/1960-first-televised-presidential-debate/.

1988 George Bush Sr. "Revolving Door" Attack Ad Campaign. n.d. Accessed October 29, 2019. https://www.youtube.com/watch?v=PmwhdDv8VrM.

"2016 Election Results: President Live Map by State, Real-Time Voting Updates." *POLITICO*, April 18, 2016. https://west.ops.politico.com/2016-election/results/map/president.

Abramsky, Sasha. 2009. *Inside Obama's Brain.* New York: Portfolio.

"Adlai Stevenson - Speech Accepting the Democratic Presidential Nomination (26 July 1952)." 2018. American Rhetoric. December 19, 2018. https://americanrhetoric.com/speeches/adlaistevenson1952dnc.html.

"Alf Landon, G.O.P. Standard-Bearer, Dies at 100." *The New York Times,* October 13, 1987, sec. Obituaries. https://www.nytimes.com/1987/10/13/obituaries/alf-landon-gop-standard-bearer-dies-at-100.html.

Al Gore Tipper Gore Kiss Convention 2000. n.d. ElectionWallDotOrg. Accessed October 29, 2019. https://www.youtube.com/watch?v=p0wDNESH-l8M&feature=youtu.be.

Allen, Jonathan, and Amie Parnes. 2017. *Shattered: Inside Hillary Clinton's Doomed Campaign.* First edition. New York: Crown.

Alter, Jonathan. 2022. "Perspective | Joe Biden Is No Jimmy Carter. He Should Wish He Was." *Washington Post,* January 14, 2022, sec. Outlook. https://www.washingtonpost.com/outlook/2022/01/14/jimmy-carter-biden-comparisons/.

Anderson, Patrick. 1968. *The Presidents' Men; White House Assistants of Franklin D. Roosevelt, Harry S. Truman, Dwight D. Eisenhower, John F. Kennedy, and Lyndon B. Johnson.* Garden City, N.Y.: Anchor Books. http://catalog. hathitrust.org/api/volumes/oclc/3911257.html.

"An Economy That Works for Everyone." n.d. The Office of Hillary Rodham Clinton. Accessed May 4, 2023. https://www.hillaryclinton.com/issues/ an-economy-that-works-for-everyone/.

Apple Jr., R. W. 1976. "FORD AND CARTER, IN FIRST DEBATE, TRADE CHARGES ON ECONOMIC ISSUE." *The New York Times,* September 24, 1976. https://www.nytimes.com/1976/09/24/archives/ ford-and-carter-in-first-debate-trade-charges-on-economic-issue.html.

Associated Press. "Transcript: Sen. Barack Obama's Announcement for President." *Fox News,* February 10, 2007. https://www.foxnews.com/story/ transcript-sen-barack-obamas-announcement-for-president.

Ayres Jr., B. Drummond. 1981. "Amid the Darkest Moments, a Leaven of Presidential Wit." *The New York Times,* April 1, 1981, sec. U.S. https:// www.nytimes.com/1981/04/01/us/amid-the-darkest-moments-a-leaven- of-presidential-wit.html.

Baker, Peter, and Michael M. Grynbaum. 2019. "Before Expected Call for Unity, Trump Laced Into Democrats at Lunch for TV Anchors." *The New York Times,* February 5, 2019. https://www.nytimes.com/2019/02/05/us/ politics/trump-lunch-news-anchors.html.

Balz, Dan. 1992. "Clinton Concedes Marital 'Wrongdoing.'" *Washington Post,* January 27, 1992. https://www.washingtonpost.com/wp-srv/politics/spe- cial/pjones/stories/pj012792.htm.

Balz, Daniel J, and Daniel J Balz. 2014. *Collision 2012: The Future of Election Politics in a Divided in America.*

"Barack Obama, Before He Was President." *The New Yorker,* May 7, 2007. https://www.newyorker.com/magazine/2007/05/07/the-conciliator.

Barack Obama on The Daily Show. 2007. The Daily Show With Jon Stewart. http://www.comedycentral.com.au/the-daily-show-with-jon-stewart/vid- eos/barack-obama-on-the-daily-show-august-22-2007.

"Barack Obama's Inaugural Address." *The New York Times,* January 20, 2009, sec. Politics. https://www.nytimes.com/2009/01/20/us/politics/20text-obama.html.

Barack Obama's Presidential Announcement. n.d. Accessed October 29, 2019. https://www.youtube.com/watch?v=gdJ7Ad15WCA.

Barber, James David. 2009. *The Presidential Character: Predicting Performance in the White House.* 4th ed. Longman Classics in Political Science. New York: Pearson Longman.

Belvedere, Matthew J. 2020. "Trump Says He Trusts China's Xi on Coronavirus and the US Has It 'Totally under Control.'" *CNBC,* January 22, 2020. https://www.cnbc.com/2020/01/22/trump-on-coronavirus-from-china-we-have-it-totally-under-control.html.

Bernhardt, Jack. 2018. "Why Lyndon Johnson, a Truly Awful Man, Is My Political Hero." *The Guardian*, January 22, 2018, sec. Opinion. https://www.theguardian.com/commentisfree/2018/jan/22/lyndon-johnson-anniversary-death-awful-man-my-political-hero.

BIDEN GAFFE: "Chuck, Stand Up, Let Them See Ya!" n.d. BlazeTV. Accessed October 28, 2019. https://www.youtube.com/watch?v=Rkr-lePr7jA.

Biden, Joe. 2017. "Joe Biden: 'We Are Living Through a Battle for the Soul of This Nation.'" *The Atlantic*, August 27, 2017, sec. Politics. https://www.theatlantic.com/politics/archive/2017/08/joe-biden-after-charlottesville/538128/.

Blake, Eubie, Noble Sissle, and Geo. J Trinkaus. I'm just wild about Harry. M. Witmark & Sons, New York, NY, 1921. Notated Music. https://www.loc.gov/item/ihas.100000004/.

Blanton, Dana. 2019. "Fox News Poll: Record Support for Trump Impeachment." *Fox News*, October 9, 2019. https://www.foxnews.com/politics/fox-news-poll-record-support-for-trump-impeachment.

Blumenfeld, Laura. 1996. "Dropping Stoicism About His War Wounds, Dole Reveals Their Strains on Daily Living." *Washington Post*, May 12, 1996. https://www.washingtonpost.com/wp-srv/national/longterm/campaign/dole/hand.htm.

Brenes, Michael. 2018. "The Tragedy of Hubert Humphrey." *The New York Times*, March 23, 2018, sec. Opinion. https://www.nytimes.com/2018/03/23/opinion/vietnam-hubert-humphrey.html.

Brown, Lara M. 2010. *Jockeying for the American Presidency: The Political Opportunism of Aspirants*. Amherst, NY: Cambria Press.

Burner, David. 2005. *Herbert Hoover: A Public Life*.

Bush, George. 2014. *All the Best, George Bush: My Life in Letters and Other Writings*. Scribner trade paperback edition. New York: Scribner.

Bush, George W. 2001. "Address to a Joint Session of Congress and the American People." WhiteHouse.Gov. September 20, 2001. https://georgewbush-whitehouse.archives.gov/news/releases/2001/09/20010920-8.html.

Bush, George W. 2010. *Decision Points*. 1st ed. New York: Crown Publishers.

Butterfield, Fox. 1988. "Dukakis." *The New York Times*, May 8, 1988, sec. Magazine. https://www.nytimes.com/1988/05/08/magazine/dukakis.html.

Byron, Jim. 2011. "The Quotable Richard Nixon." Richard Nixon Foundation. April 25, 2011. https://www.nixonfoundation.org/2011/04/the-quotable-richard-nixon/.

Califano, Joseph A. 2015. *The Triumph & Tragedy of Lyndon Johnson: The White House Years*. First Touchstone trade paperback edition. New York: Touchstone.

Candidacy for Presidency: Ronald Reagan's Announcement of Candidacy for President of U.S. 11/13/79. n.d. Reagan Foundation. Accessed October 29, 2019. https://www.youtube.com/watch?v=fAtYMD-H2UY.

Carroll, Joseph. 2001. "Seven out of 10 Americans Accept Bush as Legitimate President." *Gallup* (blog). July 17, 2001. https://news.gallup.com/poll/4687/Seven-Americans-Accept-Bush-Legitimate-President.aspx.

Carson, Dr. Ben. 2016. "Op-Ed: Dr. Ben Carson on the Donald Trump Video." *The Hill*, October 8, 2016. https://thehill.com/blogs/pundits-blog/presidential-campaign/300014-op-ed-dr-ben-carson-on-the-donald-trump-video.

Cawley, Janet, Chicago, and Linda P. Campbell. 1990. "REAGAN HAZY ON IRAN-CONTRA." *Chicago Tribune*, February 23, 1990. https://www.chicagotribune.com/news/ct-xpm-1990-02-23-9001160156-story.html.

CBS News Archives: Carter's Famous "Malaise Speech." n.d. Accessed October 28, 2019. https://www.youtube.com/watch?v=0tGd_9Tahzw.

Chernow, Ron. 2011. *Washington: A Life.* New York: Penguin Books.

Chin, Caitlin. n.d. "Social Media and Political Campaigns." Georgetown Public Policy Review. Accessed October 28, 2019. http://www.gpprspring.com/social-media-political-campaigns.

"Chronology of America's Freight Railroads." n.d. Association of American Railroads. Accessed May 4, 2023. https://www.aar.org/chronology-of-americas-freight-railroads/.

Clinton, Bill. 2004. *My Life.* New York: Knopf.

Clinton, Hillary Rodham. 2018. *What Happened.* First Simon & Schuster trade paperback edition. New York: Simon & Schuster Paperbacks.

Cohen, Michael A. 2016. *American Maelstrom: The 1968 Election and the Politics of Division.* Pivotal Moments in American History. New York: Oxford University Press.

Concha, Joe. 2017. "Trump Administration Seen as More Truthful than News Media: Poll." *The Hill*, February 8, 2017. https://thehill.com/homenews/media/318514-trump-admin-seen-as-more-truthful-than-news-media-poll.

Cook, Rhodes. n.d. "Registering By Party: Where the Democrats and Republicans Are Ahead." *Sabato's Crystal Ball* (blog). Accessed January 13, 2020. http://centerforpolitics.org/crystalball/articles/registering-by-party-where-the-democrats-and-republicans-are-ahead/.

Corn, David. 2012. "SECRET VIDEO: Romney Tells Millionaire Donors What He REALLY Thinks of Obama Voters." *Mother Jones*, September 17, 2012. https://www.motherjones.com/politics/2012/09/secret-video-romney-private-fundraiser/.

Cornog, Evan, and Richard Whelan. 2000. *Hats in the Ring: An Illustrated History of American Presidential Campaigns.* 1st ed. New York: Random House.

Crouse, Timothy. 1972. "George McGovern: The Machine That Won in Wisconsin." *Rolling Stone*, April 27, 1972. https://www.rollingstone.com/politics/politics-news/george-mcgovern-the-machine-that-won-in-wisconsin-121863/.

C-SPAN.org. 1960. *Richard Nixon 1960 Acceptance Speech*. https://www.c-span.org/video/?4016-1/richard-nixon-1960-acceptance-speech.

———. 1980. *Mondale 1980 Acceptance Speech*. https://www.c-span.org/video/?74531-1/mondale-1980-acceptance-speech.

———. 1992a. *User Clip: Message: I Care*. https://www.c-span.org/video/?c4579269/user-clip-message-care.

———. 1992b. *Clinton Appearance on Arsenio Hall Show*. https://www.c-span.org/video/?26472-1/clinton-appearance-arsenio-hall-show.

———. 1992c. *Perot Campaign Commercial 1992*. https://www.c-span.org/video/?34277-1/perot-campaign-commercial-1992.

———. 1995. *Senator Bob Dole Presidential Campaign Announcement*. https://www.c-span.org/video/?64455-1/senator-bob-dole-presidential-campaign-announcement.

———. 1996. *Bob Dole on Letterman 1996*. https://www.c-span.org/video/?c4495192/bob-dole-letterman-1996.

———. 2019. *President Trump Rally in Battle Creek, Michigan*. https://www.c-span.org/video/?467146-1/president-trump-rally-battle-creek-michigan.

———. 2019. *Senator Bernie Sanders Presidential Campaign Announcement*. https://www.c-span.org/video/?458403-1/senator-bernie-sanders-launches-presidential-bid-brooklyn-york.

———. n.d. *Hubert Humphrey 1968 Acceptance Speech*. Accessed October 29, 2019. https://www.c-span.org/video/?3424-1/hubert-humphrey-1968-acceptance-speech.

Cummins, Joseph. 2015. *Anything for a Vote*. Philadelphia, PA: Quirk Books.

"Daisy" Ad (1964): Preserved from 35mm in the Tony Schwartz Collection. 2016. Library of Congress. https://www.youtube.com/watch?v=riDypP1KfOU.

Dallek, Robert. 1999. *Flawed Giant: Lyndon Johnson and His Times, 1961 - 1973*. New York: Oxford Univ. Press.

@deanfortythree. 2016. "Biden: Ok Here's the Plan." Tweet. November 11, 2016. https://twitter.com/deanfortythree/status/797124765299318784/photo/1.

DeGregorio, William A., and Sandra Lee Stuart. 2013. *The Complete Book of U.S. Presidents*. Eighth edition. Fort Lee, NJ: Barricade Books.

Dickerson, John. 2017. *Whistlestop: My Favorite Stories from Presidential Campaign History*.

Dickerson's Debate History: George Bush Caught in the Cutaway in 1992. n.d. Face the Nation. CBS News. Accessed October 29, 2019. https://www. youtube.com/watch?v=T293aYx3uw0.

Dole, Bob. 2012. "Bob Dole on Life after Losing the 1996 Presidential Election." *Washington Post*, September 28, 2012, sec. Opinions. https:// www.washingtonpost.com/opinions/bob-dole-on-life-after-losing-the-1996-presidential-election/2012/09/28/eaef4102-f78e-11e1-8398-0327ab83ab91_story.html.

Dole, Robert J. 2001. *Great Presidential Wit: I Wish I Was in This Book*. New York: Scribner.

Domonoske, Camila. 2018. "2018 Election Voter Turnout Hit 50-Year High." *NPR*, November 8, 2018. https://www.npr.org/2018/11/08/665197690/ a-boatload-of-ballots-midterm-voter-turnout-hit-50-year-high.

Dowd, Maureen. 1999. "Liberties; President Frat Boy?" *The New York Times*, April 7, 1999, sec. Opinion. https://www.nytimes.com/1999/04/07/opin-ion/liberties-president-frat-boy.html.

Drogin, Bob. 1988. "How Presidential Race Was Won-and Lost : Michael S. Dukakis." *Los Angeles Times*, November 10, 1988. https://www.latimes. com/archives/la-xpm-1988-11-10-mn-299-story.html.

Eisenhower, Dwight D. 1944. "'In Case of Failure' Message Drafted by General Dwight Eisenhower in Case the D-Day Invasion Failed," June 5, 1944. Eisenhower, Dwight D: Papers, Pre-Presidential, 1916 - 1952. Dwight D. Eisenhower Library(LP-DDE). https://catalog.archives.gov/id/186470.

———. n.d. "D-Day Statement to Soldiers, Sailor, and Airmen of the Allied Expeditionary Force, 6/44." Collection DDE-EPRE: Eisenhower, Dwight D: Papers, Pre-Presidential, 1916-1952; Dwight D. Eisenhower Library. National Archives and Records Administration. Accessed October 28, 2019. https://www.archives.gov/historical-docs/todays-doc/?-dod-date=606.

Elder, Richard L. Berke With Janet. 2000. "THE 2000 CAMPAIGN: PUB-LIC OPINION; Poll Shows Bush Ahead of Gore, With Leadership a Crucial Issue." *The New York Times*, May 16, 2000, sec. U.S. https://www.nytimes.com/2000/05/16/us/2000-campaign-public-opinion-poll-shows-bush-ahead-gore-with-leadership-crucial.html.

"Election 2020: Halloween Mask Index." 2020. *Zettacap*. October 13, 2020. http://www.blog.zettacap.com/election-2020-halloween-mask-index/.

Epstein, Joseph. 1968. "Adlai Stevenson in Retrospect." *Commentary*, December 1968. https://www.commentarymagazine.com/articles/adlai-stevenson-in-retrospect/.

Farhi, Paul. 2019. "Democratic National Committee Rejects Fox News for Debates, Citing New Yorker Article." *Washington Post*, March 6, 2019. https://www.washingtonpost.com/lifestyle/style/democratic-national-committee-rejects-fox-news-for-debates-citing-new-yorker-article/2019/03/06/a0bdf55c-402e-11e9-922c-64d6b7840b82_story.html.

Farkas, Mark, dir. 2011. "The Contenders." C-SPAN. https://www.c-span.org/series/?theContenders.

Farrell, John A. 2017. "When a Candidate Conspired With a Foreign Power to Win An Election." *POLITICO Magazine*, August 6, 2017. https://politi.co/2VjVdvr.

FDR Discusses His Dog Fala. n.d. Historycomestolife. Accessed October 29, 2019. https://www.youtube.com/watch?v=qqt7b9veFo8.

FDR on Elections (Funny). 2016. Best of Humans. https://www.youtube.com/watch?v=uufXM_wVqO0.

File, Thom. 2017. "Voting in America: A Look at the 2016 Presidential Election." The United States Census Bureau. Accessed October 28, 2019. https://www.census.gov/newsroom/blogs/random-samplings/2017/05/voting_in_america.html.

Flegenheimer, Matt. 2020. "Around the Country in 17 Hours With Michael Bloomberg." *The New York Times*, January 9, 2020, sec. U.S. https://www.nytimes.com/2020/01/09/us/politics/michael-bloomberg-2020-campaign.html.

Flegenheimer, Matt, and Sydney Ember. 2019. "How Amy Klobuchar Treats Her Staff." *The New York Times*, February 22, 2019, sec. U.S. https://www.nytimes.com/2019/02/22/us/politics/amy-klobuchar-staff.html.

"For Most Trump Voters, 'Very Warm' Feelings for Him Endured." 2018. *Pew Research Center*, August 9, 2018. https://www.people-press.org/2018/08/09/for-most-trump-voters-very-warm-feelings-for-him-endured/.

"Founders Online: Thomas Jefferson to Walter Jones, 2 January 1814." n.d. Founders Online, National Archives. [Original Source: The Papers of Thomas Jefferson, Retirement Series, Vol. 7, 28 November 1813 to 30 September 1814, Ed. J. Jefferson Looney. Princeton: Princeton University Press, 2010, Pp. 100–104.]. University of Virginia Press. Accessed May 4, 2023. http://founders.archives.gov/documents/Jefferson/03-07-02-0052.

Frady, Marshall. 2002. "The Big Guy." *The New York Review of Books*, November 7, 2002. https://www.nybooks.com/articles/2002/11/07/the-big-guy/.

Frank, Justin A. 2018. *Trump on the Couch: Inside the Mind of the President.* New York: Avery, an imprint of Penguin Random House.

Funke, Daniel. 2020. "In Context: What Donald Trump Said about Disinfectant, Sun and Coronavirus." PolitiFact. April 24, 2020. https://www.politifact.com/article/2020/apr/24/context-what-donald-trump-said-about-disinfectant-/.

Gardner, Amy, and Paulina Firozi. 2021. "Here's the Full Transcript and Audio of the Call between Trump and Raffensperger." *Washington Post*, January 5, 2021. https://www.washingtonpost.com/politics/trump-raffensperger-call-transcript-georgia-vote/2021/01/03/2768e0cc-4ddd-11eb-83e3-322644d82356_story.html.

Gardner, Gerald. 1986. *All the Presidents' Wits: The Power of Presidential Humor.* 1st ed. New York: Beech Tree Books.

"Gentlemen, You Have Come Sixty Days Too Late. The Depression Is Over." 2015. Quote Investigator. October 12, 2015. https://quoteinvestigator.com/2015/10/12/depression/.

George, Alexander L., and Juliette L. George. 1998. *Presidential Personality and Performance.* Boulder, Colo: Westview Press.

Gerald Ford Inaugural Address: August 9, 1974. 2017. CBS News. https://www.youtube.com/watch?v=WBAXPomW-cg.

"Gerald R. Ford Speech - On Taking Office." 1974. The History Place. August 9, 1974. http://www.historyplace.com/speeches/ford-sworn.htm.

Gillman, Todd J. 2018. "John Kerry's Cool Demeanor Played a Role in 2004 Presidential Race — and He Once Gave a Hamster CPR." *The Dallas Morning News*, October 17, 2018. https://www.dallasnews.com/news/politics/2018/10/17/john-kerry-s-cool-demeanor-played-a-role-in-2004-presidential-race-and-he-once-gave-a-hamster-cpr/.

Glaister, Dan. 2008. "Richard Nixon Recordings Confirm Popular View." *The Guardian*, December 4, 2008, sec. US news. https://www.theguardian.com/world/2008/dec/04/richard-nixon-recordings.

Goldwater, Barry. 2015. *The Barry Goldwater Story*. BN Publishing. https://www.audible.com/pd/The-Barry-Goldwater-Story-Audiobook/B004N-QTUEY.

"GOLDWATER — HIS PERSONALITY AND HIS BELIEFS." *The New York Times*, July 19, 1964, sec. Archives. https://www.nytimes.com/1964/07/19/archives/goldwater-his-personality-and-his-beliefs-senators-conservative.html.

Goldwyn, Robin. 2016. "How Stocks Can Predict the Presidential Elections." *Barron's*, September 24, 2016. http://www.barrons.com/articles/how-stocks-can-predict-the-presidential-elections-1474693201.

Gomez, Luis. 2016. "R.I.P. Polls. Retailer Says Mask Sales Predict Presidential Elections." *San Diego Union-Tribune*, October 25, 2016. https://www.sandiegouniontribune.com/opinion/the-conversation/sd-can-this-halloween-costume-index-predict-presidential-election-20161024-htmlstory.html.

Goodwin, Doris Kearns. n.d. "Franklin D. Roosevelt Essay." Character Above All: Essays. Accessed October 28, 2019. https://www.pbs.org/newshour/spc/character/essays/roosevelt.html.

Greenberg, Jon. 2022. "Most Republicans Still Falsely Believe Trump's Stolen Election Claims. Here Are Some Reasons Why." *Poynter* (blog). June 16, 2022. https://www.poynter.org/fact-checking/2022/70-percent-republicans-falsely-believe-stolen-election-trump/.

Greenstein, Fred I. 2009. *The Presidential Difference: Leadership Style from FDR to Barack Obama*. 3rd ed. Princeton, NJ ; Oxford: Princeton University Press.

Greider, William. 1984. "Walter Mondale: Learning to Live With Fritz." *Rolling Stone*, March 1, 1984. https://www.rollingstone.com/politics/politics-news/walter-mondale-learning-to-live-with-fritz-63316/.

Gringlas, Sam, Scott Neuman, and Camila Domonoske. 2020. "'Far From Over': Trump Refuses To Concede As Biden's Margin Of Victory Widens." *NPR*, November 7, 2020, sec. Updates: 2020 Election Results. https://www.npr.org/sections/live-updates-2020-election-results/2020/11/07/932062684/far-from-over-trump-refuses-to-concede-as-ap-others-call-election-for-biden.

Grynbaum, Michael M. 2013. "Bloomberg Shares a Few Secrets of His Success: Be Early, Stay Late and Hold It In." *The New York Times*, August 23, 2013, sec. New York. https://www.nytimes.com/2013/08/24/nyregion/bloomberg-shares-a-few-secrets-to-success-be-early-stay-late-and-hold-it-in.html.

Haberman, Clyde. 2018. "George Wallace Tapped Into Racial Fear. Decades Later, Its Force Remains Potent." *The New York Times*, April 1, 2018. https://www.nytimes.com/2018/04/01/us/george-wallace-tapped-into-racial-fear-decades-later-its-force-remains-potent.html.

Hamby, Alonzo L. 1995. *Man of the People: A Life of Harry S. Truman*. New York: Oxford University Press.

Hansen, Hal. n.d. *Why Presidents Win: A Viewer's Guide to the Greatest Show on Earth, 1960-2012*.

Harper, Lauren. 2013. "President Carter Reflects on the Camp David Accords." *UNREDACTED* (blog). November 15, 2013. https://unredacted.com/2013/11/15/president-carter-reflects-on-the-camp-david-accords/.

Harris, David. 1983. "Understanding Mondale." *The New York Times*, June 19, 1983, sec. Magazine. https://www.nytimes.com/1983/06/19/magazine/understanding-mondale.html.

Harris, Scott. 1996. "Bob Dole Needs to Put the 'I' in Identity." *Los Angeles Times*, March 10, 1996. https://www.latimes.com/archives/la-xpm-1996-03-10-me-45347-story.html.

Hazen, Don. 2016. "Robert Reich: Don't Worry, Hillary Clinton Will Win the Election." *Salon*, November 8, 2016. https://www.salon.com/2016/11/08/robert-reich-dont-worry-hillary-clinton-will-win-the-election/.

Heilemann, John, and Mark Halperin. 2010. *Game Change: Obama and the Clintons, McCain and Palin, and the Race of a Lifetime*. 1st ed. New York: Harper.

Heineman, Ben W., Jr. 2012. "The Gallant Idealism of George McGovern." *The Atlantic*, October 21, 2012. https://www.theatlantic.com/politics/archive/2012/10/the-gallant-idealism-of-george-mcgovern/263909/.

History.com Editors. 2019. "The Kennedy-Nixon Debates." HISTORY. June 19, 2019. https://www.history.com/topics/us-presidents/kennedy-nixon-debates.

Holan, Angie D. 2019. "In Context: Donald Trump's 'Very Fine People on Both Sides' Remarks (Transcript)." *PolitiFact* (blog). April 26, 2019. https://www.politifact.com/article/2019/apr/26/context-trumps-very-fine-people-both-sides-remarks/.

Homer, Aaron. 2016. "Hillary Clinton Will Win The 2016 Election By A Landslide: FiveThirtyEight's Poll Guru Nate Silver Predicted Obama, Will The Trump Prediction Be True?" *Inquisitr*, October 12, 2016. https://www.inquisitr.com/3590671/hillary-clinton-will-win-the-2016-election-by-a-landslide-fivethirtyeights-poll-guru-nate-silver-predicted-obama-will-the-trump-prediction-be-true/.

Hook, Janet. 2019. "Joe Biden's Childhood Struggle with a Stutter: How He Overcame It and How It Shaped Him." *Los Angeles Times*, September 16, 2019. https://www.latimes.com/politics/story/2019-09-15/joe-bidens-childhood-struggle-with-a-stutter.

Hoppe, Hannah. 2015. "St. Cloud Times." *St. Cloud Times*, August 8, 2015. https://www.sctimes.com/story/opinion/2015/08/08/trump-driven-narcissistic-dreams-glory/31332299/.

How Hillary Clinton Responded to the Gennifer Flowers Scandal. n.d. The Choice 2016 | FRONTLINE. Frontline PBS. Accessed October 29, 2019. https://www.youtube.com/watch?v=PvR62T1gO0w.

Hume, Mike. 2008. "A BRIEF HISTORY OF THE PHRASE 'MANNY BEING MANNY.'" *ESPN*, October 15, 2008. https://www.espn.com/espnmag/story?id=3644816.

IM Editors. 2015. "Exclusive Post-Retirement Interview with David Letterman." *Indianapolis Monthly*, June 12, 2015. https://www.indianapolis-monthly.com/arts-and-culture/sports/exclusive-post-retirement-interview-david-letterman.

"Improviser In Chief: Clinton Text Vs. Audio." 2012. *NPR,* September 5, 2012. https://www.npr.org/2012/09/05/160643183/transcript-bill-clintons-convention-speech.

"In Their Own Words: Why Voters Support – and Have Concerns About – Clinton and Trump." 2016. *Pew Research Center*, September 21, 2016. https://www.people-press.org/2016/09/21/in-their-own-words-why-voters-support-and-have-concerns-about-clinton-and-trump/.

"Increase in Unemployment Rate in January 2009." 2009. U.S. Bureau of Labor Statistics. February 10, 2009. https://www.bls.gov/opub/ted/2009/feb/wk2/art02.htm?view_full.

"Is Hillary Clinton Facing an Enthusiasm Gap?" 2016. *Erin Burnett Out Front.* CNN. https://www.cnn.com/videos/politics/2016/11/08/obama-enthusiasm-hillary-clinton-schneider-dnt-ebof.cnn.

Isenberg, Nancy, and Andrew Burstein. 2019. *The Problem of Democracy: The Presidents Adams Confront the Cult of Personality.* New York, NY: Viking.

Ivcevic, Zorana, and Nalini Ambady. 2012. "Personality Impressions from Identity Claims on Facebook." *Psychology of Popular Media Culture* 1 (1): 38–45. https://doi.org/10.1037/a0027329.

Jackson, Dan. 2018. "Craziest Daniel Day Lewis Method Acting Stories." *Thrillist*, January 19, 2018. https://www.thrillist.com/entertainment/nation/daniel-day-lewis-method-acting-stories.

Jamieson, Kathleen Hall. 1996. *Packaging The Presidency: A History and Criticism of Presidential Campaign Advertising.* Oxford: Oxford University Press, USA. https://search.ebscohost.com/login.aspx?direct=true&scope=site&db=nlebk&db=nlabk&AN=2096298.

JFK Election Ad Knocks Nixon (1960s) - Classic Political Campaign Commercial. 2012. All Classic Video. https://www.youtube.com/watch?v=6-0UgeBU-_A.

Joe Biden For President: America Is An Idea. 2019a. Joe Biden. https://www.youtube.com/watch?v=VbOU2fTg6cI.

"Joe Biden Says He's the 'Antithesis' of President Trump." 2020. CBS News. https://www.youtube.com/watch?v=7o2e_gu7XOg.

Jones, Alex S. 1992. "Al Gore's Double Life." *The New York Times*, October 25, 1992. https://www.nytimes.com/1992/10/25/magazine/al-gore-s-double-life.html.

Jones, Jeffrey M. 2021. "Last Trump Job Approval 34%; Average Is Record-Low 41%." *Gallup*, January 18, 2021, sec. Politics. https://news.gallup.com/poll/328637/last-trump-job-approval-average-record-low.aspx.

Judis, John. 2001. "Al Gore and the Temple of Doom." *The American Prospect*, December 19, 2001. https://prospect.org/api/content/6993c4b5-57f2-52d1-a916-da2a8951b5e2/.

Kalan, Elliott, and Alexis Coe. n.d. "Presidents Are People Too!" https://podcasts.apple.com/us/podcast/presidents-are-people-too/id1168237590.

Kansas Historical Society. 2017. "Alfred Landon's Acceptance Speech." Kansapedia. December 2017. https://www.kshs.org/kansapedia/alfred-landon-s-acceptance-speech/14501.

Kettle, Martin. 2016. "Hillary Clinton Will Win. But What Kind of President Will She Be?" *The Guardian*, October 27, 2016, sec. Opinion. https://www.theguardian.com/commentisfree/2016/oct/27/hillary-clinton-will-win-what-kind-of-president-white-house-obama.

Klein, Nadav, and Ed O'Brien. 2018. "People Use Less Information than They Think to Make up Their Minds." *Proceedings of the National Academy of Sciences* 115 (52): 13222–27. https://doi.org/10.1073/pnas.1805327115.

Kolbert, Elizabeth. 1996. "Dole Campaign Will Be Bringing Out Its Secret Weapon: The Candidate's Sense of Humor." *The New York Times*, October 4, 1996, sec. U.S. https://www.nytimes.com/1996/10/04/us/dole-campaign-will-be-bringing-its-secret-weapon-candidate-s-sense-humor.html.

Krawczyk, Kathryn. 2019a. "Joe Biden: 'I Want to Be Clear, I'm Not Going Nuts.'" *The Week*, August 26, 2019. https://theweek.com/speedreads/861039/joe-biden-want-clear-im-not-going-nuts.

———. 2019b. "Trump Is Now Averaging 36 Tweets a Day." *The Week*, October 14, 2019. https://theweek.com/speedreads/871559/trump-now-averaging-36-tweets-day.

Kuehl, Rebecca A. 2019. "Fireside Chats." Encyclopedia Britannica. March 5, 2019. https://www.britannica.com/event/fireside-chats.

Lee, Bandy X., ed. 2017. *The Dangerous Case of Donald Trump: 27 Psychiatrists and Mental Health Experts Assess a President*. First edition. New York: Thomas Dunne Books, St. Martin's Press.

Lehrer, James. 2011. *Tension City: Inside the Presidential Debates, from Kennedy-Nixon to Obama-McCain*. 1st ed. New York: Random House.

"Life of John F. Kennedy." n.d. John F. Kennedy Presidential Library and Museum. Accessed October 28, 2019. https://www.jfklibrary.org/learn/about-jfk/life-of-john-f-kennedy.

Little, Becky. 2018. "JFK Was Completely Unprepared For His Summit with Khrushchev." HISTORY. August 26, 2018. https://www.history.com/news/kennedy-krushchev-vienna-summit-meeting-1961.

Loftus, Geoff. 2010. *Lead like Ike: Ten Business Strategies from the CEO of D-Day*. Nashville, Tenn: Thomas Nelson.

Lydon, Christopher. 1972. "McGovern's Route to the Top." *The New York Times*, June 11, 1972, sec. Archives. https://www.nytimes.com/1972/06/11/archives/mcgoverns-route-to-the-top-how-mcgovern-rose-to-the-top-in-primary.html.

"Lyndon Johnson and the 'Johnson Treatment.'" 2009. Text. *Facetoface | A Blog from the National Portrait Gallery* (blog). May 28, 2009. https://npg.si.edu/blog/lyndon-johnson-and-johnson-treatment.

Manchester, Julia. 2018. "83 Percent Say the President Should Be Consoler in Chief after National Tragedies." *The Hill*, December 4, 2018. https://thehill.com/hilltv/what-americas-thinking/419689-83-percent-say-the-president-should-be-the-consoler-in-chief/.

Marcus, Ruth. 2016. "This Election Is an Unpopularity Contest for the Ages." *Washington Post*, April 19, 2016, sec. Opinions. https://www.washingtonpost.com/opinions/an-unpopularity-contest-for-the-ages/2016/04/19/7e-1d25a2-0663-11e6-a12f-ea5aed7958dc_story.html.

Margolick, David. 1985. "Former Aides Remember Dewey, the Prosecutor, as a Loyal Mentor." *The New York Times*, April 27, 1985, sec. New York. https://www.nytimes.com/1985/04/27/nyregion/former-aides-remember-dewey-the-prosecutor-as-a-loyal-mentor.html.

Marston, William Moulton. 2014. *Emotions of Normal People*. Place of publication not identified: Routledge.

Maysles, Albert. 2016. *John F. Kennedy Rallies the Crowd in PRIMARY*. CriterionCollection. https://www.youtube.com/watch?v=wLkT7z0C5Bc.

McCain, John, and Mark Salter. 2018. *The Restless Wave: Good Times, Just Causes, Great Fights and Other Appreciations*. First Simon & Schuster hardcover edition. New York, NY: Simon & Schuster.

McCammond, Alexi. 2019. "Focus Group Women like Elizabeth Warren's Policies More than Her." *Axios*, September 23, 2019. https://www.axios.com/elizabeth-warren-focus-group-wisconsin-swing-voters-f5d1d420-3076-4b49-99eb-fecfa93a97c2.html.

McCarthy, Justin. 2019. "High Enthusiasm About Voting in U.S. Heading Into 2020." *Gallup*, November 7, 2019. https://news.gallup.com/poll/268136/high-enthusiasm-voting-heading-2020.aspx.

———. 2019. "Trump Job Approval Higher Than Approval of Him as a Person." *Gallup*, October 3, 2019. https://news.gallup.com/poll/267182/trump-job-approval-higher-approval-person.aspx.

McCullough, David G. 2002. *Truman*. Simon & Schuster Paperbacks. New York: Simon & Schuster.

———. n.d. "Harry S. Truman." Character Above All: Essays. Accessed October 28, 2019. https://www.pbs.org/newshour/spc/character/essays/truman.html.

McKeever, Porter. 1989. *Adlai Stevenson: His Life and Legacy*. 1st ed. New York: Morrow.

McLaughlin, Seth, and S.A. Miller. 2019. "Trump's 'Sleepy Joe' Taunt Strikes Chord with Democrats: 'I Want to Be Excited about Someone.'" *The Washington Times*, June 20, 2019. https://www.washingtontimes.com/ news/2019/jun/20/sleepy-joe-biden-taunt-strikes-chord-democrats/.

McNally, Katie. 2017. "Presidential Fuming: 7 Historic Outbursts, From Jackson to Obama." *UVA Today*, August 3, 2017. https://news.virginia.edu/ content/presidential-fuming-7-historic-outbursts-jackson-obama.

Merica, Dan, Jeff Zeleny, and Arlette Saenz. 2020. "'Amtrak Joe' Could Arrive for His Inauguration by Train." *CNN*, December 7, 2020. https://www. cnn.com/2020/12/07/politics/biden-amtrak/index.html.

Millett, Allan R. 2001. "Dwight D. Eisenhower and the Korean War: Cautionary Tale and Hopeful Precedent." *Journal of American-East Asian Relations* 10 (3–4): 155–74. https://doi.org/10.1163/187656101793645515.

Moore, Alexander. 2019. *The Democrats: Biographies of Joe Biden, Bernie Sanders, Elizabeth Warren, Kamala Harris, and Cory Booker*. Independently published.

Moorhead, Molly. 2012. "Mitt Romney Says 47 Percent of Americans Pay No Income Tax." PolitiFact. September 18, 2012. https://www.politifact.com/ truth-o-meter/statements/2012/sep/18/mitt-romney/romney-says-47-percent-americans-pay-no-income-tax/.

Morrissey, Charles T. 1963. General Harry H. Vaughan Oral History Interview, January 14, 1963. Harry S. Truman Library. https://www.trumanlibrary.gov/library/oral-histories/vaughan1#note.

Munger, Sean. 2015. "Biggest Losers: Alf Landon and the Election of 1936." *SeanMunger.Com* (blog). February 11, 2015. https://seanmunger. com/2015/02/10/biggest-losers-alf-landon-and-the-election-of-1936/.

Murphy Jr., Bill. 2018. "You Won't Believe What President George H.W. Bush's Nickname Was During World War II. Here's the Story." *Inc. Magazine*, December 3, 2018. https://www.inc.com/bill-murphy-jr/heres-story-behind-very-strange-nickname-president-george-hw-bush-picked-up-during-world-war-ii.html.

PERSONALITY WINS

Nadeem, Reem. 2021. "Behind Biden's 2020 Victory." *Pew Research Center*, June 30, 2021. https://www.pewresearch.org/politics/2021/06/30/behind-bidens-2020-victory/.

NCC Staff. 2019. "The Nixon Pardon in Constitutional Retrospect." *Constitution Daily | National Constitution Center* (blog). September 8, 2019. https://constitutioncenter.org/blog/the-nixon-pardon-in-retrospect.

Newport, Frank. 2000. "Most Americans Know Al Gore Well." *Gallup*, August 17, 2000. https://news.gallup.com/poll/2626/Most-Americans-Know-Gore-Well.aspx.

Nix, Elizabeth. n.d. "'Dewey Defeats Truman': The Election Upset Behind the Photo." HISTORY. Accessed October 28, 2019. https://www.history.com/news/dewey-defeats-truman-election-headline-gaffe.

Nixon 1960 Campaign Ad. n.d. Accessed October 29, 2019. https://www.youtube.com/watch?v=j3cpQnVvXSs.

"Nixon's First Watergate Speech." 1973. Watergate.Info. April 30, 1973. https://watergate.info/1973/04/30/nixons-first-watergate-speech.html.

Noonan, Peggy. n.d. "Ronald Reagan." Character Above All: Essays. Accessed October 28, 2019. https://www.pbs.org/newshour/spc/character/essays/reagan.html.

"Obama's Health Care Speech to Congress." *The New York Times* September 9, 2009, sec. Politics. https://www.nytimes.com/2009/09/10/us/politics/10obama.text.html.

"October 6, 1976 Debate Transcript." n.d. Commission on Presidential Debates. Accessed October 28, 2019. https://www.debates.org/voter-education/debate-transcripts/october-6-1976-debate-transcript/.

O'Donnell, Lawrence. 2017. *Playing with Fire: The 1968 Election and the Transformation of American Politics*. New York: Penguin Press.

Offner, Arnold A. 2018. *Hubert Humphrey: The Conscience of the Country*. New Haven, CT: Yale University Press.

Okimoto, Tyler G., and Victoria L. Brescoll. 2010. "The Price of Power: Power Seeking and Backlash Against Female Politicians." *Personality and Social Psychology Bulletin* 36 (7): 923–36. https://doi.org/10.1177/0146167210371949.

Olorunnipa, Toluse, and Josh Dawsey. 2019. "'What I Said Was Accurate!': Trump Stays Fixated on His Alabama Error as Hurricane Pounds the Carolinas." *Washington Post*, September 5, 2019. https://www.washingtonpost.com/politics/what-i-said-was-accurate-trump-stays-fixated-on-his-alabama-error-as-hurricane-pounds-the-carolinas/2019/09/05/32597606-cfe7-11e9-8c1c-7c8ee785b855_story.html.

Osgood, Charles, ed. 2008. *A Funny Thing Happened on the Way to the White House: Humor, Blunders, and Other Oddities from the Presidential Campaign Trail.* 1st ed. New York: Hyperion.

Otterbein, Holly. 2019. "'I Am Back': Sanders Tops Warren with Massive New York City Rally." *POLITICO*, October 19, 2019. https://www.politico.com/news/2019/10/19/bernie-sanders-ocasio-cortez-endorsement-rally-051491.

Peltz, Perri, and Matthew O'Neill, dirs. 2020. "President Trump Interview." *Axios.* HBO. https://play.hbomax.com/page/urn:hbo:page:GXvzUDAeAe5piwwEAAAGH:type:episode.

Perry, Mark. 2016. "Maps of the Day: Travel Times from NYC in 1800, 1830, 1857 and 1930." *American Enterprise Institute* (blog). October 5, 2016. https://www.aei.org/carpe-diem/maps-of-the-day-travel-times-from-nyc-in-1800-1830-1857-and-1930/.

Peters, Gerhard, and John T Woolley. n.d. "Address Accepting the Presidential Nomination in Elwood, Indiana." The American Presidency Project. Accessed October 28, 2019. https://www.presidency.ucsb.edu/documents/address-accepting-the-presidential-nomination-elwood-indiana.

"Presidential Approval Ratings -- Bill Clinton." 2008. *Gallup*, March 11, 2008. https://news.gallup.com/poll/116584/Presidential-Approval-Ratings-Bill-Clinton.aspx.

"Presidential Approval Ratings -- Donald Trump." 2016. *Gallup*, November 16, 2016. https://news.gallup.com/poll/203198/presidential-approval-ratings-donald-trump.aspx.

"Presidential Approval Ratings -- George W. Bush." 2008. *Gallup*, January 20, 2008. https://news.gallup.com/poll/116500/Presidential-Approval-Ratings-George-Bush.aspx.

"President Trump Goes One-on-One with Chris Wallace." Fox News. https://www.youtube.com/watch?v=W6XdpDOH1JA.

"Progressive Development of U.S. Railroads - 1830-1890." 2014. Central Pacific Railroad Photographic History Museum. 2014. http://www.cprr.org/Museum/RR_Development.html.

Rabbe, Will. 2011. "George Bush, Meet the Barcode Scanner." *Will Rabbe* (blog). January 8, 2011. http://willrabbe.com/microblog/2011/4/8/george-bush-meet-the-barcode-scanner.html.

Reagan, Ronald. 1986. "Explosion of the Space Shuttle Challenger Address to the Nation." NASA History Division. January 28, 1986. https://history.nasa.gov/reagan12886.html.

Reagan's Joke Lead To Red Alert. 2014. Flashback | NBC News. https://www.youtube.com/watch?v=CFCABnWlN8E&feature=youtu.be.

Reeve, Elspeth. 2012. "How Romney Really Blew the Election, Even by His Own Strange Scoreboard." *The Atlantic*, December 17, 2012. https://www.theatlantic.com/politics/archive/2012/12/how-romney-really-blew-election-even-his-own-strange-scoreboard/320377/.

Reid, Claire. 2018. "Robin Williams Improvised One Of The Funniest Scenes In 'Good Will Hunting.'" LAD Bible. September 24, 2018. https://www.ladbible.com/entertainment/film-and-tv-robin-williams-ad-libbed-this-scene-from-good-will-hunting-20180923.

"Remarks by President Biden in a CNN Town Hall with Don Lemon." 2021. The White House. July 22, 2021. https://www.whitehouse.gov/briefing-room/speeches-remarks/2021/07/22/remarks-by-president-biden-in-a-cnn-town-hall-with-don-lemon/.

Revesz, Rachael. 2016. "The Man Who Predicted 49 out of 50 States in 2012 Has Said Who Will Win on Tuesday." *The Independent*, November 5, 2016. http://www.independent.co.uk/news/world/americas/sam-wang-princeton-election-consortium-poll-hillary-clinton-donald-trump-victory-a7399671.html.

Richardson, James D., and 1834 President Jackson's Message of Protest to the Senate; April 15. n.d. "A compilation of the messages and papers of the presidents." Text. New York : Bureau of National Literature Inc., [c1897-1915]. Accessed May 4, 2023. https://avalon.law.yale.edu/19th_century/ajack006.asp.

Rogan, Joe. 2019. "Bernie Sanders." *The Joe Rogan Experience*. Accessed October 28, 2019. https://www.stitcher.com/s?eid=63052691.

Ronald Reagan: "I Am Paying for This Microphone" (1980). n.d. New Hampshire Institute of Politics (NHIOP). Accessed October 29, 2019. https://www.youtube.com/watch?v=Rd_KaF3-Bcw.

Ronald Reagan TV Ad: "Its Morning in America Again." n.d. Accessed October 29, 2019. https://www.youtube.com/watch?v=EU-IBF8nwSY.

Ronald Reagan TV Ad: "The Bear." n.d. Accessed October 29, 2019. https://www.youtube.com/watch?v=NpwdcmjBgNA.

Rosenbaum, David E. 2012. "George McGovern, a Liberal Trounced but Not Silenced, Dies at 90." *The New York Times*, October 21, 2012, sec. Politics. https://www.nytimes.com/2012/10/22/us/politics/george-mcgovern-a-democratic-presidential-nominee-and-liberal-stalwart-dies-at-90.html.

Rubenzer, Steven J., and Thomas R. Faschingbauer. 2005. *Personality, Character and Leadership in the White House: Psychologists Assess the Presidents.* Washington, D.C: Potomac Books.

Rule, Nicholas, and Nalini Ambady. 2010. "First Impressions of the Face: Predicting Success: Predicting Success from the Face." *Social and Personality Psychology Compass* 4 (8): 506–16. https://doi.org/10.1111/j.1751-9004.2010.00282.x.

Rule, Nicholas O., and Nalini Ambady. 2008. "The Face of Success: Inferences From Chief Executive Officers' Appearance Predict Company Profits." *Psychological Science* 19 (2): 109–11. https://doi.org/10.1111/j.1467-9280.2008.02054.x.

———. 2009. "She's Got the Look: Inferences from Female Chief Executive Officers' Faces Predict Their Success." *Sex Roles* 61 (9–10): 644–52. https://doi.org/10.1007/s11199-009-9658-9.

Rutz, David. 2018. "Cory Booker's Split Personality." *The Washington Free Beacon*, July 27, 2018. https://freebeacon.com/politics/cory-bookers-split-personality/.

S, Pangambam. 2014. "Steve Jobs IPhone 2007 Presentation (Full Transcript)." *The Singju Post*, July 4, 2014. https://singjupost.com/steve-jobs-iphone-2007-presentation-full-transcript/.

Scheer, Robert. 1976. "The 1976 Playboy Interview With Jimmy Carter." *Playboy Magazine*, November 1, 1976. https://www.playboy.com/read/playboy-interview-jimmy-carter.

Schreiber, Hermann. 1964. "Goldwater Interview With Der Spiegel." *The New York Times*, July 9, 1964, sec. Archives. https://www.nytimes.com/1964/07/09/archives/goldwater-interview-with-der-spiegel.html.

Schroeder, Alan. 2008. *Presidential Debates: Fifty Years of High-Risk TV*. 2nd ed. New York: Columbia University Press.

Seelye, Katharine Q. 1996. "War Wounds Shape Life, and Politics, for Dole." *The New York Times*, April 14, 1996, sec. U.S. https://www.nytimes.com/1996/04/14/us/war-wounds-shape-life-and-politics-for-dole.html.

"Senator Richard Nixon's Checkers Speech." n.d. Watergate.Info. Accessed October 28, 2019. https://watergate.info/1952/09/23/nixon-checkers-speech.html.

Shafer, Ronald G. 2016. *The Carnival Campaign: How the Rollicking 1840 Campaign of "Tippecanoe and Tyler Too" Changed Presidential Elections Forever*. Chicago, Illinois: Chicago Review Press.

Shirley, Craig. 2016. "How Gerald Ford Beat Ronald Reagan at the Last Contested GOP Convention." *Washington Post*, April 22, 2016, sec. Opinions. https://www.washingtonpost.com/opinions/how-gerald-ford-outmaneuvered-ronald-reagan-at-the-last-contested-gop-convention/2016/04/22/6bed14ec-07cf-11e6-b283-e79d81c63c1b_story.html.

Siddiqui, Sabrina. 2012. "Mitt Romney's 47 Percent Remark Hurts Him In Swing States." *The Huffington Post*, September 26, 2012. https://www.huffpost.com/entry/mitt-romney-47-percent_n_1916159.

"Siena's 6th Presidential Expert Poll 1982 - 2018." 2019. Siena College Research Institute. February 13, 2019. https://scri.siena.edu/2019/02/13/sienas-6th-presidential-expert-poll-1982-2018/.

Silver, Nate. 2017. "How Popular Is Donald Trump?" FiveThirtyEight. March 2, 2017. https://projects.fivethirtyeight.com/trump-approval-ratings/.

———. 2021. "How Popular Is Joe Biden?" FiveThirtyEight. January 28, 2021. https://projects.fivethirtyeight.com/biden-approval-rating/.

MERRICK ROSENBERG

Slisco, Aila. 2020. "56% of Joe Biden Voters Are Voting Because 'He Is Not Trump,' New Poll Says." *Newsweek*, August 14, 2020, sec. News. https://www.newsweek.com/56-joe-biden-voters-are-voting-because-he-not-trump-new-poll-says-1525259.

Smith, Hendrick. 1984. "REAGAN'S GAFFE." *The New York Times*, August 16, 1984. https://www.nytimes.com/1984/08/16/world/reagan-s-gaffe.html.

Smith, Jean Edward. 2009. "Obama, F.D.R. and Taming the Press." *100 Days* (blog). February 2, 2009. https://100days.blogs.nytimes.com/2009/02/02/obama-fdr-and-taming-the-press/.

Snopes Staff. 2001. "Was President George H.W. Bush 'Amazed' by a Grocery Scanner?" Snopes.Com. April 1, 2001. https://www.snopes.com/fact-check/bush-scanner-demonstration/.

Sterling, Christopher H. 2002. "'The Fireside Chats'—President Franklin D. Roosevelt (1933-1944)." Library of Congress | National Recording Preservation Board. 2002. http://www.loc.gov/static/programs/national-recording-preservation-board/documents/FiresideChats.pdf.

Stern, Andrew. 2010. "George Bush, Promoting Book, Laughs It up on Oprah." *Reuters*, November 9, 2010. https://www.reuters.com/article/us-bush-book-oprah-idUSTRE6A840J20101109.

Stone, Alan. 2018. "The Psychiatrist's Goldwater Rule in the Trump Era." *Lawfare* (blog). April 19, 2018. https://www.lawfareblog.com/psychiatrists-goldwater-rule-trump-era.

Stone, Irving. 1966. *They Also Ran*. Place of publication not identified: Doubleday.

Strauss, Daniel, and Lauren Gambino. 2020. "Joe Biden: From a Campaign That Almost Collapsed to Fighting Trump for the Presidency." *The Observer*, November 1, 2020, sec. US news. https://www.theguardian.com/us-news/2020/nov/01/joe-biden-campaign-us-election.

Tauberg, Michael. 2019. "Which 2020 Candidate Is the Best at Twitter?" *Medium* (blog). August 28, 2019. https://towardsdatascience.com/which-2020-candidate-is-the-best-at-twitter-fd083d13fb4e.

Tavernise, Sabrina, and Robert Gebeloff. 2018. "They Voted for Obama, Then Went for Trump. Can Democrats Win Them Back?" *The New York Times*, May 4, 2018. https://www.nytimes.com/2018/05/04/us/obama-trump-swing-voters.html.

Taylor, Ryan. n.d. "Donald Trump 2020 Election Night Speech Transcript." *Rev.* Accessed May 4, 2023a. https://www.rev.com/blog/transcripts/donald-trump-2020-election-night-speech-transcript.

———. n.d. "Joe Biden 2020 Election Night Speech Transcript." *Rev.* Accessed May 4, 2023b. https://www.rev.com/blog/transcripts/joe-biden-2020-election-night-speech-transcript.

The Center for Responsive Politics. n.d. "Sen. Bernie Sanders - Campaign Finance Summary." OpenSecrets. Accessed October 28, 2019a. https://www.opensecrets.org/members-of-congress/summary?cid=N00000528.

———. n.d. "Summary Data for Donald Trump, 2016 Cycle." OpenSecrets. Accessed October 28, 2019b. https://www.opensecrets.org/pres16/candidate?id=N00023864.

The Editorial Board. 2019. "Bloomberg's 'Stop and Frisk' Apology." *Wall Street Journal*, November 19, 2019, sec. Opinion. https://www.wsj.com/articles/bloombergs-stop-and-frisk-apology-11574122365.

"The Origins of Modern Campaigning: 1860-1932." 2014. See How They Ran! FDR & His Opponents: Campaign Treasures From the New-York Historical Society. December 2, 2014. http://www.roosevelthouse.hunter.cuny.edu/seehowtheyran/portfolios/origins-of-modern-campaigning/.

"The Nobel Peace Prize 2009." 2009. NobelPrize.Org. October 9, 2009. https://www.nobelprize.org/prizes/peace/2009/press-release/.

"The Smoking Gun Tape." 1972. Watergate.Info. June 23, 1972. https://watergate.info/1972/06/23/the-smoking-gun-tape.html.

"Thomas Dewey." n.d. The Mob Museum. Accessed October 28, 2019. https://themobmuseum.org/notable_names/thomas-dewey/.

Thomas, Evan. 2016. *Being Nixon: A Man Divided*. Random House trade paperback edition. New York: Random House.

Thrush, Glenn. 2012. *End of the Line: Romney vs. Obama: The 34 Days That Decided the Election: Playbook 2012 (POLITICO Inside Election 2012), Obama: The 34 Days That Decided the Election: Playbook 2012 (POLITICO Inside Election 2012),*. Random House. http://www.myilibrary.com?id=449445.

Todorov, A. 2005. "Inferences of Competence from Faces Predict Election Outcomes." *Science* 308 (5728): 1623–26. https://doi.org/10.1126/science.1110589.

Tolchin, Martin. 1990. "How Johnson Won Election He'd Lost." *The New York Times*, February 11, 1990, sec. U.S. https://www.nytimes.com/1990/02/11/us/how-johnson-won-election-he-d-lost.html.

"Top 10 Joe Biden Gaffes." *Time*, January 31, 2007. http://content.time.com/time/specials/packages/article/0,28804,1895156_1894977_1644536,00.html.

"Town Hall with Bernie Sanders." 2019. Fox News. April 15, 2019. http://video.foxnews.com/v/6026527843001/.

"Transcript of Debate Between the Vice-Presidential Candidates." *The New York Times,* October 16, 1976, sec. Archives. https://www.nytimes.com/1976/10/16/archives/transcript-of-debate-between-the-vicepresidential-candidates-dole.html.

"Transcript of Nixon's Question and Answer Session With A. P. Managing Editors." *The New York Times,* November 18, 1973, sec. Archives. https://www.nytimes.com/1973/11/18/archives/transcript-of-nixons-question-and-answer-session-with-a-p-managing.html.

"Transcription: Washington's Inaugural Address." 1789. National Archives and Records Administration. April 30, 1789. https://www.archives.gov/exhibits/american_originals/inaugtxt.html.

"Trump Seen Marginally as Decisive Leader, but Not Honest." 2019. *Gallup*, July 10, 2019. https://news.gallup.com/poll/260495/trump-seen-marginally-decisive-leader-not-honest.aspx.

University of New Hampshire Survey Center. 2019. "CNN 2020 NH Primary Pol." CNN. July 16, 2019. http://cdn.cnn.com/cnn/2019/images/07/16/rel1_nh_.2020.pdf.

Updegrove, Mark K. 2017. "Lyndon Johnson's Vietnam." *The New York Times*, February 24, 2017, sec. Opinion. https://www.nytimes.com/2017/02/24/opinion/lyndon-johnsons-vietnam.html.

US Census Bureau. 2021. "2020 Presidential Election Voting and Registration Tables Now Available." Census.Gov. Accessed May 4, 2023. https://www.census.gov/newsroom/press-releases/2021/2020-presidential-election-voting-and-registration-tables-now-available.html.

"U.S. Senate: Senate Censures President." n.d. Accessed May 4, 2023. https://www.senate.gov/about/origins-foundations/parties-leadership/censure-president-jackson.htm.

USA TODAY Staff. 2020. "Read the Full Transcript from the First Presidential Debate between Joe Biden and Donald Trump." *USA TODAY*, September 30, 2020. https://www.usatoday.com/story/news/politics/elections/2020/09/30/presidential-debate-read-full-transcript-first-debate/3587462001/.

Waldman, Paul. 2016. "Why Did Trump Win? In Part Because Voter Turnout Plunged." *Washington Post*, November 10, 2016. https://www.washingtonpost.com/blogs/plum-line/wp/2016/11/10/why-did-trump-win-in-part-because-voter-turnout-plunged/.

Walter Mondale TV Ad: "House." n.d. Accessed October 29, 2019. https://www.youtube.com/watch?v=ebXAcfyhmfk.

Walter Mondale TV Ad: "More." n.d. Accessed October 29, 2019. https://www.youtube.com/watch?v=e07vlQNz88c.

Walsh, Deirdre. 2020. "Trump And Biden Had A Real Debate, And 4 Other Takeaways." *NPR*, October 23, 2020, sec. Politics. https://www.npr.org/2020/10/23/926844747/trump-and-biden-had-a-real-debate-and-4-other-takeaways.

Warner, Margaret Garrard. 1987. "Bush Battles the 'Wimp Factor.'" *Newsweek*, October 19, 1987. https://www.newsweek.com/bush-battles-wimp-factor-207008.

Waxman, B., and Merrill Fabry. 2018. "From an Anonymous Tip to an Impeachment: A Timeline of Key Moments in the Clinton-Lewinsky Scandal." *Time*, May 4, 2018. https://time.com/5120561/bill-clinton-monica-lewinsky-timeline/.

Weisberg, Jacob. 2016. "Ronald Reagan's Disarmament Dream." *The Atlantic,* January 1, 2016. https://www.theatlantic.com/politics/archive/2016/01/ronald-reagans-disarmament-dream/422244/.

Weisenthal, Joe. 2012. "This Is What The Economy Did The Last Time A President Didn't Win Re-Election." *Business Insider,* July 8, 2012. https://www.businessinsider.com/the-economy-under-george-hw-bush-2012-7.

Weisman, Steven R. 1984. "The President and the Press." *The New York Times,* October 14, 1984, sec. Magazine. https://www.nytimes.com/1984/10/14/magazine/the-president-and-the-press.html.

Westen, Drew. 2007. *The Political Brain: The Role of Emotion in Deciding the Fate of the Nation.* New York: PublicAffairs.

"Who Is John Kerry?" *The Economist,* July 22, 2004. https://www.economist.com/special-report/2004/07/22/who-is-john-kerry.

Willie Horton 1988 Attack Ad. n.d. Accessed October 29, 2019. https://www.youtube.com/watch?v=Io9KMSSEZ0Y.

Wilstein, Matt. 2016. "Trevor Noah Rips Hillary Clinton's Racist Joke: 'Why Would You Do This, Hillary?'" *The Daily Beast,* April 13, 2016, sec. entertainment. https://www.thedailybeast.com/articles/2016/04/13/trevor-noah-rips-hillary-clinton-s-racist-joke-why-would-you-do-this-hillary.

Zenko, Micah. 2017. "Obama's Final Drone Strike Data." *Council on Foreign Relations* (blog). January 20, 2017. https://www.cfr.org/blog/obamas-final-drone-strike-data.

Zipp, Samuel. 2019. "The Lost Internationalism of Wendell Willkie." *The Nation,* March 14, 2019. https://www.thenation.com/article/wendell-willkie-david-leavering-lewis-review/.

About the Authors

Merrick Rosenberg is a keynote speaker and the leading personality expert in corporate America. He is the award-winning author of five books about the power of your personality, including *The Chameleon*, *Taking Flight!*, *Which Bird Are You?*, and *Flight School*.

Since 1991, Merrick has worked with more than half of the Fortune 100 companies and has reached hundreds of thousands of people around the world through his speaking engagements. He has been named the CEO of the Year for New Jersey and his company, Take Flight Learning, has been selected as the NJ Business of the Year, one of the Best Places to Work, and one of the Fastest Growing Companies in the Philadelphia area.

A regular guest on news and entertainment programs, Merrick has been interviewed by NBC, PBS, and more than 100 radio stations. Publications that regularly seek Merrick's input include The New York Times, Fast Company, Fortune, The Huffington Post, Forbes, Herald Tribune, The Wall Street Journal, InformationWeek, Inc., Parents, and Glamour.

Merrick earned a B.A. in Political Communications from George Washington University and an MBA from Drexel University, which recently selected Merrick as its Entrepreneur of the Year. Look for Merrick on the news and talk shows discussing how personality plays out in our relationships, careers, and presidential elections.

For more information about Merrick Rosenberg and the services offered by Take Flight Learning, visit MerrickRosenberg.com or TakeFlightLearning.com.

Richard Ellis is a strategist and writer based near Park City, UT. Since launching Pen & Path in 2013, he has served as a trusted advisor to more than 350 investors, entrepreneurs, and executives. They turn to Rich when credibility and capital are on the line. From Forbes columns and TechCrunch op-eds to product launches and brand messaging to IPO disclosure documents and private placement memorandums, Rich delivers when words matter most.

Rich believes in telling meaningful stories, raising controversial issues, and questioning assumptions. Towards that end, he has saved more than 10,000 drafts and broken five backspace keys in the last decade. When interviewing clients, he is known for asking unfair questions like, "What does that mean?" and "Can you give an example?"

Rich graduated *summa cum laude* from Yale University in 2011 with a B.A. in History. His thesis on Israel's Six Day War earned the Alfred D. White Senior Essay Prize in American History. To learn more about Rich, visit penandpath.com.

www.ingramcontent.com/pod-product-compliance
Lightning Source LLC
Chambersburg PA
CBHW062116020426

42335CB00013B/987